PRAISE FOR
Is Your Story Making You Sick?
BY MARK PIRTLE

"Mark Pirtle has provided an original, profound, and deeply insightful work that reframes the source of our central challenges and outlines the critical work we must all undertake to heal ourselves, the people around us, and the world. It is impossible to overstate the significance of Mark's perspective. He has fundamentally changed how I think about trauma, recovery, and the way forward."

— Harry Nelson, Chair, Behavioral Health Association of Providers (BHAP), and author of *The United States of Opioids: A Prescription For Liberating A Nation In Pain*

"In his book . . . Mark Pirtle shows us how to combine mindfulness training (for emotional maturity) with proven psychological techniques (for enhancing reasoning and skillful action). He outlines the steps and points to a path from healing one's story to healing the world. This book is a tangible message of tempered optimism for difficult times."

— Shinzen Young, founder of Unified Mindfulness, co-director of the Sonication Enhanced Mindful Awareness (SEMA) Lab at the University of Arizona, and author of *The Science of Enlightenment: How Meditation Works* and *Break Through Pain: A Step-by-Step Mindfulness Meditation Program for Transforming Chronic and Acute Pain*

"Mark's relentless, honest, and at times painful search for truth, healing, and perspective in his own life, which has been influenced through a lifetime of helping others, reveals a universal wisdom that illuminates a path forward for all of us who seek peace in an increasingly complicated world. *Is Your Story Making You Sick?* is a rare gem!"

— Frances Causey, Emmy Award winning Director of
The Long Shadow and *Heist: Who Stole the American Dream?*

"How we heal is an ancient question. Dr. Mark Pirtle has devoted his life's work to exploring it. *Is Your Story Making You Sick?* highlights both ancient and newly developed techniques—supported by both research and his personal experience—to help readers heal from myriad stress illnesses and chronic disease. . . . This guide is a wonderful compendium for anyone interested in self-care and healing."

— Dr. Ann Marie Chiasson, MD, director of the
Fellowship in Integrative Medicine at the University of
Arizona's Andrew Weil Center for Integrative Medicine,
and author of *Energy Healing: the Essentials of Self-Care*

"Science increasingly tells us that the true biology of sickness far transcends the overly reductionist models and behaviors that drive much of modern medical practice. It is more and more apparent that the stories we tell ourselves have strong biological effects that can cause illness or aid in healing. Tackling this head-on, Mark Pirtle in *Is Your Story Making You Sick?* contributes invaluably to making these truths more widely available."

— Charles Raison, MD, co-author of
The New Mind-Body Science of Depression

"*Is Your Story Making You Sick?*, by Mark Pirtle, draws from the wisdom of many fields to provide roadmaps to health and development. You'll enjoy the stories, and benefit from any of the practices and insights that attract you in this far-reaching work."

— Keith Witt, PhD, author of
Integral Mindfulness and *Shadow Light*

"Mark Pirtle leads us on an exquisite journey through virtually all things that make us human and divine—separates them in their elegant granularity with colorful life stories, and then integrates them all together with both agility and grace. Included are practical processes that one can learn as well as the discovery of categories of self that most people never know are there. I highly recommend this book to serious readers who are interested in all phases of the self."

— Terri O'Fallon, PhD, founder of Stages International

"*Is Your Story Making You Sick?* shows that healing is possible by courageously transforming adversity into the path towards psychological growth."

— Eric Garland, PhD, LCSW, ; Distinguished Professor & Associate Dean for Research University of Utah College of Social Work and director if the Center on Mindfulness and Integrative Health Intervention Development

"We will never solve the epidemic of stress-related illness that is overburdening our healthcare system unless those who suffer learn and practice self-care. Although there is no replacement for the support of wise and kind people, individuals must discover within themselves healthier ways to cope with their challenges. That's the greatness of what Mark Pirtle's book is offering: a way for readers to become their own best therapists."

— Howard Glasser, creator of The Nurtured Heart Approach and Founder of the Nurtured Heart Institute

"In his breakthrough book *Is Your Story Making You Sick?*, Mark Pirtle teaches us how we can change deeply ingrained stories, thoughts, and behaviors, to heal our pain and re-make our life story. Pirtle's 'how-to' approach for skillful meditation is based in science and broken down into actionable steps and exercises. This book is truly life changing!"

— Karen Malkin, certified health & wellness coach, founder of Karen Malkin Health Counseling

"We are witnessing a remarkable resurgence of people searching for spiritual ways to heal their lives and be in service to the planet. That's what *Is Your Story Making You Sick?* is all about. Stories from our past anchor us to unhealthy relationships and ways of living. It not only hurts us individually but all of us collectively. There is a tremendous amount of hope to gain if we learn to attune and stay present to all life brings to us—both the joys and the challenges. Mark Pirtle inspires us to find our way back to our authentic selves and serve a larger mission."

— Sandra Ingerman, MA, shamanic teacher and author of
The Book of Ceremony and *The Hidden Worlds*

"*Is Your Story Making You Sick?* is one of those books you read when you want to understand how to heal trauma on a deeper level. Of course, traditional medicine can treat the symptoms. But working with the root causes and recovering one's soul is where true healing begins."

— Cheryl S. Sharp, MSW, exclusive consultant to the
National Council for Mental Wellbeing Trauma-Informed
Services and Suicide Prevention Efforts

"I highly recommend *Is Your Story Making You Sick?* to anyone who is interested in healing—body, mind, spirit, and soul. We are living at a time of challenge and transformation. To heal ourselves, our relationships, and the world we must change our stories. Mark Pirtle offers clear direction and guidance on how to do that. Asking the question, 'Is your story making you sick?' can be the beginning of your healing journey."

— Jed Diamond, PhD, LCSW, author of
*The Irritable Male Syndrome: Managing the Four Key Causes
of Depression and Aggression* and *12 Rules for Good Men*

"Affected as we are by the ripple effects of the systems in which we live, Mark Pirtle, in his book, *Is Your Story Making You Sick?* gifts us with an engaging, personal reflection on self-awareness, healing, and growth, for ourselves, our families, and a larger world."

— Frederic Craigie, PhD, visiting associate professor, Andrew Weil Center for Integrative Medicine, University of Arizona College of Medicine, and author of *Positive Spirituality in Health Care: Nine Practical Approaches to Pursuing Wholeness for Clinicians, Patients, and Health Care Organizations*

"Mark Pirtle's book is a powerful source of self-realization and healing. Drink deeply from it, craft a new character and narrative to change your story, and then change your life."

— Ryan Blair, founder of AlterCall and author of *Nothing to Lose, Everything to Gain*

"In his book, *Is Your Story Making You Sick?*, Mark Pirtle slides the camel through the eye of the needle, slipping complex information in through easy-to-read story telling. Honest, vulnerable, rich, and alive, Mark takes you on the ultimate journey of your own self-story, guides you through deeply human struggles, and leaves you standing on the precipice of human potential."

— Kim Barta, MA, co-founder of Stages International

"Mark Pirtle's book provides a thorough introduction to meditation, with step-by-step instructions on how to practice. By integrating stillness and self-reflection into your everyday life, you can heal negative thinking patterns and develop new healthier ones that can result in a happier life."

— Danét Palmer, host of the Yummy Way Podcast and author of *Coffee with the Divine: A Yummy Guide to Daily Miracles* and *Baptized by Love: How I Found Present Joy and Never Let It Go*

"The stories we tell ourselves about how drugs hijack the brain, thereby creating an addiction, allow us to ignore the true causes of distress. If the intervention isn't addressing root causes, then it's probably yet another fairytale. Dr Pirtle's book addresses the root causes of our pain."

— Carl L. Hart, PhD, Ziff Professor (psychology and psychiatry) at Columbia University, and author of *Drug Use for Grown-ups: Chasing Liberty in the Land of Fear*

"Is Your Story Making You Sick?" is an important book about mind-body connectedness. It explores the deeper causes of sickness beyond what is traditionally recognized in western medicine."

— Bruce Lipton, PhD, cellular biologist and author of *The Biology of Belief* and *Spontaneous Evolution*

IS YOUR

HEAL YOUR STORY

STORY

HEAL YOUR LIFE

MAKING

HEAL YOUR WORLD

YOU SICK?

Mark Farris Pirtle

© 2022 Mark Farris Pirtle

First Edition

Published in the United States of America

Lojong Publishing
2506 E. Drachman Street
Tucson, Arizona 85716

ISBN: 978-1-7377777-0-0

Library of Congress Control Number: 2021916809

Original Design, Font & Layout of Cover Image by Susanne Weihl
Cover Illustration by Nick Schaefer
Book Cover Design by ebooklaunch.com
Book Interior Design by Ampersand Bookery

All rights reserved. No part of this book may be used or reproduced by any means, graphic, electronic, or mechanical, including photocopying, recording, taping or by any information storage retrieval system without the written permission of the publisher except in the case of brief quotations embodied in critical articles and reviews.

To my dearest daughter Alana. You're there to see me when my story is making me sick, and when it's not. Thank you for your grace. Striving for the light to be your best dad is my one true calling.

CONTENTS

Introduction 1

PART 1: MEDITATION 101 17

Sacred Space 20
    Your Altar................................. 20
    Sacred Objects 21
    Seating Options 23
    Meditation Posture.................. 24
    Sitting Meditation 25

The Finer Points of Sitting Posture 27

Walking Meditation 29

Lying-Down Meditation 30

About Breathing 31

Time of Day 32

How Much and How Long? 33

Special Practices and Rituals 34

Preparatory Practice: Relaxation Breathing 37

Beginning a Mindfulness Meditation Practice...... 39

Set a Conscious Intention 41

Four-Step Transition 41

Breath Counting 43

Mental Noting and Labeling................... 44
Loving-Kindness Meditation 45
A Simple Heart-Centered
Loving-Kindness Practice 46
Cycle through This Five-Phase Process and
You're Meditating Perfectly 47

PART 2: IS YOUR STORY MAKING YOU SICK?........................55

Chapter 1: The "Effauses and Caufects" of Healthful Change................................. 57

Chapter 2: The Three Transcendentals 73

Chapter 3: All About Karma.................. 89

The Three Virtues of Mind 104
Four Virtues of Speech 104
Three Virtues of Body 106

Chapter 4: Bewegungsmuster.................109

Chapter 5: The Mind System 133

Chapter 6: Disrupted Development 163

Chapter 7: Is Your Story Making You Sick?......185

Chapter 8: Becoming SkillfullyAware 211

SkillfullyAware 219
Acceptance 221
Care.................................. 226

A Wish for a Higher Good 228
Becoming SkillfullyAware 229
Attention and Awareness 230
Three Domains of Awareness:
World, Body, Mind 231
In Truth, There Is Only One Whole Space
of Awareness 233
Six Objects of Attention 235
SkillfullyAware Spaces and Objects 238
   Space of the world. 238
   Space of the body 238
   Space of the mind 239
The SkillfullyAware Instructions 239
Five Fundamental Techniques of
Becoming SkillfullyAware 241
   1. Focus on Positive. 242
   2. Prime Ahead of Time 243
   3. Name It to Tame It 244
   4. Shift Open Stay 245
   5. Zooming 245
SkillfullyAware in Action. 247

Chapter 9: Slaying the Dragon 251

Chapter 10: Chasing Shadows 263

Know Thyself—the Many
Benefits of Shadow Work. 264
Shadow at the Boundaries .265

  Half of Shadow Work—Balancing
  Shadow Energies 272
  The Other Half of Shadow Work—Meeting
  Your Shadow 276

Chapter 11: Raising Your Window: the Concrete Tier 289
  1.0 Impulsive. 295
  1.5 Egocentric 300
  2.0 Rule-Oriented 305
  2.5 Conformist 309

Chapter 12: Raising Your Window: the Subtle Tier 315
  3.0 Expert 315
  3.5 Achiever. 322
  4.0 Pluralist. 330
  4.5 Strategist 337

Chapter 13: Raising Your Window: the Metaware Tier. 347
  5.0 Construct-Aware 348
  5.5 Transpersonal. 355
  6.0 Universal and 6.5 Illumined. 359

Epilogue. 369
Endnotes 377
Acknowledgements 387
About the Author 389

IS YOUR STORY MAKING YOU SICK?

INTRODUCTION

Sometimes, doing one right thing can magically change everything for the better. Ever heard of a trophic cascade?

A trophic cascade is a natural, unpredictable, and synergistic process of reformation that ripples through a system. A good example is what happened when wolves were reintroduced into Yellowstone Park. There were no wolves in Yellowstone's ecosystem for more than seventy years, and because they were absent those many decades, deer populations swelled. Whole areas of Yellowstone were almost entirely denuded of vegetation as deer spread into every corner of the park, overgrazing on grasses and saplings. The park's ecosystem was in decline, and most animal species were struggling to survive because the system in which they lived was sick and out of balance. Then the wolves were reintroduced.

The first unpredictable consequence of their reintroduction was that deer behavior immediately changed. Deer began avoiding specific areas of the park to evade wolf attacks. The tight valleys, gorges, and slot canyons became much too dangerous, as in those locations they were easy prey for the small bands of cooperative wolves. With no deer to graze on the small and delicate saplings, trees of all kinds began to sprout up and retake root. As soon as the forest reestablished itself, an array of bird species moved back in.

Not only did migratory and songbirds return, but so did beavers. Beavers require trees for food and shelter, so whole areas of the park that were previously inhospitable to beavers were now open again. The presence of beavers and their ponds provided food and habitats for otters, muskrats, ducks, fish, reptiles, amphibians, mollusks, and more.

The wolves also preyed on coyotes, thinning and balancing their populations as well. Consequently, the populations of rabbit and mice increased. More rodents drew in birds of prey. Weasels, foxes, and badgers also returned to repopulate their old niches in the park. The leftover carcasses of wolf predation became food for ravens and bald eagles. Additionally, bear populations also started to rise, due to the increasing abundance of wild berries and carrion.

Incredibly, reintroducing wolves even changed the geology of the park. The abundant regrowth of vegetation markedly reduced erosion, which improved the quality of the water. More important, the protective blanket of foliage caused rivers' banks to stabilize. The rivers meandered less, and channels formed and deepened. Those changes produced abundant pools, which further supported the industrious beavers. Ever more livable habitats were the by-product. Such awe-inspiring synergy was a further boon to flora and fauna of all kinds.

We humans live in a biopsychosocial ecosystem. By almost every measure, our system is as out of balance and sick as Yellowstone was without its wolves. The stress of these times is virtually unprecedented. Many of us were just treading water before the

COVID-19 hit. Since then, more of us have been pushed under. The Yellowstone example shows that all parts of a system connect to all other parts and that when one part is ill, a disease will spread. An out-of-balance ecosystem is a stressed and sick one.

Political unrest, climate crisis, ecosystem collapse, overpopulation, transgenerational poverty, racial inequality, social injustice—these and other system problems all arise out of our collective ignorance and inaction. We were suffering with all these issues well before the coronavirus pandemic of 2020. The COVID outbreak was just the next manifestation of the blight we were living through. But the virus was unique in that it forced us to isolate more, which worsened many people's anxiety and depression. Addictions flared across the world as people struggled to cope. Economies teetered on the brink of collapse. In so many ways, COVID pushed us to the edge.

But the virus was qualitatively different from every other global systemic problem to date. For the first time in human history, one challenge got all our attention. It tested whether we had the will and creativity to mobilize and do something about it. It's been astonishing how COVID put a focus on our collective pain. If there's a silver lining, let it be that many more of us wake up to our mutual interdependence. The solutions that will change the world for the better will be integral and systemic. Unless you wield the power of a president, you can't act on the larger system—it's too big—but that doesn't mean you can't do your part. You can, and if enough of us do, we will make a difference.

So, imagine opening your heart and mind to the idea of unleashing a "trophic cascade" in your life. None of these larger global issues are stopping us from creating just such a torrent of positivity. National parks are not the only places where the power of trophic cascades are felt. Trophic cascades are examples of the way all living systems behave.

Your mind-body is a living system. The family you grew up in is a living system. The culture and nation you come from is a living system. The economy in which you participate is a living system. The global biosphere is a living system. Systems nested within systems is the way the universe manifests itself, all the way up from the smallest particle to the most massive galactic clusters. The rules that govern large-scale systems like Yellowstone Park are also present and active in smaller systems like you, your family, your workplace, and your community.

A crucial point to make is that all systems are open to each other. For example, your family system directly influences your mind-body for better or for worse. That influence is also true of the people with whom you work. The influence adds up and flows up and through our economy and culture as well. We, as individuals, are not separate from the systems in which we live.

Human systems are interdependent. Positive and negative influences travel in both directions, up and down the chain. For example, let's say you want to improve your relationships. You realize that what you think, say, and do matters, so you set a conscious intention to be kinder. As a result, during the day, this intention reminds you to closely monitor your word choice and tone of voice when speaking to others. In the back of your mind, you also consciously filter what you say to amplify clarity and kindness. Because you do this, you positively influence the people with whom you interact. Because emotions are contagious, your consideration changes them, and they, in turn, are kinder in their subsequent interactions. From you, the positivity spreads outward and upward to affect a broader system.

Downstream, your kindness penetrates deep down into your mind-body system as well. A positive intention feels good. That good feeling turns into biochemicals in your body and brain, such as the "connection" chemicals serotonin, oxytocin, and endorphins. Thanks to open systems, every cell of your body is positively affected by your initial intention to improve your relationships.

All systems work this way, from physical systems like Yellowstone and your family unit to metaphysical systems of stories and emotion. Indeed, it was just such a system dynamic that led to the creation of this book.

My close friends know that I experienced emotional and physical trauma growing up. I was mostly ignorant of the havoc that trauma was wreaking as it worked its way through the system of my young life. Unconscious obsessions and compulsions drove my thoughts and behavior. In other words, I was blind to the signs and symptoms of the trauma, and there were many. If you live with pain long enough, such dysfunction can end up feeling normal, even when it isn't. The way we normalize our troubles is through the stories we tell ourselves.

I'm going to tell you a story now, the story that made me sick. In the '90s, I worked as a physical therapist and businessman. I owned a clinic, and by all outward measures, I was successful. But I also lived with a gaping maw of insecurity. Who I was and what I had were never good enough. Craving money and status as I did, I was perpetually on the lookout for more and better opportunities.

Seek and ye shall find, right? Providence graced me with an introduction to two people equal to me in opportunism. Drunk as we were on the dream of the even larger business we could build together, we divided the physical and intellectual assets three ways. What could go wrong?

We operated a national orthopedics education company and clinics in two states. Within two years, revenues increased by 1,000 percent. But behind-the-scenes resentments sparked and smoldered. None of us had the emotional maturity to work through our issues skillfully. Eventually, the partnership imploded. I went from having a net worth (on paper) of about three million dollars to being a net debtor. In addition to the business, I lost my title, savings, income stream, equity, reputation, and, most profoundly, my sense of who I was. The breakup left me lost, bitter, and consumed with venomous hate.

Have you ever tried to get to sleep while plotting someone's murder? Spoiler alert: it doesn't work. That's what I found myself doing in the weeks, months, and even years following what felt like the biggest betrayal of my life. The stickiness of that woeful story captured all of my attention. I was completely invested in it. How could I not endlessly ruminate on such a compelling narrative? After all, I was the main character.

In addition to becoming a raging insomniac, I eventually developed chronic pain, heart palpitations requiring hospitalization, and severe depression. To soothe myself, I picked up a few addictive behaviors, too. I was a total mess. My medicine cabinet overflowed with bottles of pills, but they offered me only marginal symptomatic relief.

It's impossible to recount how much time and effort I spent searching for healing by following the conventional medicine route. That fruitless pursuit was draining in so many ways. Then, after two full years of intense suffering, it wasn't a doctor but a movie that changed my life. Late one night while home alone, I turned to Netflix for consolation.

Have you seen *Forrest Gump*? If so, you might remember the white feather that floats freely on the breeze in both the opening and closing scenes. That symbol of providential serendipity sailed right over my head, but I did sit up and take notice of Lieutenant Dan. I saw in his story a reflection of my own. Like me, he had a preconceived plan for his life. He was also unwaveringly attached to his story line. Just like me, he was so utterly committed to it that when the script changed, it threw him into confusion and chaos. Years after Forrest carried him out of the jungle, Lieutenant Dan found himself sitting in a wheelchair, alone and drunk, locked behind the closed door of a dank apartment. Worse, he was mad as hell! Watching the movie, I realized I was Lieutenant Dan. That night, I cried myself to sleep.

The next morning, I woke up and put on my running shoes. Running was the way I coped. To that point in my life, I'd never known how to work with emotions effectively. I always just ran when I needed some headspace. That morning was no different. As I write this some twenty years later, I want to convey the total implausibility of what happened to me on that fateful run. I was forty years old at the time and had been running a few times a week since high school, so I'd logged many thousands of runs.

But that day was different. As I ran I began plotting my ex-partner's demise, not even thinking about the movie I'd watched the night before, when suddenly a white feather fell out of the sky and hit me right in the chest.

It is exceedingly rare to see a turning point in one's life as it occurs. I'd been bouncing along the bottom for so long I'd given in to hopelessness. But there it was, the pivot point delivered to me with grace and irony—knocked *conscious* by a feather. I finally got the message! Indeed, until that feather so thoroughly penetrated my fixation, I'd never been able to see how my story was making me sick.

My story *had* me, instead of me having it. But the feather changed all that. I finally saw that the incessant rumination made me an accomplice to my own self-destruction. Before, I wanted to blame my ex-partners, but I couldn't anymore. The feather revealed how I'd kept myself stuck by repeatedly indulging that victimizing story of injustice.

Tears erupted. Overtaken by sobs, I hid my face and staggered home. But the message got through! From that moment on, I knew that pills and procedures weren't the path forward. Instead, the universe was calling me on a journey of self-discovery and reclamation.

The first thing I did when I got home was to plan a trip. (I can't call it a vacation, because I still didn't have a job.) I needed the perspective that fresh scenery provides. As it happened, I ended up in a New Age bookstore in Flagstaff, Arizona. Intuiting that I needed to learn to work with my mind, I bought a book on meditation. I credit this book with starting me on the path of using meditation and self-reflection to peer into the subtle workings of my mind. Fast-forward twenty years, doing just a few skillful things consistently, I've cultivated practices that have yielded some pretty excellent results. These practices will work for you, too.

So, what is this book about exactly? Most people think that because I teach meditation and mindfulness, this book is going to be about how to use meditation and mindfulness therapeutically—so you feel better. Sure, this book will help you learn to meditate and be mindful. If you diligently engage in the practices I describe, positive change and healing will undoubtedly take root in your life. But feeling better is not the sole purpose of this book. The objective is broader than just helping you change and heal yourself, although we want to start there.

The larger purpose of this book is to create a positive system effect that ripples out from your mind and heart to not only positively affect your mental and physical health but also your relationships and your local community. When added to the good works of others, it will all amplify to positively affect our culture, political system, economy, and eventually the global ecosystem. That's the big-picture purpose of this book.

I realize this may sound aspirational, grandiose, and maybe even delusional, but what I describe is a potential butterfly effect accomplished by leveraging the power of living systems. Connected systems can amplify feedback to create far-reaching and unimaginable effects. If you, I, and enough other people start fundamentally changing our thoughts and behaviors, that collective action will modify what we value, which will, in turn, transform how we feel. Feeling better, we'll start to relate differently to ourselves, others, and the world. Such a virtuous re-valuation will also change how we raise our children, how we make our food choices, how we use energy, the way we do business, how we vote, what we purchase, and how we create and spend our human capital in every imaginable way. When that happens, we'll create a tipping point where the whole system transforms for the better, just like what happened in Yellowstone.

So, where do we start? What's the one thing we could all do that could initiate a global positive trophic cascade analogous to reintroducing wolves to Yellowstone? Quite unbelievably, there is an answer to that question. The most important thing to learn and practice right now is *attunement*. "What is attunement?" you may ask. My friend and colleague Keith Witt defines it this way: "The act and art of connecting to yourself and others with acceptance and caring intent, and always doing so in service of a higher good."[1]

Attunement has gotten a lot of attention lately in positive-psychology and conscious-parenting circles. Most of us have had the experience of someone attuning to us. You know it because you can feel it. When someone genuinely attunes to you, he or she carefully tracks and aligns with your body language. They show a sincere interest in what you have to say. They monitor their motivations, so as to keep them clear and clean. They reflect your words back to you and ask open-ended questions. They do all that because they genuinely want to connect with you.

When people are in attunement with each other, they relax and engage. It happens down at the subconscious cellular level, too—your body feels safe, which enables you to drop your defenses and soften. That rarified state of resonance with another person opens all concerned to growth and positive influence. Attunement, done skillfully and by enough people, could initiate system-wide effects that could amplify into something like a trophic cascade.

Another way you can attune is by spending time in nature. Have you ever stood in an open landscape and sensed the paradox of expansive intimacy you share with it? You're not only a part of it, you come from it. At such times, all boundaries between you and Mother Nature fall away, and your stories can't help but drop away, too. There's nothing but presence. That's also attunement.

Attunement not only feels good but is also vital for health and well-being. Humans are utterly hardwired for connection. Of all the factors associated with poor health outcomes, isolation and loneliness top the list. Even cigarettes won't kill you as fast as disconnecting from yourself, loved ones, and nature. For this reason, your life won't go well, in any respect, unless you learn to better attune to yourself and others.

It seems reasonable to assume that some people drawn to this type of book came from families that did not prioritize emotional skillfulness. If that's true for you, it's also reasonable to assume that when you were a child, your parents and others didn't provide you with adequate attunement. Equally likely, as an adult, you might be suffering some downstream adverse system effects involving your health and relationships. What's left for those of us who didn't receive competent attunement as children? We must begin the process of examining the stories we tell ourselves, which includes the act of attuning to, and compassionately re-parenting, ourselves now.

You *can* recover your health and restore your relationships. But it must start with attunement. In practical terms, this means becoming ever more aware of the subtle but powerful emotional energy that subconsciously drives all of your judgments, moods, and reactions. For example, anger is a powerfully destructive emotion. It can set a person on fire. Lacking requisite attunement, people often don't recognize their simmering anger before they spread it onto others. People who learn to attune to their internal emotional states can gain influence over this potent emotion. Every sort of emotionally charged circumstance is workable when mindful attunement skillfully guides your responses. Attuning is how you'll learn to make sense of and rewrite your story so that instead of making you sick, it becomes the basis for emergent health and happiness.

Showing up with acceptance and caring intent in service of a higher good can cause all the hot-button issues in your life to cool. Soon, attuning to yourself and others will become second nature. Once you learn to mindfully attune to yourself while at the same time approaching any situation or person with loving-kindness, your stories will lose their power. Their grip on you will loosen, and you can sit back and watch goodness begin to blossom.

This book comes in two parts. The first is a basic how-to on beginning a meditation practice. If you're feeling well enough to start meditating, I'll teach you to do it skillfully, which has the potential to accelerate your spiritual development. The second part is the meat of the book. There are thirteen chapters in Part 2. Each chapter explores one big idea that relates to mindful attunement. At first glance, some of the chapter topics may seem quite divergent from attunement. But from a higher perspective, especially once you've read the whole book and put the entire program together, their connection to attunement will become abundantly clear.

Nothing comes from nothing; everything is constructed of other things. In other words, before anything can exist, there must be the causes and conditions necessary for its existence. For this reason, Chapter 1, "The Effauses and Caufects of Healthful Change," takes a systems approach to broadly explain what actions you'll need to take before you can expect more health and happiness to arise in your future.

I will detail "The Three Transcendentals"—beauty, goodness, and truth—in Chapter 2. Be advised that enhanced attunement to and amplification of beauty, goodness, and truth are the foundational activities of your reclamation project.

Chapter 3 is titled "All about Karma." In it, I set the record straight. Karma is not something that happens to you. Instead, karma comes *from* you. There really is a moral dimension to healing and feeling better. Also in that chapter, I outline the ten karmic actions that will give you the biggest bang for your spiritual buck.

In Chapter 4, "Bewegungsmuster," not only will you learn some incredibly long German words, but I'll "map" the science of living systems onto karma to strengthen the thesis: that doing good outwardly leads to feeling better inwardly.

In Chapter 5, "The Mind System," you will learn what mind is, how it functions, and how to influence it. That's exceedingly important information given that everything you experience arises in, cycles through, and is colored by your mind.

In Chapter 6, "Disrupted Development," I illustrate how early childhood trauma leads to stress and illness later in life. To awaken your empathy, and also so the science hits home, I recount the story of "Sophie" as a cautionary tale. Never give up on yourself!

In Chapter 7, "Is Your Story Making You Sick?" you'll learn about Jim, a highly sensitive artist who, despite his innate penchant for overthinking, learns to cope in ways that enrich both himself and his patrons.

In Chapter 8, "Becoming SkillfullyAware," I teach you the science and practice of the mindful attunement method I created and practice. Not only will you learn how to balance your awareness and attention, but you'll also learn five simple interrelated, evidence-based techniques that, when practiced together, will markedly accelerate your process.

Navigating toward a truer version of yourself is neither easy nor effort-free. At times you will need to exercise some aggression. There are thresholds ahead you'll need to pass through. Some will demand a pound of flesh. Chapter 9, "Slaying the Dragon," explains why it's imperative you know this, so you can prepare mentally and physically for the challenges to come.

The bulk of the work along the spiritual path is making the unconscious conscious. That requires acknowledging, working through, and integrating shadow aspects of yourself. Chapter 10, "Shadow Dancing," explains much of the process of shadow work and how re-scripting your story fits into the process.

The last three chapters of the book explain how a person's perspective influences their worldview and, to some extent, their story. I use the metaphor of looking out an apartment window: the view from the ground floor is limited, whereas the view from the penthouse apartment offers much peace and perspective. If changing and healing are your goals, then understanding the approximate level of the window through which you view yourself and the world can help you to focus on practices that are appropriate for your level. Additionally, just reading about the stages of consciousness can have the effect of raising the window. So, relish those three chapters.

In the pages that follow, I intend to write candidly about my efforts to clean up, wake up, and grow up. If I'm to persuade you to remake your life into a spiritual practice, you deserve to know that it's not been easy for me either. That said, I wouldn't change the past for anything. Growing into a better version of myself has been more than worth the effort. Now, no matter the challenges I face, I am resourced with psycho-emotional skills that help me cope. I still have pain in my life, but I don't spiral downward anymore. Thus I am as emotionally resourced as a person can be, which enables me to handle the pain without making it worse. It's a gift I'm truly grateful for.

My hope is to provide you with a broad and versatile tool kit for transformation that can remake your life, like it did mine. This book will help you explore, challenge, and begin to rewrite your story. When you do, you'll unleash the cascading magic of systemic changes in your life. I invite you to read on.

PART 1

Meditation 101

"Meditation dissolves the walls unconsciousness has built."

Sadhguru

Why meditate? The answer is simple. Everything you experience happens within the space of your mind. Understanding what mind is and how it works requires specific training. Meditation is that training. The meditation technique you'll learn in this book, Shamata-Vipassana, is also referred to as mindfulness meditation. When done by the right person the right way and in a favorable setting, it will reveal both the nature of your mind and how it functions. That's important because once you familiarize yourself with your mind's inner workings, you'll also begin to better understand how to effect personal change and healing.

But be warned: skillful meditation undertaken with the intention of deepening your understanding and influence over your mind is, by its nature, an extremely subtle activity. With meditation, missteps are easy to make, which is why it's especially important that anyone unfamiliar with the practice start off on the right foot. So, before you jump right into it, a word of caution: mindfulness meditation is not right for everyone.

Mindfulness meditation focuses the mind. In doing so it shines a light on what is already there, in the mind. Therefore, if you are currently experiencing extreme stress or feeling psycho-emotionally unstable, the hyper-focus of mindfulness meditation may cause you to feel worse.[2] It's not that mindfulness meditation cannot help—it very well might—but to be safe, anyone suffering from any intense behavioral health challenge should first learn and practice mindfulness meditation in a supervised setting, with the support of a well-trained teacher.

Very broadly, if you are currently experiencing acute distress, which prohibits you from observing your thoughts and feelings with a reasonable amount of emotional detachment, this is probably not the right time for you to start a mindfulness meditation practice. If you're still unsure about whether you should start practicing mindfulness meditation, review the questions below. If you answer yes to any of them, please don't start a mindfulness meditation practice without the support of a trained professional in a supervised setting.[3]

- Have you had a manic or hypomanic episode within the past six months?
- Are you currently self-harming or experiencing suicidal thoughts?
- Are you currently drinking a lot of alcohol or using other drugs?
- Are you currently depressed to such an extent that it is difficult for you to manage your everyday affairs?

- Are you currently grieving to the point where you are overwhelmingly preoccupied by it?
- Are you currently suffering from severe anxiety, or panic disorder?
- Are you currently under care for psychosis, borderline personality disorder, or PTSD?
- Are you currently suffering with, or being treated for, *any* other intensely preoccupying psycho-emotional condition?
- Do you have a history of brain trauma or suffer from a seizure disorder?

I hope I didn't scare you away. Indeed, studies show that the vast majority of people struggling with stress and chronic illness are psychologically well enough to start a modest mindfulness meditation practice and that they derive significant benefits from it.[4, 5, 6]

Raising your awareness of the inner workings of your conscious experience will help you better attune to yourself, others, and the world. That's why I'm encouraging readers to learn and practice mindfulness meditation.

If you're certain you can safely handle learning to sit and watch your thoughts and sensations without getting carried away by them, give it a go. If not, don't dismay. There is another powerful meditation practice that poses no known psychological risks yet may help alleviate some of the various negative symptoms associated with the conditions mentioned above.[7] That meditation practice is referred to as loving-kindness meditation, or *metta* practice. I'll teach you that meditation, too. The choice is yours—mindfulness, loving-kindness, or both. Whatever works for you.

But before you can properly begin practicing either type of meditation, let me answer some basic questions about starting a meditation practice. Let's begin with the question of where to meditate.

SACRED SPACE

If you want to begin to transform your life through daily spiritual practice, the simplest and most tangible way to start is by seeking out and dedicating a space in your home for your nascent practice. In this way, you immediately create something real in the world—an actual place for the new you to come into being. I firmly believe that this first step is imperative if you want to keep a consistent meditation practice going over the long haul. The space you choose should ideally be relatively quiet, uncluttered, allow for privacy, and have a spiritual "feel." You will know it when you see/feel it. Your sacred space should call you to it.

EXERCISE 1

Before reading any further, walk around your house and begin to imagine where you might create a sacred space where you'll come every day to sit, read, pray, and meditate.

Your Altar

This piece of furniture can come in many forms, shapes, and sizes. And it's perfectly okay for you to change your mind and allow it to evolve over time. At this early stage, do not pour every last ounce of your energy into getting just the right thing. The point is to start while you're feeling inspired. My first altar was downright inelegant. It was a small prefabricated wooden bookshelf. That suited me just fine for a few years, but as it happens, now my altar is a handmade antique low-top Chinese table. I purchased it at an Asian trader's shop, but I didn't consciously go looking for it; it just showed up when the time was right. That is the way it can happen for you, too. Your altar may evolve as you do. The altar should be the right height, about mid-belly, for a meditator sitting on a cushion, or higher if you are planning on meditating while sitting in a chair. Make sure your altar has space enough on top to place several sacred objects as well.

EXERCISE 2

Wander through your house again. Does a piece of furniture you already own seem right to use as your first altar? If so, will it fit well in the sacred space you have chosen? Again, it is a feel thing. As a last resort, and if there is nothing that immediately calls to you, go on an outing to a secondhand store. Look for a piece of furniture that is a close match to what you're picturing in your mind.

Sacred Objects

Here's where this process gets fun. Sacred objects are objects you declare to be unique, significant, and spiritually relevant to you. These objects sanctify your altar and set the spiritual tone for your space. In that regard, the sacred objects you choose to put on your altar will conjure feelings of love, connection, nostalgia, sacredness, safety, comfort, and belonging. Some may, of course, symbolize your highest spiritual aspirations. Because of that, make sure they are personal. Pick objects that feel right to *you*. Avoid worrying about what others might want or think. Remember, this is your space and no one else's. Feel out objects that carry with them spiritual energy that enlivens *you*. You sanctify your spiritual place with these objects, and they in turn bid you to come and sit.

Crosses, statues of Buddha, rosary and mala beads, or other religious symbols may immediately spring to mind, but I encourage you not to stop with the obvious religious iconography. Many people are also inclined to place pictures on their altar. The subjects can range from happy times to loved ones living or departed to spiritual teachers or sacred places. My altar holds many sacred rocks, feathers, and other personal treasures as well. I have a rock from Omaha Beach, Normandy, France. It is one of my most sacred possessions. Every time I look at that rock, it reminds me that the enjoyments of my life are dependent on the sacrifice of others. Family heirlooms or any emotionally and spiritually moving objects have a place on your altar.

EXERCISE 3

Now go treasure-hunting. Spend some time poring through photo albums, drawers, closets, and memorabilia.

> *Find those things that will most inspire you to grow, change, and heal, and then bring them back to your altar and arrange them in an artful way. Enjoy.*

Seating Options

Meditators need a place to sit. Seating accommodations vary widely, as do individual meditators' meditation styles and physical capacity. If you think you want to start meditating by sitting in a cross-legged position, the mats and cushions you will want to check out are zabutons and zafus. Keep in mind that these vary in price, material construction, thickness, height, and comfort. Your ultimate choice will come down to personal preference.

When I started meditating, I knew I could not sit comfortably cross-legged even for five minutes. I gave up the idea of a zafu immediately. Instead, I chose what is called a seiza bench. Later, as I sat more and became used to cross-legged sitting, I switched to sitting on a small zafu made of buckwheat hulls. Please understand, though, that you won't find anything perfectly comfortable. I think the meditation masters of old planned it this way. The discomforts that you will inevitably experience during meditation teach patience and equanimity. But at the same time, do your best to find seating that allows you to meditate as comfortably as possible.

Meditating in a chair is a perfectly acceptable option, too. If you do choose to meditate in a chair, it is essential to pick a firm, straight-back chair. It can have a cushion but only a modest one. If the chair is too doughy and comfortable, you will sink into it and fall fast asleep. Try to sit up straight and avoid leaning back against the backrest. This will aid in keeping your mind bright and alert as you meditate.

EXERCISE 4

Now get on the Internet and start researching meditation-seating options. Search for "meditation supplies," "zabuton," "zafu," and/or "seiza bench." If you know of a meditation center nearby, stop in and sit on their cushions or benches. You will want to be comfortable, but remember—no cushion, bench, or seat is perfectly comfortable. Make the choice that works best for you.

Meditation Posture

The three basic meditation postures are sitting, walking, and lying down. These positions vary in terms of enhancing concentration, mental clarity, and wakefulness. I'll explain each of these in turn. If you are a beginner, and especially if you are coming to meditation because of a stress illness, give yourself a little leeway. In the beginning, make sure to account for your present condition. Your comfort is important. You will find it harder to focus and benefit from the meditation if you are too uncomfortable. But also realize that meditating is naturally relaxing. If you are too comfortable, because you are slouching or lying down, you will probably struggle to concentrate and instead fall asleep. Meditating is a "middle way" practice, meaning you must try to find the balance between the two extremes of comfort and discomfort. In all of the following postures, try to find the middle between too rigid and too relaxed.

Sitting Meditation

The sitting posture is what most readily springs to mind when one thinks of formal meditation. Meditators the world over sit still because stillness offers two distinct benefits: it aids alertness and supports tranquility. Alertness and tranquility foster increased clarity and concentration. As mentioned above, sitting can be done either in a cross-legged position or seated. If you are going to sit with crossed legs, here are your choices:

BURMESE STYLE—The meditator's ankles do not cross in this position. Instead, the legs are folded one in front of the other, and the shins rest comfortably on the mat. Your bottom and two shins form a tripod, with the weight distributed evenly between each. This is my preferred position.

QUARTER LOTUS—The meditator crosses their legs at the ankles, and each foot fits comfortably under the opposite thigh

HALF LOTUS—In this position, the meditator puts one foot on top of their opposite thigh while the other foot rests underneath

FULL LOTUS—This is the classic hard-core meditator's posture, with both feet placed on top of the opposite thigh. If you are super-flexible or totally into pain, this is the posture for you!

THE FINER POINTS OF SITTING POSTURE

- If you're using a meditation cushion, sit with your hips higher than your knees. Go for an upright, relaxed back posture, with your pelvis tipped slightly forward. Sitting that way will allow unrestricted belly breathing. If in a chair, uncross your legs and put your feet flat on the floor. Whether sitting on a cushion or chair, avoid slouching.
- Position your arms slightly away from your torso while at the same time keeping them relaxed. Holding the arms this way helps to control sweating. Relax your shoulders and allow your arms to hang in a natural position.

- Place your hands facing either up or down on your thighs, or in a "mudra" (sacred position). The "cosmic" mudra places the back of the right hand in the palm of the left while creating what looks like an arch, with the tips of the thumbs touching over the top. Thumb-touching this way is a handy mindfulness feedback device. If you get tired and lose focus, the bottom will fall out of your mudra, which then alerts you to energize your mind. In this way, mindfully maintaining awareness of your mudra helps to keep you alert.

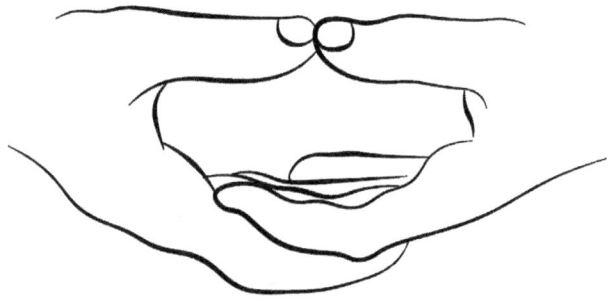

- Hold your head upright, but tuck your chin ever so slightly downward. The relative position of your chin enables you to find the right balance between mental dullness and overactivity. Lowering your chin calms the mind, while raising it increases mental energy. If your mind is racing, dip your chin. On the other hand, if you find yourself falling asleep, raise your chin.
- Keep your jaw relaxed. You may hold your lips closed or just slightly opened, whichever works best for you. Touch

the tip of your relaxed tongue against the back of your front two teeth and soft palate.
- Depending on your choice of a meditation object—breath, a candle, a mantra, etc.—you may close, halfway open, or fully open your eyes. In all cases, however, relax the muscles of the face and eyes. When meditating with the eyes open, allow yourself to blink naturally.

WALKING MEDITATION

The Theravadin Buddhist tradition of Southeast Asia is known for emphasizing walking meditation. But mindful movement is also found in other Asian spiritual traditions like yoga, tai chi, qigong, archery, and Zen. The aim of all of these practices is to increase a practitioner's mindfulness while in motion.

A walking meditation begins with standing. Notice the slight automatic effort your body makes to keep you erect and balanced. Notice, also, what happens to these natural righting responses when you close your eyes. Be still and relax while standing. Breathe into your belly. After half a dozen centering breaths, begin to walk slowly. At first, bring all of your attention to your feet and ankles. Walking slowly and smoothly can be challenging. If you find it so, see if you can become curious about the process of economizing your effort. Move smoothly, consciously, like a cat creeping. As you get more deeply concentrated, become aware of your calves, knees, and upper legs. Feel the fact that slow, smooth motion requires coordination and concentration. Keep your breath relaxed and in your belly. Arms and shoulders participate in the movement only minimally. Hands are traditionally held together, clasped at the waist, either in the front or behind the back. The head faces downward with eyes trained on the ground a few feet ahead to limit distracting sights. Focus your attention both inward on thoughts and sensations and outward on sights and sounds. Most walking meditators find a path or track that repeats itself and then walk it over and over.

LYING-DOWN MEDITATION

If pain or some other physical limitation prevents you from sitting, a lying-down meditation is a viable option. Do it by lying on your back with your knees bent. The slight effort it takes to keep your knees together will aid in keeping you alert and awake. No promises, however. Lying-down meditation often results in the meditator's falling blissfully asleep.

I enjoy doing another variation of the traditional lying-down meditation. I start meditating every time I get into bed at night or if I wake up in the middle of the night. I also frequently meditate just after waking in the morning, when still resting in bed. Meditating as I lie down to sleep often helps me fall asleep more quickly. I think it also promotes a deeper sleep. Late night and early morning lying-down meditations increase the likelihood of my having a lucid dream, and meditating at these times also helps me to remember my dreams. You'll find you notice other incredibly interesting subconscious activity you wouldn't normally have been aware of. I do these lying-down meditations positioned on either my back or my sides.

ABOUT BREATHING

If you are sitting and meditating, keep your back straight and your pelvis tipped slightly forward. This posture helps you breathe, without restriction, all the way down into your belly. If your chest rises, it should do so only at the very end of each in-breath. At the start of a particular meditation, you may find it helpful to count slowly to six on each in-breath and to eight or more on each out-breath. Set a goal of making each cycle last twelve or more seconds. Then pause at the end of each full expiration. Focus on the stillness. Carefully watch the turn of each breath. Then, with as little conscious control as possible, let your body initiate the next in-breath. In other words, place your awareness at the precise point where your body seems to regulate itself. I call this way of breathing "relaxation breathing." It will help concentrate and relax you; it can also be done lying down. More on relaxation breathing later.

After consciously breathing slowly, lightly, and deeply for a few minutes, allow the rate and depth of your breathing to regulate itself. You may find that your breath becomes very shallow at that point, and that is okay. Quiet, shallow breathing will strengthen your concentration. The subtlety of changing breath sensations at the nose makes it an excellent meditation object. In fact, watching one's breath sensations at the nose is by far the most traditional and favored of all meditation objects.

TIME OF DAY

Students ask me about this element of practice all the time. "Is it best to meditate in the morning? What about before bed? Is it okay if I do not meditate at the same time every day?" Yes, yes, and yes. The point is to find a way to meditate every day. If you can, try to create a little structure around your practice. Try not to let the chaos of your daily life keep you from practicing. Practice in spite of it—because of it!

Morning is indeed a fabulous time to meditate. The mind is fresh after a good night's sleep, so sitting in a quiet spiritual space is a great way to start your day. However, mornings can also be a time of intense household activity, especially if you have young children. If that is your case, maybe the time that works best for you is late evening when all the kids have gone to bed. I like both times. There is a vast brightness to the mind in the morning, but I enjoy experiencing the natural energy of thoughts and sensations flowing through my mind-body at the end of the day as well. Meditating at night, before bed, is also an excellent way to allow that buzz of the day to run itself through and out of your nervous system. That way, you do not take all that turmoil to bed with you.

There is also the option of learning to meditate during the normal activities of your daily life. Some of the practices you will learn in this book allow you to do just that. Modern life is stressful. Taking your practice with you "on the road," so to speak, will bring the greatest benefits. Practicing in daily life is called *informal practice*. Formal practice, on a cushion, in your home allows mental clarity and concentration to develop. The goal of formal practice is to "awaken" to such an extent that you are informally practicing all the time. Informal practice allows for emotional regulation and wise action. Both forms of training are necessary and beneficial. However, if you are just beginning your meditation practice, there is no substitute for a formal sit each day. Formal practice is important, but it will never be urgent. If it's not on your calendar, you'll forget to do it. For that reason, schedule it so it becomes a habit.

HOW MUCH AND HOW LONG?

When considering how much time to meditate, it is helpful to think of meditation as medicine. As you know, all medication must be taken in the proper dose for it to have any effect. The same holds true for meditation, meaning one must practice with enough frequency and duration to make a difference. Meditating once a day is adequate, and fifteen to thirty minutes seems to be a sufficient duration. But to many people new to meditation practice, fifteen to thirty minutes seems too big an expectation, so they don't even try. If that's you, do this: Imagine sitting for ten minutes. How does that feel? If ten minutes still feels too long, what about five? Still too long? How about a minute or two? What I'm trying to get you to do is find the minimum amount of time that seems doable so that you can at least get started. The first hurdle to get over is making meditation practice a daily habit. If you choose to sit for only two minutes, repeat that practice at least six times a day. Meditating for twelve minutes a day for eight weeks is the minimum amount of time needed to grow wisdom-producing gray matter in your brain.

Once you're meditating daily and the practice is feeling familiar and doable, if you feel like extending the time, go for it. Ultimately, you'll want to increase your time to get to the fifteen-to-thirty-minute minimum dose. But if in the beginning a few minutes is all you can muster, give it your all. As soon as you sit, generate a determined and focused attitude, like you are about to study for an important exam. One of my teachers, Shinzen Young, says to "start on a dime." What he means is that as soon as you settle into your posture, become aware, pick an object, and be mindful.

As you progress in your practice, you may find yourself sitting for an hour or more, sometimes more than once a day. If that happens, great. Of course, be flexible in how you respond to the demands of your life. But remember—if you want to generate a positive change in your life, formal practice must find its way to the upper half of your priority list.

SPECIAL PRACTICES AND RITUALS

Religious practitioners from all around the world make widespread use of rituals. Participating in formal ceremonies exemplifies one's personal intention to take careful and deliberate steps to grow spiritually. The key concept is that it is *personal*. Rituals are for your benefit—to help you change your thoughts and actions. They are meant to remind you of your intention to evolve and put that intention into action.

Some teachers advise their students to keep their spiritual practice private. That is good advice. Keeping one's practice to oneself supports evolution beyond one's ego. It also saves explaining and justifying your process to others. Not everyone will understand. Or worse, some people may feel the need to question or admonish you for your spiritual choices. I am not saying that if you live with someone safe and supportive that you keep your practice a secret. Your spiritual practice may be something that you begin to develop and share with someone else. If that happens, it is a beautiful thing. I wish that for all my readers. But if you find yourself living with people who don't support your meditation practice, keep it to yourself.

The following are a few common rituals that you may want to include in your practice.

> OFFERINGS—Offerings are your gift to the Divine. There are many forms of traditional offerings, such as flowers, milk, pure water, fruit, leaves, and rice. If you are inclined to make offerings a part of your practice, create space on your altar for that purpose. When presenting your offering each day, consider giving it with a sense of gratitude and a wish to open up and be led to your divine purpose—as in "not my will but yours."

> PRAYER AND MANTRA—Prayer is universally associated with religious and spiritual practice. Mantra, or

chanting, is an abbreviated form of prayer. The meaning of the ancient Sanskrit word *mantra* is a sound, syllable, word, or group of words that are considered capable of "creating transformation." Every religious tradition employs prayer, chanting, or mantra as part of its devotional practices. Prayers and mantras have become part of my practice as well.

While on retreat at Chenrezig, a Tibetan Buddhist Center in Eudlo, Australia, I was introduced to many Tibetan prayers. I was impressed by their thoughtfulness, breadth, and depth, so I brought a prayer booklet home with me, intending to create a personal and comprehensive spiritual guidance system. I used those Tibetan prayers as a template. Then I arranged them in what seemed a logical order, modifying them slightly to reflect my spiritual inclinations better. It took me a while, but eventually I memorized them. Now I enjoy reciting the whole collection of prayers, either as part of my formal practice or at other times during my day when I feel the need for a spiritual tune-up. If you're interested, I'm happy to share my revision of those Tibetan prayers with you. Just contact me through my website.

ROSARY OR MALA BEADS—A familiar symbol of Catholicism is the beaded rosary. Malas are the Buddhist analogue of these Christian prayer beads. In each case, people use them to count prayers, chants, or mantras. Prayer counting and strings of beads are not confined to the Christian and Buddhist faiths, however. Jews, Hindus,

Taoists, and Muslims also use strands of beads to count prayers, chants, and mantras. The physical act of counting with beads can produce a high state of concentration and cause a sense of peace to arise in the spiritual aspirant.

PREPARATORY PRACTICE: RELAXATION BREATHING

After setting up your sacred space and before you start practicing mindfulness or loving-kindness meditation, it's imperative you learn a proper preparatory breath practice. The habit of breath awareness has the potential to transform your life all by itself! I cannot overstate the importance of breath awareness throughout your day. Simply become aware of your breath and regulate it by breathing slowly, lightly, and deeply. A number of best-selling books have been dedicated to this topic alone.[8, 9]

Breathing slowly, lightly, and deeply through your nose produces many positive health benefits, from quickening lymph drainage (filtering toxins) to causing a tranquilizing heart/brain response (lowering heart rate and blood pressure). It can reduce pain as well.

I call the breath practice you are about to learn relaxation breathing. You can relaxation-breathe lying down, sitting, or standing. If you're sitting or standing, do so with your back straight and your pelvis tipped slightly forward. Tipping your pelvis forward will allow each breath to naturally flow without restriction down into your belly.

Relaxation breathing is slow, light, and deep. Each breath cycle should last longer than twelve seconds. What you're trying to do is breathe five or fewer times per minute. To start, simply exhale all of the air in your lungs. As you do, you'll want to feel your belly pulling in, toward your spine. Don't over-force it, but do your best to empty your lungs of air. Then allow the natural impulse to breathe to take over. You should feel a "bounce" of air streaming back into your belly once you start the inhale. But after the bounce, control the in-breath a bit—slow and light. Also, breathe only through your *nose*. See if you can make the inhalation last four to six seconds. But don't try too hard and over-fill your lungs. Your belly should expand, but your chest not so much. Be mindful that you don't exaggerate the inhalation and engage your secondary breathing muscles in your upper chest and neck. Over-breathing like that can cause you to feel anxious. So, nice and easy. This is *relaxation* breathing, after all.

Then at the turn of the breath again, watch it, and with as little conscious control as possible, let your body initiate the next exhalation. Slow it down. The exhalation can last longer than the inhalation. Breathing this slowly, you may feel like you're on the edge of oxygen debt. Don't make breathing this way uncomfortable. Simply put your awareness at the precise point where your body seems to regulate itself. Another thing I do when I relaxation-breathe is put a slight smile on my face. Doing that amplifies the pleasure of the practice.

Whatever type of meditation you do, mindfulness or loving-kindness, start your session with this breathing technique. It will help to concentrate your mind and relax your body. Just a few minutes of relaxation breathing is sufficient. Afterward, you may choose to allow the rate and depth of your breathing to regulate itself. You may find that your breath becomes shallow at that point, and that is okay. Quiet, shallow nose breathing will strengthen your concentration. The subtlety of breath sensations at the nose makes them an excellent meditation object.

Last, when you are not formally meditating, see if you can bring mindful attention to your breath as much as possible throughout your day. Let relaxation breathing be a go-to practice that keeps you attuned to your body and emotions. Endeavor to breathe through your nose only. As many authors and fitness gurus have said, the nose is for breathing and the mouth is for eating.

BEGINNING A MINDFULNESS MEDITATION PRACTICE

Search Google Scholar for "benefits of mindfulness meditation" and you'll get more than 100,000 results. Indeed, in the past few decades there has been an explosion of research documenting the mental and physical benefits of the practice. It's almost incomprehensible that just sitting and watching your breath can reduce physical pain, increase immune function, decrease anxiety and depression, increase your sense of well-being, and lead to greater happiness and emotional self-regulation. But it's true. Why? Because when you practice mindfulness meditation you balance the right and left hemispheres of your brain and activate and enhance brain regions associated with attention, self-awareness, emotional self-regulation, and decision-making. At the same time, you dampen activity in brain areas associated with emotional reactivity. Your whole brain-body system benefits from attuning to yourself in this way.

On the surface, mindfulness meditation seems like a reasonably uncomplicated activity—just sit and watch the breath. As you develop more skill as a meditator, however, the complexity of the activity ramps up quite a bit.

Very basically, a person starts mindfulness meditation by attempting to hold their attention as still as possible while maintaining an open awareness. As you balance your attention and awareness, you also open yourself, nonjudgmentally, to sights and sounds, thoughts, and sensations flowing through the world-body-mind system. Traditional mindfulness meditation uses sensations of breath at the tip of the nose as the "object" of attention. What you're doing when you watch the breath is trying to discern the momentary changes in the *qualities* of breath sensations, like warmth, coolness, tingling, pressure, expansion, and contraction.

But be warned, your attention is not under your control. Indeed, you'll quickly discover that your attention has a mind of its own. Try as you might to pay attention to the changing qualities of breath sensations at the tip of the nose, you'll often find that you're paying attention to something else entirely. Don't get discouraged or make your wandering attention into a problem, however. Instead, as soon as you're aware that your attention has wandered, gently refocus it on the changing sensations of breath again. The following techniques have been found to help beginning meditators stabilize their attention. Practicing these techniques will change your brain so that possessing a stable, focused attention becomes a reality for you.

SET A CONSCIOUS INTENTION

The first technique may not seem like a technique at all, but it's absolutely imperative you practice it if you ever hope to gain any traction in your meditation practice. This technique also goes along with one of the primary themes of this book, which is that intention always precedes change and healing. In other words, before you can change or heal, you need to set a conscious intention. The same applies to your meditation practice. Any skill or benefit you hope to develop will require that you set a conscious intention first. Whether you practice mindfulness meditation or loving-kindness, here is the intention you should set when you start to meditate: *I will do my best to pay attention to the changing sensations of breath at the tip of my nose and try to limit the time that my mind wanders.* After strongly setting that skillful intention, you should then employ these additional techniques.

FOUR-STEP TRANSITION

This procedure will narrow your attention to breath sensations at the tip of your nose in a series of four steps.

1. Start your meditation by closing your eyes, relaxation breathing, and staying fully aware of everything you hear. Listen to the whole space of the room in which you are sitting. Use your body to feel into the whole space of the room, too. Hear out and feel out. Don't rush. Settle in.

2. Next, as you continue to listen and feel into the whole space of the room, narrow your attention to *all* the sensations in your body. Include all physical sensations, like warmth, coolness, tingling, pressure, comforts, and discomforts. Also, pay attention to all emotional-type feelings that may be present. Fully feel all of your bodily sensations, on the outside and on the inside. Accept all of your sensations and feelings without resistance.
3. Next, narrow your attention once more, this time restricting your focus to include only *breath* sensations. Let sounds and all the other bodily sensations remain in the background of your awareness, globally, but your local attention should now only focus on breath sensations.
4. Finally, once you think you've got that, narrow the scope of your attention once more, this time to just the changing sensations of breath at the tip of your nose. Employ this same four-step transition each time you meditate. Make it a habit.

Here are the same four steps again, in abbreviated bullet form:

- Open your awareness to the whole space of the room, hear out and feel out.
- Staying fully aware, narrow your attention to *all* body sensations in and out.
- Staying fully aware, narrow your attention to *all* breath sensations.

- Staying globally aware of the room and your body, narrow the focus of your attention to changing qualities of breath sensations at the tip of your nose.

BREATH COUNTING

To further assist you, after the above four-step transition, start counting your breaths. Pick the end of any out-breath to start counting. Your goal will be to continuously follow the various breath sensations at your nose, without significant interruption, for a full count of ten. When I practice breath counting, I divide the activity into two cycles in my mind. The first cycle is the *micro*-cycle, which lasts from one out-breath to the next out-breath. The second cycle of which I remain aware is the *macro*-cycle, which lasts from the first count of one to the last count of ten. If you get distracted at any time during the ten-count macro-cycle and forget your breath, start the process over again beginning with one.

If you're new to meditation, employ the four-step transition and breath counting as a way to develop a more stable attention. As you count and watch the breath sensations, see if you can identify all aspects of your breath. Notice the in-breath, the out-breath, the turn of each, and the various feelings that arise between. Do your best. Notice what you notice.

MENTAL NOTING AND LABELING

Mental noting is a valuable technique to use when you are having a hard time concentrating. For example, if an itch arises on your face, you may dispassionately make note of it, but then return your attention to your breath sensations. That's mental noting. If the itch persists and turns into a gross distraction, you may want to employ the more potent form of the technique, referred to as labeling. *Labeling* is thinking or saying a word related to what you are noting. If we continue with the example of the itch, you might mentally say "itch" to yourself, then go back to the breath sensations. Every time you notice your attention focused on the itch instead of the sensations of breath, say the label "itch" again and replace your attention. That's labeling.

Meditators soon discover that potentially innumerable objects can arise to distract them from their breath. I've found that coming up with just the right label for each distraction is a distraction in and of itself. For example, if I get distracted by the thought "What's for dinner?" what label should I employ? "Thinking"? "Hungry"? To make labeling thought-free, my solution is to give every disruption just one label, "distraction." But that's just me. As long as you understand how and when to use the techniques of mental noting and labeling, you can figure out the way that works best for you.

LOVING-KINDNESS MEDITATION

The Buddha defined karma as "intention." By his definition, he meant that a moral essence imbues *all* of your actions. In other words, the spiritual product, or *felt sense*, of all your actions *is* your karma. Practically speaking, how you relate to people, objects, and even to your own thoughts and feelings can't help but affect you emotionally. Therefore, if you want to change your karma so you feel better inside, you'll have to consciously relate to everything more affirmatively. Which is why the practice of inclining your mind toward love and compassion is one of the most powerfully transformative acts you can engage in.[10]

Loving-kindness meditation, also known as *metta*, is a practice that sits at the center of ethically based mindful attunement. Metta practice is a "constructive" meditation. *Constructive*, in this sense, means using one's imagination to construct a positive feeling state centered around what Buddhists call the *Brahmaviharas*, or the *Four Immeasurables*.[11]

The first of the four immeasurables is loving-kindness, which means benevolence, goodwill, and wanting others to be happy. The second is compassion, defined as a desire to lessen the suffering of others. The third immeasurable is sympathetic joy, which refers to the feeling of joy in yourself when others are happy. The last of the four is equanimity. Equanimity is feeling emotionally balanced and serene despite external circumstances. A person feels equanimity when they treat others and their life circumstances with imperturbable impartiality. Metta practice seeks to consciously construct the felt sense of each of these four immeasurables in the heart of the meditator.

A SIMPLE HEART-CENTERED LOVING-KINDNESS PRACTICE

Find a reasonably private, reasonably quiet place to meditate. Close your eyes if you like, and commit to meditating for ten or more minutes. Begin this meditation by first engaging in a few minutes of relaxation breathing and then employ the four-step transition, breath counting, and finally noting and labeling if necessary.

After you feel relaxed and concentrated, focus broadly on all the physical and emotional sensations in your chest. Let a slight smile emerge on your face. Then cross your hands over your heart and bring to mind a beloved person or pet. Through this mental image, initiate feelings of love and compassion that you have for your beloved. Once you are successful in initiating feelings of love and compassion, see if you can amplify them. Last, while sustaining the feelings of loving-kindness, begin to repeat these four lines:

- May you be healthy.
- May you be happy.
- May you be free of suffering.
- May you live with ease.

After generating feelings of love and compassion for your beloved, see if you can shift your focus and shine some of that same loving-kindness on a neutral person—someone you know but for whom you don't have any strong feelings of attachment.

Keep in mind that that person, just like you and your loved ones, wants to be happy and free from suffering. The wish for this is universal.

Once you're able to generate and send love and compassion to a neutral person, see if you can broaden the scope of your practice even more by bringing to mind a person or group of people onto whom you project feelings of dislike or ill will. Can you wish them well also? I know, this is a heavy spiritual lift, but as you will learn, karma comes *from* you. So, if you truly want to feel good without restriction in a world where you and other people exhibit bad behavior, you have to train yourself to wish everyone well.

Last and most important, don't forget to include yourself in this practice as well. Some people have a reflexive aversion to wishing themselves well, but remember—you're a spark of the divine, too. Love and feel compassion for yourself, and include all of your hurt and as yet unrefined parts. Those parts of you want to be loved and happy, too!

CYCLE THROUGH THIS FIVE-PHASE PROCESS AND YOU'RE MEDITATING PERFECTLY

If you're a beginning meditator, your mind will cycle through a progression of five phases. The first is setting a firm ***conscious intention***. Meditating is like navigating toward a goal. Every time you sit down to meditate, remind yourself of what you're trying to accomplish. *I'm going to place my attention on the sensations of breath at the tip of my nose and try to limit the time that my mind wanders.* That's the appropriate intention for beginners, because no untrained person can stay focused on breath sensations without their attention unconsciously jumping to something else. What happens to novice meditators is that shortly after they set a conscious intention to remain aware of breath sensations and limit mind-wandering, their attention becomes distracted and attaches to something else. Meditators call this moment ***forgetting***.

Forgetting is the second occurrence in the five-phase process of beginning meditation. Forgetting happens to every beginning meditator, and it happens by itself. A person never says, "Hey, I'm going to forget my breath." They just forget, and most often, they are entirely unaware of it. So, please, don't be hard on yourself when you forget the breath.

Immediately after forgetting, your mind will wander off and start worrying, thinking, planning, or fantasizing. Attention attaches to whatever is the worry, thought, plan, or fantasy of the moment. That period of reverie, however long it lasts, represents the third stage in the process, called ***mind-wandering***.

Mind-wandering can last for an indeterminate amount of time. It can be long or short, depending on some combination of the strength of your initial conscious intention, energy level, and motivation. Assuming you set a robust conscious intention to pay attention and have sufficient energy and motivation, mind-wandering will be self-limiting. That's because a firm opening intention will eventually spark a mini "awakening." The moment when you pop out of your foggy trance to realize that your mind has wandered is called ***remembering***, which is the fourth point in the process.

Strangely, remembering is also unconscious. You won't decide to remember. Like forgetting, remembering just happens. While you meditate, the remembering function of mindfulness works in the background of your subconscious. It compares what's happening in your mind to your initial conscious intention. If your mind starts wandering, this background-comparing function of mindfulness will notice that your attention is off task. Then a subconscious mental process will trigger the mini-epiphany of remembering. One last note about remembering: when it happens, rejoice! This is you getting it right, catching your off-task attention.

After remembering, reaffirm your original intention and then replace your attention on breath sensation. **Replacing** is the fifth and final phase of the cycle. Once attention is set back on breath sensations, the five-step process starts over again. That's the "video game" you play in your head: setting the conscious intention, forgetting, mind-wandering, remembering, and replacing. With practice, you can get to the point where you stop forgetting the breath altogether. Once that happens, you will be able to do something no untrained person can do: stay focused on the breath for over twelve minutes without forgetting the breath. That's a laudable accomplishment.

How quickly you cycle through these five phases depends. If you are preoccupied or emotional or your conscious intention is weak, forgetting will happen almost immediately, which will lead to prolonged periods of mind-wandering, followed by very little remembering and replacing. People who don't set a robust intention to watch breath sensations and limit mind-wandering will eventually get frustrated. I've heard so many people say, "I can't meditate." Of course, that's not true. The primary reason for their sloppy meditation is their weak initial intention. There can be reasons for this—sleepiness, restlessness, insufficient motivation, or perhaps lack of belief in themselves. However, with sufficient energy, will, and confidence, correctly channeled into setting a robust intention, even a novice meditator can begin to limit the frequency of forgetting and the time spent mind-wandering.

If you're a beginner, the cycle of conscious intention, forgetting, mind-wandering, remembering, and replacing will often repeat many times throughout each meditation session. Indeed, this cycle characterizes the experience of beginning meditation practice. It's the process by which you train your attention to stay focused on its intended target. For beginners, therefore, the primary goal is to set a strong initial intention. That alone will become sufficient cause for training your attention and awareness. You *can* do it—it just takes a strong conscious intention and practice. Improving your ability as a mediator corresponds to fewer moments of forgetting and less mind-wandering. Those are the goals you're shooting for as a beginning meditator.

Whether you get discouraged or not comes down to how you *relate* to the moments in which you "remember." Meeting the moment of remembering with gladness will shorten the time it takes you to accomplish the aforementioned goals. So, every time you remember to replace your attention, pat yourself on the back. You did it! That's what beginning practice is all about.

Never admonish yourself at the time you remember. Many people do and then quickly come to the false conclusion that they can't meditate. Please, forgetting, mind-wandering, and remembering is the nature of a beginner's practice. So, hold yourself in compassion and then move on to the last phase of the process. The tragic mistake many beginners make is shaming themselves for forgetting the breath in the first place. They blame themselves for "not doing it right." Negatively appraising the moment when they notice their attention has wandered amplifies pessimism. Rather than viewing remembering as something positive, they chastise themselves for not meditating correctly. That corrosive attitude derives from a false belief that they were in control and *allowed* their minds to wander in the first place. Caustic self-criticism like that becomes the reason many people give up.

The moment you remember your breath is a precious moment! It means you're doing it right. You caught your attention wandering, and in catching it, you were able to influence it. If you want to evolve, change, and grow, accept that meditation training requires that you forget breath sensations a million times over. That's just the way it is. You're not in control. So please, do not ever say, "I can't meditate." That story always has a bad ending. You *can* learn to meditate, but you must accept that meditation is a process, one that involves setting a firm conscious intention, forgetting, mind-wandering, remembering, and replacing. Repeat that straightforward sequence in your mind over and over again for years, and you, too, will receive the gift of positive emotional transformation that comes with sincere and skillful practice.

Carol Dweck is a Stanford-trained psychologist who has done some groundbreaking work in the area of motivation and success. Her book *Mindset* puts forth the simple idea that people who possess a "growth" mindset, as opposed to a "fixed" mindset, do better in nearly every facet of their lives.[12] The areas in which they benefit include physical and mental health, athletics, the quality of their relationships, worldly achievements, financial success, and overall positive self-regard. All that success adds up. People with a growth mindset feel happy and satisfied. Crucially, a person with a growth mindset understands that they are *in process*. They know that they are not perfect *yet* but that if they keep working on self-development, they can and will get better. People with growth mindsets believe in their *potential to become*. A growth mindset helps them cultivate more patience and persistence as well.

People with fixed mindsets, on the other hand, see limitations everywhere. Such a person is often arguing for and thus solidifying their weaknesses. They will tell you why something *can't* happen, like why they can't meditate. Opportunities for growth are seen as obstacles. They don't have enough self-determination to push into the discomfort of their challenges. The immobilizing effect of a fixed mindset keeps them stuck, and then their life becomes even more difficult.

If this book is trying to teach you anything, it's that you are a *changing thing*. Nothing is fixed. Everything is evolving, including you. So push into the resistance when it's time to meditate and then focus on what's positive. Slow things down and start appreciating the coolness of the air entering your nostrils and swirling behind the bones of your face. Feel into those parts of your body where you don't feel anything. These are examples of simple pleasures and peacefulness that exist in every moment of your experience. There are plenty more examples. It's all there; you just have to tune in, acknowledge, and appreciate.

The next time you meditate, set your intention to attend to breath sensations and try to limit the time your mind wanders.

Then watch your mind cycle through forgetting, mind-wandering, remembering, and replacing. As you do, stay aware of all the positive aspects of your experience. Make a concerted effort to acknowledge and amplify all that goodness, especially when it comes to the moment of remembering. Every time you remember, rejoice! That simple act will help you cultivate a growth mindset toward your meditation practice, which will keep you going.

Sitting and watching the flow of energy and information passing through your world-body-mind network is a game-changer. You can't read about meditation and gain any deep understanding of the intricate workings of your living system—you have to do it! The insights you gain by meditating will then alter how you relate to yourself, others, and the world. In this way, meditation, done right, is self-therapy.

So set the intention to meditate today. With a sense of energetic eagerness, start with relaxation breathing and the four-step transition. As you meditate, watch your mind carry you through the five phases of beginning meditation. Allow yourself to appreciate all the positive aspects of the experience.

I've now laid out all the basics you need to start on the path to becoming a meditator, but if you'd feel more comfortable beginning your practice with guided meditations, visit my website (www.drmarkpirtle.com) or my YouTube channel (Dr. Mark Pirtle Meditation for Stress Relief). I have a thirteen-month sequential guided meditation program specifically designed to teach you how to become a skillful meditator. Enjoy!

PART 2

Is Your Story Making You Sick?

CHAPTER 1

The "Effauses and Caufects" of Healthful Change

"This being, that becomes; from the arising of this, that arises; this not being, that becomes not; from the ceasing of this, that ceases."

Samyutta Nikaya, 11.28,65

I don't want to dampen your spirits, but statistics suggest that most people will not work hard enough on mindful attunement to attract the changes they're hoping to engender.

Why am I telling you this? Isn't my job as a self-help author to keep you inspired all the way to the end of the book? Well, sure, maybe. But if I'm to be honest with you, I have to give it to you straight. Knowing that everything could improve if you just attuned better won't motivate most people to change. That's because when things are "good enough," the vast majority of people will take their foot off the gas and coast.

I don't want to imply we're lazy. Most of us are quite busy doing the same old trivial stuff over and over. So busy, in fact, that when the time comes to open our minds and calendars to make room for something else—anything else—we balk.

Let's face it—changing is hard work. It takes initiative and follow-through, both of which are difficult, overburdened as we are with other responsibilities. Besides, we're not going to give up our precious screen time. Forget that! And yet there is one aspect of life that's powerful enough to get us off the couch to do what we need to do to stimulate growth and change. The most consistently motivating factor for anyone, anywhere, anytime, is—wait for it—pain! Yes, dreaded pain is the perfect motivator to get someone to do something different in service of a greater good.

How fast did world governments shift gears and close economies down when COVID-19 spread across the globe? And just wait—when New York, Boston, Miami, New Orleans, Houston, Los Angeles, Seattle, and countless other coastal communities start slipping beneath the surface of rising oceans, watch how fast we'll all band together, mobilize, and start working earnestly to solve the global climate crisis. I'll bet when that day comes and it finally dawns on us that we'd better take action, even the climate deniers will chip in and help. Just like with COVID, the "in-your-face" pain of real, rather than hypothetical, crisis is what will trigger collective action.

Pain is a fantastic motivator. I'm convinced that without it, we'd still be living in caves. Every living creature is motivated to avoid pain, and humans are no exception. We dislike pain so much that for millennia we've used the superpowers of our imagination and ingenuity to devise all manner of remedies to lessen it. But there's more to life than reducing pain. The other half of life is seeking psychological, emotional, and spiritual fulfillment.

So why not put your pain to work in service of a higher good? If you're struggling with some form of pain right now, be it physical, emotional, or spiritual, you've got your motivator. As lousy as your present condition or situation may be, your pain can goad you forward. It can push you to devote more time and energy into making changes happen. Your pain got you to read this book, didn't it? You're here because there are things you want to change, work through, heal, or transcend. Allow yourself to feel the dissatisfaction that comes from those things. Then turn that dissatisfaction into the rocket fuel that launches you into a robust change process.

What will this change process look like? Strangely, although each person's path is unique, the substance of the process is the same in every case. Evolution happens the way it happens, through *inclusion and transcendence*. Nature takes what came before and includes it in the making of its next creation. Past *being* is always included in future *becoming*. That's how evolutionary influence carries forward.

Your development is no different. You'll include and transcend your current self as you develop your future self. Personal growth always means working through emotionally charged triggers, thoughts, and sensations until they lose their potency. You'll grow past current triggers not by shielding yourself from them but by working with them. In the process, you'll remake yourself.

You have a story. Right now, it is what it is. You have to *include* it even as you seek to *transcend* it. The "writing" of your new story happens as you attune to yourself in the moments when you're most triggered. Accepting what is, with care, opens you up to higher perspectives with additional opportunities for self-reflection, correction, reconciliation, and insight. Sure, easy to say, much harder to do, but attuning in this way is how you make meaning out of your suffering. For example, you could ask, "How can I turn this painful condition or situation into the best thing that ever happened to me?" Questions like that and sitting bravely with your stuff generate insights that can change the direction of your life. It's from those wiser and more compassionate insights that your new story writes itself. That's how a new "you" comes into being.

I want to point out another fundamental concept inherent to the process of development: *interdependence*. Interdependence means that everything connects to everything else.

Have you ever heard the term *portmanteau*? *Portmanteau* is a word mash-up, which blends the sounds and meanings of two words into one, like brunch. *Infomercial* is another example. Want more? Check out a Taco Bell menu sometime. At Taco Bell, the same five ingredients combine to produce all the menu items, and the names of these same menu items are similarly blended. Enchirito, anyone?

It is with great excitement and delight that I add two *portmanteaus* to the ever-expanding English lexicon: *effauses and caufects*. If you're wondering about their meaning, *effauses* and *caufects* are synonyms. Although we conventionally speak of causes *and* effects, in actuality they are not separate phenomena. Life exists as one endless entangled flow of activity—a movement of energy, information, and matter through systems that are nested like Russian dolls where causes are effects and vice versa.

I've combined the words *cause* and *effect* to signify a mutual concurrence related to both evolution and life itself. There is only one simultaneous flow. Thus, effauses and caufects. What we're going to attempt to shift is the direction of this single flow and turn it in a more favorable direction.

Think of *effauses* as another word for recursive feedback—swirling cycles of information feeding back into a system to affect the system's output in chaotic and unpredictable ways. It's not exactly accurate to say that reintroducing the wolves back into the Yellowstone ecosystem was the *only* reason it healed. More precisely, their reintroduction unleashed a symbiotic flow of automatic and energetic feedback loops that, in total, got the job done.

The process by which you will transcend your current issues will happen the same way. Energy and information will flow and recycle in ways that change the output of your system (mind, body, spirit, family, community, nation, world) in unpredictable ways. The trick is learning to coax the effause-and-caufect stream in a more positive direction.

Effauses and caufects reflect the true nature of the entangled universe in which we find ourselves. There is a bi-directional flow of energy and information between you and the people and events in your life. Whatever happens outside of you instantly affects you on the inside. Similarly, what goes on inside of you also leaks out to influence what is happening on the outside.

This two-way current also includes the past and future. You're carrying the influence of both inside you right now. Your past experiences sensitize you to present circumstances. Your past is far more responsible for your current emotional state than you can imagine. How you imagine your future impinges on your current emotional state as well. In systems, all the information drawn from each of these directions cycles back on itself and drives evolution.

I'm harping on interdependence because it is utterly consequential in determining the after-effects of your present-moment thoughts, speech, and behavior. Your interior thoughts and feelings intimately connect to everything you relate to on the outside. What you do now affects the thoughts, sensations, and feelings that will come from you later. That's the karma of it. (More on karma in Chapter 3.)

Now let's effause and caufect our way back to whatever pain roused you to pick up this book. There are no magic bullets when it comes to evolving beyond it. The first step in the direction of your recovery must come from you. So check in. Can you identify any faith or inspiration inside you that's driving you forward? If so, great, because you'll need the little push of both faith and inspiration to get an effause-and-caufect stream going.

The beginning is always bootstrap time. There's a great quote by the late French author and poet Marcel Proust that speaks to this point: "We do not receive wisdom, we discover it, after a journey through the wilderness, which no one can make for us, which no one can spare us." When that white feather hit me in the chest years ago, I intuitively knew there was no other way to heal my life. I had to rise to the challenge and start a positive effause-and-caufect stream for myself. You can, too, and it starts with just one step forward.

The requisite faith and inspiration must therefore come from you, too, or more specifically, from your "warrior self." Words are potent. I write "warrior self" to conjure a powerful image in your mind. Warriors symbolize latent potentials we all carry—potentials for courage, persistence, resilience, and serving a higher purpose. Warriors step forward to face what's coming. You have a warrior inside of you, too, a fighter who is ready to meet the current challenge and who won't give up.

Warriors don't look back either; they press ahead, not requiring or expecting perfect circumstances. They accept what is, even discomfort and uncertainty. The conditions you find yourself in are the ones you'll have to work through. But your warrior can handle it. Everyone starts their reclamation project feeling weak and robbed. I know I did. For this reason, we all deserve compassion. But that doesn't mean we can't connect to our inner warrior's strength and start kicking some ass.

Give yourself a great gift. Activate the strength of your warrior. Let go of any unacknowledged longing to turn back the clock to a time when your life and circumstances were easier to handle. For me to rewrite my story, and ultimately heal my life, I had to let go of all the what-ifs. You'll have to do the same. What the present moment requires of you is full-on, forward-facing, radical acceptance of what is. When you accept what is, you'll be able to move ahead with faith and inspiration. As a result, a commitment to growing in service of yourself, your relationships, and a greater good will surface.

Allow yourself to dream of who you might become. Give your warrior self an enticing mission to which they can commit their vast energies. What I'm asking you to do is exercise your autonomy—an aspect of your personal power. The effauses and caufects of faith and inspiration will arise when you search inside yourself and find a compelling reason to grow. Could there be a vague whisper of longing in the background of your awareness? One that, until now, has been too faint to hear? Listen carefully. Maybe take a whole retreat day or even week to turn inward, introspect, and journal about it. Whatever comes up, make that the foundation of your work. Cultivate the image of your healed future self. Breathe life into that subtle stirring, nurturing it to the point where you can claim it as *yourself*. When that longing integrates with your personhood and you begin to identify with it, faith and inspiration will gush forth freely. Indeed, faith and inspiration are all that warriors need to start their quest. Armed with these, can you accept your current circumstances?

I feel confident that you'll be able to conjure the gumption, galvanize your warrior, and bootstrap yourself into action. But after that, what's next in the effause-and-caufect loop? The answer is simple. You're already doing it. You're reading this book. Others might find different routes, like doing an Internet search, taking a class, entering rehab, seeking out a therapist or spiritual adviser, or going on an extended retreat. However you do it, your path forward will require learning something new. The new information and experiences will have the effect of opening your mind to new thoughts and perspectives, which in turn will alter your physiology. Learning is, therefore, psychoactive. It's an effause-and-caufect loop where information flows into your system and changes it at the same time. Though you're not aware of it, just by reading this sentence right now, you're linking and unlinking millions of neurons in your brain! You are never the same person after learning something new.

That's exactly how it worked for me when I was so sick and angry those many years ago. When I read that first book on meditation, it initiated an organic and virtuous effause-and-caufect stream in me. I had no way of knowing where it was taking me ahead of time, but I stayed with it. There were many times when

I picked up that book feeling like I was going to explode with rage, but then, after reading just a few pages, I would notice the salutary effects that the enlightened ideas had on my body, mind, and spirit. The *meaning* embedded in the words shifted my emotional state toward the positive end of the spectrum. That positive shift simultaneously initiated a chemical cascade in my brain. Those generative chemicals stimulated me. My brain cells connected and formed ever more complex networks. Energy and information flowed to my heart and gut. Within a few minutes of picking up the book, my heart rate would slow and the intense pounding would stop. The better and safer I felt, the more my digestion would regulate itself. My mind would quiet down and peace would arise. Recollecting those moments now, the dejection and fear I frequently sat down with often evaporated as more wholesome thoughts and feelings took their place.

But that peace was only a state change. Often, back then, five minutes after closing my book, I found myself unconsciously fixated on my story of betrayal again. Sadly, it may be the same for you. You'll have to keep dipping into the well of spiritually uplifting ideas and practices to eventually change yourself enough that feeling good again becomes not just a state but a trait.

After finishing that first book on meditation, I felt inspired and eager to investigate further. I responded to an ad in the back of the book to start a yearlong class on meditation. Through that class, I connected with a meditation teacher, Thubten Yeshe ("TY"), who lived at Chenrezig, a Tibetan Buddhist monastery in Eudlo, Australia.[13]

Over the course of that year, I listened to a progressive program of guided meditations. As I remember it, I didn't miss a day. More important, though, after finishing the program, I identified myself as a *meditator*. Through my inspiration, investigation, effort, and practice, I eventually effause-and-caufected my way into being a different person—new understandings, new skills, and—voilà—a new me!

But even then I wasn't finished. At that early point in recovery, I still had a long way to go. But I successfully leaped over the first and most challenging hurdle: letting go of one way of living and picking up another. That early and consistent effort gave my spiritual practice legs.

I credit that new spiritual practice with relieving some of my stress-related symptoms as well. Mentally, physically, and spiritually I was on the right track and desperate to keep the positive effause-and-caufect stream flowing. One day, after an encouraging phone call with TY, I bought a plane ticket and flew to Australia to spend two months in retreat at Chenrezig, and those two months were one of the highlights of my life. I still reflect on how near-immediate the shift in my mood was. Flying to the opposite side of the planet changed me. Getting upside down turned me inside out. Going from a southwestern desert to a semitropical forest was a profound contextual shift as well. That's the power of contexts—they change who we are and how we show up. There was also the fact that apart from TY, no one at Chenrezig knew me or my story. That condition alone provided the opportunity for me to reinvent myself. Everyone there greeted me with warmhearted friendliness, opening up the possibility for me to enact and embody new conceptions of myself. What a relief it was not having to push back against other people's hardened projections just as I began to reinvent myself.

The daily schedule at Chenrezig was loose but rich. I busied myself with frequent meditation, Dharma instruction, contemplation, writing, and exercise. My downtime was spent hanging out with friends at the Big Love Café, debating the hows and whys of suffering and the incomprehensibility of karmic causality. Heavy, I know. I ate nutritious food at every meal, hiked through the bush, laughed a lot, and rested as much as I needed. If I had to choose between an extended retreat and a western medicine approach to treating stress-related illnesses, I'd do a retreat every time.

Novelty is also a vital component of the process. Only with sufficient novelty, like traveling to a foreign country, meeting new people, and learning new skills, can a weak impulse (wanting to feel better) amplify into a new pattern! That's how I started to change and become healthier. All the experiences I attracted sprang from a sincere desire to feel better. The stream took me, and I flowed from one learning experience to the next, deepening my intention to better myself. It hasn't all been easy, but all the teachings and experiences eventually produced profound changes in me. Ask anyone who knew me twenty years ago—I'm not the same person anymore.

When a person is stuck, it's because they close themselves off to new ideas, information, and experiences. To paraphrase Mark Twain, the man who does not read has no advantage over the man who *can't* read. Thus "stuckness" results when potential effauses and caufects of healthful change, initiated by new information, can't form feedback loops and amplify. A person who does not read is not taking advantage of their latent capacity. And the same old thoughts and feelings that created their troubles keep cycling through their system, producing the same sorry results.

It's a fact: the more novel and spiritually nourishing ideas you can introduce, the lower the volume of the negativity in your system. That's the foundation of the bibliotherapy you're now engaged in. But you can't just sit at the foot of a teacher or read your way to the end of your suffering. Investigating information alone is not enough to unstick yourself and form new habits. If that were the case, we could all have six-pack abs and buns of steel by merely reading fitness magazines. Wish we could, but it doesn't work that way. Legitimate teachers and books will inevitably suggest actual practices or exercises, and then it's up to you. You'll need to put in effort on a daily basis before you begin to experience signs of improvement. I had to practice for months before I began to feel better. But just knowing you've opened yourself up to growth, and having faith in your practice, will give you the energy to continue. One step forward, then the next.

It's also critical to realize that the spiritual activities you practice, like meditation and mindfulness, are not an end in themselves. We're all connected, so use them in service of a higher good. Take the mundane example of a basketball player. Any good basketball player needs to practice free throws, but practicing free throws is not the end goal. Consistently hitting free throws during the game so your team wins is the end goal. The same is true regarding all manner of spiritual practices. They enable skillful attunement with oneself, others, and situations in service of a higher purpose. That is the reason we practice what we practice. Spirituality is a hollow exercise unless you put it into action for the betterment of yourself, other people, and a larger whole. Eventually, a basketball player may wind up at the free-throw line at the end of a tie game, with no time left on the clock. So, too, may you find yourself in a pressure-packed and consequential situation. How will you perform? The quality of your awareness and composure at that pivotal moment will determine the result.

I can recall hundreds of situations involving work, parenting, marriage, and life where I rose to the occasion. Assisted by awareness and composure, I metaphorically swished my free throws. I can also recall hundreds of instances where, due to unconsciousness and reactivity, I choked and clanked the ball off the proverbial rim. It's a *practice*. No one's perfect. But if your life *becomes* a practice, then "missing a shot" provides the feedback you need in order to do better next time. So, incrementally, you track closer to your goal. There's a lot of satisfaction in living this way.

That's the life of a spiritual warrior. You take the good with the bad and know that the path of development is never linear, straight from where you are now to where you want to be. Development, instead, is a jagged yet gradually rising incline, involving many ups and downs. But with enough consistent effort over time, you can achieve an outcome that's ultimately gratifying. The natural developmental rhythm initiated by attunement ends up purifying you. Practice helps you integrate past traumas, shadow impulses, and neuroses into a singularly unique, healthy, well-balanced, mature, wise, kind, (and yet imperfect) person. Service to others and your mission will consistently result in you feeling a sense of wholesome triumph. Warriors, basketball players, and anyone you can think of, including yourself, love the feeling of victory.

In the early stages at least, the sweet taste of triumph is the juice that will keep your spiritual warrior going. Honestly, one of the best reasons to rise and fight to reclaim yourself is because it feels so good. When you shed that victim mentality and step into your power, it feels great. Then, as you accumulate new experiences, you'll start to grow beyond the old narratives. The process itself generates transformative insights. Remember what Marcel Proust wrote: "We do not receive wisdom, we discover it, after a journey through the wilderness, which no one can make for us, which no one can spare us." It's only because of all your hard psycho-emotional-spiritual work that new capacities and positive patterns emerge. That emergence, then, *is* the change at which you're aiming.

Imagine the joy a butterfly feels when it breaks out of its cocoon and wakes up to its newfound beauty and freedom. Especially when it remembers that not long ago, it lived with the limitations inherent in the life of a caterpillar. No matter where you're starting your journey, this same sense of triumph and freedom is available to you, too.

But you'll have to cultivate your own insights. Transformation will arise out of iteration. You'll need to practice the same skills in the same situations with the same people over and over. Sometimes it takes years to overcome an old habit and evolve, but as you progress in your practice, you won't have to rely on faith so much. Instead, you'll generate something better: *verified* faith. What I mean is that you won't have to cross your fingers and hope and pray for a lucky break or divine intervention anymore. Verified faith comes from *self*-empowerment. As long as you keep the virtuous effause-and-caufect stream flowing, goodness is on the way.

Take a look at the diagram below. Notice the "Start Here" in the upper right corner. Right under it, it reads "Pain Experience." Next, follow that diagram clockwise around, full circle. Notice the effause loops, starting with *Faith* and *Inspiration*, moving on to *Investigation and Information, Effort and Practice, Awareness and Composure, Insight* and *Change* and finally feeding back into the cycle again at *Verified Faith*.

There it is, a map of upwardly spiraling, system-wide trophic cascading, produced by the recursive feedback of effauses and caufects. That is the way the new pattern of you will develop. So start paying attention to all the granular moments in your life. See if you don't begin to notice the effause-and-caufect loops feeding back on themselves now, revealing flashes of insight in the blink of an eye, patterns emerging and dissolving. Stay aware, too, as you enact the practices you learn in this book. Watch as the effause-and-caufect loops manifest newer healthier behaviors over days, weeks, months, and years. Let your practice unfold, and stay aware of it *as* it unfolds.

EFFAUSES OF HEALTHFUL CHANGE

Start at **Pain Experience** in the upper right corner and move clockwise around the inner circles. *Faith* and *Inspiration* lead to *Investigation* of new forms of Information (what you are doing now).

New ideas gained through study then lead to working on new practices. *Practice* and *Effort* then increase your *Awareness* of and *Composure* during stressful events, which leads to better outcomes and personal *Insight,* which leads to *Change.*

Then the cycle starts again, **Verified Faith.** The second time around, you know that you are on the right track. This cyclic process shows you how you will change and/or heal yourself.

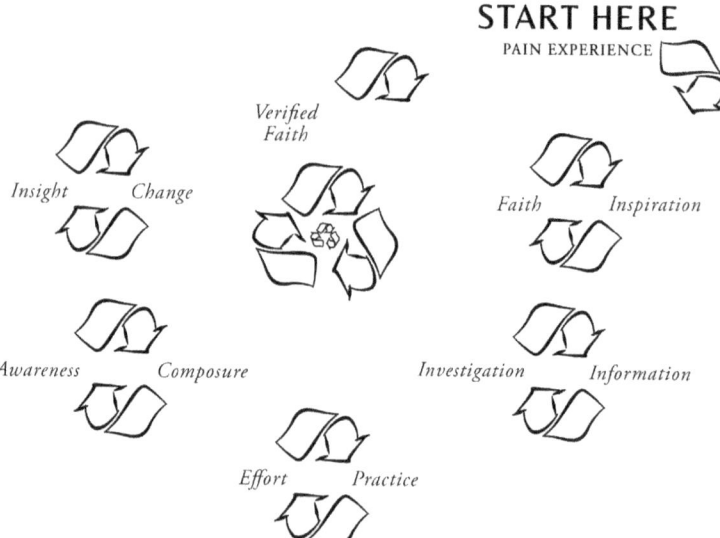

CHAPTER 2

The Three Transcendentals

"The ideals which have always shown before me and filled me with joy are beauty, goodness, and truth."

Albert Einstein

Startled by the noise, he looked up from his map. Peering out the driver's side window, he saw mailboxes rattling back and forth on their stands. Some unseen force was causing the mailbox doors to clamorously flip open and closed. Inside his truck, gravity seemed to turn sideways, spilling out the contents of the glove box and whirling them around the cab. Horrified by what was happening, Roy Neary stuck his head out the window and looked up to investigate. Squinting up into the dark night sky, he was hit by a dazzling flash of light from above.[14] Days later, sitting at the dinner table with his family, he lost himself in a bedeviling preoccupation, trying to sculpt mashed potatoes into ... what? He didn't know. Finally, the full weight of three pairs of staring eyes penetrated his reverie. Struggling to meet his family's gaze, he sheepishly tried to explain his behavior. "I guess you've noticed there's something a little strange with Dad. It's okay, though.

I'm still Dad. I can't describe it, what I'm feeling and what I'm thinking." Looking down at the mashed potatoes again, he muttered, "This means something. This is important."[15]

These are two iconic scenes from Steven Spielberg's 1977 science fiction classic *Close Encounters of the Third Kind*. When the alien light hit Roy, it affected him so powerfully that his life was never the same again. From that moment forward, he was unable to resist a compulsive mission-driven urge to resolve his confusion. Roy Neary's quest for adventure was born!

Early one Saturday morning in November 2014, an equivalent obsession seized my psyche. As if whispered in my ear, the following words woke me from a restless sleep: "Make a documentary!" Flat on my back, I opened my eyes wide and sat upright. I remember scratching my head and looking around. "Make a documentary? What?" Yet even though the drowsiness, this much was clear: this meant something; this was important!

It was 3 a.m., and my mind fixed on the idea. I threw off the covers and got out of bed. At the time, it seemed to make perfect sense. For more than a decade I'd made a career out of understanding the drivers of stress-related illnesses and how to use mindfulness-based attunement to ease people's pain. With all the unnecessary suffering I saw around me, I desperately wanted to do more to help. A documentary to raise awareness seemed like a perfect solution. I slipped on my house shoes and shuffled over to the espresso machine, made a cup, and sat down at my computer. Before I was fully aware of what I was doing, I was well into writing a business plan for a documentary about the causes and remedies of stress illnesses.

There was nothing rational about the idea. I had no business producing a film. But the enlivening energy that took me over that night wouldn't relent. Indeed, not a single thought of the sheer improbability of completing the project ever entered my head. When I think back on it now, it seems utterly crazy. Producing a film takes a team of people. At that time, I knew not a single person who could produce, write, direct, shoot, edit, and distribute a film. Even more central to the venture, who was going to pony up all the money to fund such an enormous undertaking? Really, what were the odds of success? And yet it happened. How do we explain such improbabilities?

The inceptive drive that infected Roy Neary at the railroad crossing was the same sort of force that had quickened in me. An idea sought to complete itself through the head and heart of a living person. Indeed, as Plato argued, ideas are real and live in a transcendental realm, beyond the physical, to manifest only when they harmonize with the right person at the right time.

In a similar vein, Elizabeth Gilbert, the author best known for the global best seller *Eat Pray Love*, dedicated another book, *Big Magic*, to the creed of living a life invigorated by divinely inspired artistic creativity. In *Big Magic*, she writes, "Ideas are alive [and] seek the most available human collaborator." But the life of an artist is not all Bohemian flair and clove cigarettes, as Gilbert makes abundantly clear. She counsels her readers to "face their fears and work like farmers."

All of which makes me think (and this may sound counterintuitive) that artists have a lot in common with warriors. In Chapter 1, I invited you to call upon your warrior spirit in support of your self-improvement. Now I'm joining a chorus of sages and self-help gurus appealing to you to kindle your distinctive artistic fires as well. There's no denying that both of these archetypes, the warrior and the artist, live in all of us. Yes, you, too! They only require that you acknowledge them before they begin to make mischief together inside you. You can tap into your inherent ache to change, to heal, and to become more, through artful grit.

Get quiet, turn inward, and *feel* what's driving you. Feel the emotion beneath the surface? That's it. Your artist and warrior are both itching to grab hold of something to start. Artists and warriors are mission-driven! Each is 100 percent motivated by challenges that test their intelligence, skill, creativity, courage, endurance, depth, and character. Don't ever tell an artist or warrior it can't be done. They'll prove you wrong.

What is it then that activates artists and warriors—these vessels of spirit—to breathe life into destiny and strive to conquer the obstacles that stand between them and their dreams? Philosophers through the ages have described three apogees of value equal to mother's milk for the spirit, three magnetizing forces that catalyze the human soul to take bold, impassioned, and evolutionary action. So far, no mortal has identified anything superior to these powerful potentiators of transformation: beauty, goodness, and truth. Beauty. Goodness. Truth. Each represents a fundamental relationship you have with the universe.

It has been said, and it's absolutely true, that beauty is in the eye of the beholder. The space from which beauty is judged will always and forever be from within one's internal space— the *intra*personal space of me, myself, and I. Beauty is subjective, recognized by you, *in* you. We typically associate beauty with something that can be seen or heard, like a beautiful smile, sunset, melody, or voice. But from here on out, I want to expand your conception of beauty to include not just sights and sounds, but beautiful tastes, smells, touches, feelings, and thoughts as well. The more sensory information you associate with beauty, the better you'll feel. The better you feel, the kinder you're likely to be to others.[16] Which leads us to the second transcendental: goodness.

Goodness arises in the heartwarming connections you share with all other living beings. As such, goodness is an *inter*personal experience. When you share the gifts of kindness, care, love, generosity, empathy, compassion, appreciation, virtue, or rightness with someone else, you're both experiencing the mutual exchange of goodness.

The last transcendental is truth. Truth discloses itself in the *external* objective domain. There is a world of facts that you and anyone else can observe. This is the domain of truth. Also, there *are* laws of cause and effect, so if you're hoping to feel better, it's best to understand and abide by these rules.

As original values, beauty, goodness, and truth represent nothing less than the highest spiritual qualities the universe offers, which is why these three inexhaustible sources of inspiration hold the exalted designation "The Three Transcendentals." If you're open, curious, and observant, these three fundamental values will guide you to know yourself better, connect with others more deeply, and harmonize your inner and outer worlds.

No one is alone in their desire to improve conditions or circumstances. Indeed, that innate drive motivates every living creature everywhere and has for all time. Like every creature, you are hardwired with "approach-avoidance" programming—to move toward pleasure and away from pain. So all-pervading is this drive to increase happiness and reduce misery that it is called the *Universal Aspiration*. It is the spirit of your artist and warrior, calling you to remake your life into one brimming with more beauty, goodness, and truth.

This book is based on the premise that the more you know about your condition, the better the choices you'll make as you navigate toward improvement. But how do you "know" something? How do we know anything? Very plainly, you came to know what you know through your senses: seeing, hearing, feeling, tasting, smelling, and thinking. I added thinking to the list of five senses because, to Buddhists, it's another way of sensing. From a Buddhist perspective, thinking is what happens in the mind space, where thoughts make more meaning.

When you equip yourself with refined senses, you become a more conscious agent of your own evolution. Developing and refining your senses increases your capacity to apprehend even subtler stirrings. That development, in turn, enhances your ability to attune to self, others, and situations. Subsequently, enhanced attunement allows you to make "better" choices, which produce increasing amounts of beauty, goodness, and truth. It's another effause-and-caufect feedback loop.

A line of a Tibetan Buddhist prayer I memorized while retreating at Chenrezig goes like this: *Awakened ones of the past realized things as they are within the circle-of-three.* The "circle-of-three" represents the subject (your sense of self), an object (any object upon which your attention can fall), and the interaction between the two. The interaction is the relationship between your past programming, your present intention, and the object of your attention. What this short and powerfully astute verse means to convey is that everything you need in order to wake up happens within this tight dynamic. One or more of the three fundamental perspectives—the *intra*subjective (beauty), the *inter*subjective (goodness), and the external objective (truth)—are involved in every movement of your attention.

Everything you've ever done and everything you ever will do happens inside this sphere. As such, the circle-of-three is our developmental crucible. In other words, the circle-of-three is our life.

Let me offer concrete examples of ways in which we can enhance beauty, goodness, and truth in our lives. As your senses mature, your bandwidth for savoring and appreciating beauty in all its expressions will increase in equal measure. When life becomes an expression of your inner artist, you'll happily realize that living attuned to the beauty in and around you will connect you to your higher calling.

Goodness, as mentioned, is revealed in our interpersonal relationships. To maximize goodness, we have to set intentions to do so. When I'm attuned to my daughter Alana, I can meet her sometimes-volatile emotions with love, calmness, and care. Of course, I'm not always attuned. No parent is. Parents reading this book know firsthand how hard it is to hold your center and model emotional stability when your kid is throwing a fit. But when we parents get it right, our spongy kids soak up the vital social-emotional learning associated with the messy project of living with other human beings. Indeed, living harmoniously with others is where the garden of goodness starts to grow.

Practicing meditation helps a person discover the truth about how the mind works. That truth, if you're open to watching it objectively, will assist you in uncovering your stuck patterns and shadow issues. You'll be able to work through past traumas and endow yourself with more humility, honesty, and accountability. Meditation is an indispensable tool for cutting through the stories we tell ourselves and cultivating the beauty, goodness, and truth that accompany clear insight.

My spiritual practice helped me rediscover my inner artist. There was a time in my life when I painted, took photographs, played the guitar, and dabbled in design. Then life got in the way and I strayed off the path and let go of all those beautiful pursuits. A decade later, it was a piece of art that reignited my artistic desires. Most readers are familiar with Al Gore's documentary about the climate crisis, *An Inconvenient Truth*. When I watched his film, I took a keen interest in the way he made his argument using a Keynote slide presentation. Gore intentionally connected truth with beauty.

What impressed me about Gore's slides was his devotion to artistry as a means of amplifying his message, and I was immediately inspired to use slide presentations myself and express the same beauty in them. Now my SkillfullyAware classes serve all Three Transcendentals. Beautiful slides communicate developmental truths that help to increase the goodness in the world. This is my unique way of uniting all three transcendental qualities. By trusting your inner artist, you'll find your own way to express the Three Transcendentals.

I didn't know what I needed after my business blew up. But even though I was angry and confused, I never stopped innately longing for improvement. The Three Transcendentals were still active inside me, beckoning to me. Thankfully, I was just aware enough to hear the call. "What's your mission?" was the burning question I had to answer. I couldn't know then what choices I'd have to make, what trials I'd have to face, or who I'd become.

You may now find yourself grappling with a similar quandary. What's next? It can be frightening to think that "the future is coming!" Even more so because who you'll be then is developing out of what you do now. Pondering such complex questions can be emotionally wrenching. So, please, relieve yourself of the burden of trying to see into an uncertain future. No one can. A better option is humbly acknowledging your confusion. Attune to yourself and the present situation with acceptance and care, but then decide to keep it simple. Remember, there's a recursive code in all of us that points toward a better future. You already know what to do. All you have to do now is get quiet and open yourself to feeling the subtle pull of beauty, goodness, and truth. Amplifying the Three Transcendentals is the easiest, surest path to improvement. That simple truth was my lifeline. It can be yours, too.

The first person I befriended after arriving at Chenrezig was a well-traveled young man named Robert. He'd been globetrotting for a few years before landing in Australia and finding his way to Chenrezig. Robert was a born seeker. At only thirty-six years old, he'd sat at the feet of many teachers and had taken enough time to process what he'd learned to develop his own distinctive outlook on life. He'd been hanging around Chenrezig long enough to absorb the essence of the teachings, and shortly after

I arrived, I asked what the big takeaway was. He put it to me very succinctly: "You reap what you sow."

Growing up in a Christian culture, I'd heard this proverb many times. Indeed, the axiom was one I thought I held close. But hanging around Robert put the lie to that conviction. Remember, I'd left for Chenrezig shortly after my business failure. The whole catastrophe was still very raw. I often inadvertently fell into the trap of retelling my story as a way to process it. I wanted others to empathize with me, to agree that I was betrayed, that I was the victim. I wanted others to know I'd been wronged. My ego was seeking validation. I was retelling my story as a way of justifying my sense of failure.

Robert was quick to disabuse me of that defense mechanism. Whenever he noticed me peddling my story of injustice, he would say, "So, that's your racket, eh?" I never had a good answer for this squelching retort. Though I hated it at the time, I knew he was right. Rationalizing was a fraud I was perpetrating on myself. It kept me stuck. By continuously retelling that story, I was allowing it to define me. Worse, I was sowing the seeds of future suffering. At the time, however, I did not know anything about the Three Transcendentals, and yet I knew I had to start focusing my attention elsewhere if I wanted to return to Tucson a changed person.

My time at Chenrezig was up before I knew it, vanishing like a dream. A week before I was to fly back home, I requested a meeting with my Dharma teacher, Geshe Tashi Tsering. Frankly, I was worried. I rightly sensed that returning to Tucson, chockfull of triggering reminders of betrayal and loss as it was, would reignite the not yet cold embers of anger that still smoldered in my psyche. Should my anger be rekindled, I'd probably fall back into despondency and thus nourish the same stress-related symptoms I was so desperate to starve. How could I go back but not backslide? I asked *Geshe-la*, "What I should do?" His answer was simple. Softly, but with conviction, he said, "Keep practicing." I set the firm intention to do so.

I'd already been meditating for more than a year before I left for Chenrezig. The place in my house where I practiced was jammed into a corner of my office. I was able to meditate reasonably well there, but it was situated close to my desk and computer, causing worldly and spiritual energies to mix in an inelegant way. Up to that point, I'd sat in front of a rickety two-shelf cabinet posing as an altar. After my return from Chenrezig, however, that location no longer fit the way I wanted to express my passion for meditation and spirituality. So I set about refashioning and reenergizing my practice space. I cleared a guest bedroom and set up a new altar, decorating it with things I'd picked up at Chenrezig and other mementos. The spiritual feel and artistic expression of the new spot reflected my increased interest in practice. Once finished, the new space brimmed with beauty, goodness, and truth.

But I had been right to worry that Tucson would be full of triggering encounters with people and places that reminded me of my past life as a successful businessman. The office building that housed my old physical therapy clinic was near my home, and it was impossible not to drive by it frequently. Each time I did, I felt resentment hit me like a gut punch. There was nothing I could do about it except try to get better at working with these jolts of emotion and discomfort. It was my journey, which no one could make for me, which no one could spare me.

I also had to work with the automatic thoughts that came with those painful feelings. If I wasn't careful, that well-worn story of resentment would hijack my attention and generate a self-spooling negative narrative. But now, after the time I'd spent at Chenrezig and with Robert's words ringing in my mind, I was alert to this potential and ready to interrupt the self-serving racket.

To get ahead of the trigger, I set an intention to prime myself before I passed by the old office building. Nevertheless, when I drove past it, the emotional belly blow still came. So, mindfully attuned, I opened to the experience. I heard myself say, "Gut punch!" out loud. Then I shifted my attention to the present moment. But because I accepted the present moment in all its fullness, my attention didn't get caught by the old story. Imagine that: mindfulness as a remedy. It really worked.

Before long, I could drive by my old office without too much emotional turbulence. That's not to say I'd fully wrested control over the automatic thoughts. They're called *automatic* for a reason. Sometimes, no matter where I was or what I was doing, those old painful memories would spontaneously arise. Triggers like those are always hard to deal with. You're blithely concentrating on something one second and enmeshed in a negative fixation the next. I could prepare for something when I knew it was coming, like driving by the old office, but it was much harder to work with spontaneously arising thoughts that weren't dependent on a context.

In those early years after my financial collapse, such thoughts would pop into my consciousness frequently and at any time. I could be lying in bed, exercising, hanging out with friends, working in the yard, or, most notably, meditating. On the meditation cushion, I had a strategy for these vexing thoughts, however. Before each sit, I would go through a preparatory routine, one step of which was to acknowledge any potential distractions. During that early recovery period, I always included those thoughts of betrayal and loss as a potential distraction. Next, I would set the intention to focus on breath sensations and try to limit the time my mind wandered.

That latter intention is a very skillful one. It concedes that attention will move and get stuck on random thoughts and perceptions. But seeding one's subconscious with the directive to *try to limit the time the mind wanders* implants an automatic wake-up mechanism into the process. With that intention in place, I could meditate without getting lost in resentment. When trauma-based thoughts arose, they were disrupted by each mini-awakening that the skillful intention inspired. Soon, the triggering distraction itself had the effect of waking me up ever more quickly. Because of that intention to limit mind-wandering, I got really good at immediately noticing the automatic thoughts and redirecting my attention back to breath sensations.

That intention worked so well that I set out to repurpose it to deal with all manner of negative automatic thoughts that troubled me off the cushion. To do this, I had to I develop rituals that reminded me to stay aware of my mental activity throughout the day. The best way I found to do that was to focus on "transitions." Transitions are times when you move from one place or task to another. For example, when I got out of bed, I'd set an intention to stay as aware as I could of triggers, thoughts, and sensations throughout the day. I developed intentions for when I sat down to eat a meal, or moved from my office into the main house. I had another for when I left the house and got into the car. I had still another for when I was getting back into bed at night. Just as intentions serve meditation, they work well during daily life.

Geshe Tashi Tsering was right: just keep practicing. I've discovered through trial and error that practicing also necessarily involves staying *in* the practice! If you want to change or heal, you'll have to stay in it and keep at it. For me, just a little effort every day did the trick. Just as I'd hoped, the spiritual practice delivered real benefits. I came to realize that although Chenrezig was on the other side of the world, my refuge wasn't the monastery anymore. My refuge had become the spiritual practice that was teaching me how to work with my triggers, thoughts, and sensations.

Inspiration, like what I felt the night I wrote the business plan for the documentary, is mysterious, mystical, and unpredictable. A muse like that can strike at any time. The opportunity we have as humans is to remain open and receive the gift of its arrival. That includes both the challenges it bears and the gifts it offers. Open yourself to the fullness of your life. In every problem there lies hidden a potential insight and prospect for growth. But to find it, you'll have cultivate a strong and resilient inner warrior. To receive these mysteries when they present themselves, we must also nurture the open-minded, creative, and inspired energy of an inner artist.

Similar values motivate both of these forces. Each is mission-driven. Both the artist and the warrior vibrate in step with the Three Transcendentals: beauty, goodness, and truth. Although there is no definitive rulebook for a virtue-based morality, you can, through practice, develop a keen sensitivity to the way you think, speak, and act, which will optimize the Three Transcendentals in your life.

In the next chapter, I'll teach you a practice that will enable you to actualize more beauty, goodness, and truth. You'll continue what you've already started by setting intentions and attuning to yourself, others, and contexts. In so doing, you'll develop habits, perceptions, and character traits that express your strength and creativity.

CHAPTER 3

All about Karma

"The creation of a thousand forests is in one acorn."

Ralph Waldo Emerson

Imagine that the Dalai Lama and Hitler are playing golf in a thunderstorm. Is one of them more likely to get hit by lightning than the other?

You've heard the word *karma* before. If you believe karma acts as some administrative function behind the curtain of reality that dishes out justice in perfect measure to those who deserve it, you probably chose Hitler. And if you did, you're in good company. That's the way the majority of those who believe in karma see it working. But is there any evidence for this oversimplified formulation of karma? If you allow yourself to think deeply about it, you'll find there isn't much. Bad things happen to good people all the time and vice versa. Case in point: If a plane crashes, does it mean that everyone on board shares the same karma? I don't think so. If karma does exist, it is unquestionably an extremely hidden phenomenon, far more complicated than the universe as judge and jury. If there is anything to karma, it may be that it acts as an organizing principle, in some way mixing with, and perhaps directing, evolution. Karma may influence the endless cycles of energy, information, and matter that mingle to form cohesive patterns in living organisms flowing through space and time.

There is a meta-science that transcends and includes physics, chemistry, biology, psychology, and the rest. The purpose of this science is to explain the way energy, information, and matter self-organize and produce life. That science is called "living systems theory" or the science of self-organizing systems. I mention it here because understanding the foundational principles of living systems theory will help you wrap your mind around the enigma of karma.

Indeed, systems science and the Buddhist doctrine of karma can help to clarify one another. The former explains the way physics, chemistry, and biology organize the external objective world. The latter helps us to understand how we, through our value-based intentions, organize our inner subjective worlds. Both share similar rules of cause and effect. As such, we are able to map them onto one another.

It is highly relevant to your development to update your notion of karma. Understanding the congruence between these two ways of explaining reality (external and internal) will shed light on why I spent a whole chapter on beauty, goodness, and truth. In this chapter I'll go further, to provide you with an ethically based karmic framework that will support your recovery. But for now, allow me to attempt to amend your conception of karma so that this old idea becomes applicable to your life today.

The concept of karma has evolved significantly over the past few millennia. Let's begin our examination of the shifting views of karma with the originators of the idea, the Vedic philosophers of ancient India.[17] The Vedas are a collection of four sacred texts of the pre-Indian culture. They are also among the oldest-known religious books written, said to date to roughly from 1500 to 1000 BCE. Many authors contributed to their production. Some were called *rishis*, sages who practiced self-development through various yogas. Other scribes were the priests and scholars of their era, collectively known as Brahmin.

Like the Bible, the Torah, and the Koran do for modern believers, the Vedas gave the devotees of their time instructions on rites and rituals. It was thought that these instructions kept the people in God's good graces and helped them maintain order in society. But unlike the aforementioned Abrahamic texts, the Vedas didn't define a set of beliefs per se. Instead, the Vedas laid out a list of specific things to *do*. The Brahmin also co-authored a group of texts that, taken as a whole, are known today as the Upanishads. The Upanishads comprehensively examine and answer questions relating to the creation of the universe, the laws of nature, and man's role in the world. Most readers are familiar with the Eastern concept of reincarnation. The Upanishads were the first texts to describe reincarnation as a cosmic mode of existence where living beings are caught in an endless procession of repeating lifetimes. That perpetual recycling through lifetimes was called *samsara*.

Being stuck on the wheel of samsara wasn't viewed as a happy existence. Instead, it implied cyclic states of relative and perpetual suffering. The Upanishads teach that a procession of reincarnations continues until a person, through ritual practice and meditation, "purifies" themself of all defilements. Then, finally, as a result of their spiritual penance, followers may merge with God. That avenue to release is somewhat analogous to the way believers of the Abrahamic religions receive entry into heaven, by the grace of God's forgiveness. In pre-Indian culture, as long as devotees had karma to purify, they were stuck on the wheel of samsara.

Two thousand six hundred years ago, pre-India was a highly stratified society, divided into four main classes, or castes. At the top of the pyramid sat the Brahmin, or priestly caste, followed by the warriors and administrators, then tradesman and farmers, and, at the bottom, the laboring class. Since the Brahmin were the primary authors of the sacred texts outlining universal creation and order, they were in the privileged position of crafting the political narrative in self-serving ways. One particularly self-serving view propagated by the Brahmin was that the Vedas and Upanishads were "revealed" texts.[18] In other words, the almighty Brahman (God) channeled these sacred writings directly through the Brahmin. All the Brahmin had to do was pay close attention and take dictation.

And what did the Lord reveal to the Brahmin? To hear them tell it, God craved order. More specifically, the orderly structure He liked best was one that put Brahmin in charge of everyone else. Just as Wall Street bankers lobby hard to influence the rules of our financial system, the Brahmin eagerly set the rights, rituals, and duties of a strictly stratified Indian society. The Brahmin wrote their ticket to the top, self-servingly defining a universe in which others were taught to accept their lot. Those multitudes so unfortunate as to not be born into the Brahmin class were discouraged from questioning the authority of the scriptures.

Thus these religious texts became the de facto handbooks for determining the social contract between the classes. The explicit message of the Vedas was this: performing the sacred rituals and duties according to one's station in life makes God happy. Indeed, it was better to do one's duty within one's class poorly than to perform the functions of another class well.[19] A poem in the *Rigveda*[20] goes so far as to say, "If one pokes his head up, chop it off."[21] Social movement between classes was canonically forbidden!

Karma is a Sanskrit word that loosely translates as "action." As outlined by the Brahmanic texts, the action that mattered the most to God was an individual's pious performance of their sacred rituals. Thus the Brahmanic version of karma amounted to a tally of all sacramental devotions, which can almost be paraphrased by the Christmas song "Santa Claus Is Coming to Town": "He (God) knows if you've been bad or good, so be good for goodness' sake!"

The universe as defined by the Brahmin was opaque, capricious, and ruled by a fickle God who liked things *His* way. If you were dissatisfied with your lot or didn't perform your rituals well, you would certainly infuriate God. That sort of "ingratitude" generated a lot of bad karma, and in your next life you'd probably find yourself born into a lower class. On the other hand, should you unquestioningly adhere to authority and to the obligations of your cast, you might well score a more favorable rebirth. Thus, if you were an ancient Indian, you needed to be patient, because if there was a reward for living a pious life, it always came in the *next* life. This inflexible worldview reinforced the idea that one's present life circumstances were set in stone and beyond one's control.

You don't have to be a cynic to see that this fatalistic karmic worldview suited the Brahmin who spread the idea. They trumpeted that to be born a Brahman was the most favorable incarnation. Indeed, it was a karmic "reward" for pleasing God by performing one's past-life rituals and duties righteously. The Vedas were explicit: the universe was giving the Brahmin a collective pat on the back for their moral rectitude. By contrast, those multitudes born into the laboring class were seen as morally impure—a consequence of not having performed sacred rituals and ceremonies excellently in a past life.

Not surprisingly, the complete social immobility that arose out of this system rubbed a lot of Indians the wrong way. As a result, many people decided to drop out of society altogether. These dropouts collectively became known as *Sramana*.[22] A Sramana is just as you might imagine a wandering spiritual aspirant to be. He or she renounced Brahmanical society and roamed, half-naked and homeless, through the forest practicing austerities. They did this in an attempt to annihilate their ego, unite with God, and finally escape the wheel of samsara.

One notable Sramana went by the name of Siddhartha Gautama. You know him today as the historical Buddha. Siddhartha was born into a princely caste, but he was tormented by the obvious suffering he saw all around him. As a result, he decided to renounce his life of comfort and luxury, leave his family, and become a wandering ascetic himself. His goal was to discover a remedy for suffering.

For six years he engaged in the process of immersive, systematic, and empirical observation of his mind through meditation. As he did, he also held the Brahmanic and Sramanic worldviews up to the light of critical analysis. Eventually, his ardent and exacting inquiry enabled him to see through the self-serving metaphysics of the Brahmin. He also noticed the ontological flaws and moral failings of his wandering comrades. These many observations accelerated the evolution of his perspective.

Siddhartha came by his conclusions honestly, by developing a heretofore-unknown method of investigation. He employed the common practice of meditation, but he used it differently. Instead of merely focusing his attention and falling into a deep trance—the leading meditation "technology" of his day—he added the extra dimension of ever-present and wakeful awareness. Today, we call his method mindfulness meditation. This novel form of meditation opened a window into the connection between the mind and the body and, more generally, into how a person's life organizes itself.

As he meditated, he watched flows of energy and information cycle through his mind-body. Taking the stance of an objective observer, he watched as feelings and thoughts organized themselves into patterns of "self" without any effort on his part at all. It was then he realized that there was only a slim prospect of altering the flow in a positive direction. He rightly understood that he didn't directly *control* physics or chemistry, his biology or psychology, or the broader culture in which he found himself. Instead, these immensely complex and intertwined streams of causality impinged on him.

But sitting in the middle of it all, meditating, he discovered a hair's breadth of agency. He found he could set *conscious intentions*, motivated by care, and a wish for a higher good. He could exercise his moral will and thus alter the trajectory of the system. Setting a conscious intention shifted the focus and quality of his *attention*. Balancing his mind that way caused the resultant procession of thoughts and feelings to shift toward the positive. Amplifying internal *beauty* led to the *truth* of less suffering.

Thus it dawned on him that setting conscious intentions was *the* way to change how thoughts and feelings organized themselves into patterns that either amplify or reduce suffering. The truth he exposed to the sunlight of his awareness was that moral values aren't handed down by divine decree but instead emerge out of the profound interconnectedness of all reality—every living thing prefers happiness over suffering. To increase the former and reduce the latter is our united task. Thus, setting conscious intentions to actualize a higher good is a way to skillfully manage creation's chaotic unfolding. Only when we recognize our mutual participation in the overall pattern-making do we reclaim and exercise our power!

Before we go any further, let me be clear and delineate the significant difference between intentional action and *consciously* intentional action. Every morning I get out of bed and wander over to the coffee maker. To be sure, this is a deliberate action, tightly screwed into the machinery of my mind-body system. But this intention is mostly *unconscious*. It's not that I'm asleep on my feet until I get a shot of caffeine to bring me online, but I don't consciously choose to walk over and make the coffee. The procedural memory of making a cup of coffee every morning is imprinted in my mind-body by repeating this behavior thousands of times. The result is that my mind-body now walks itself into the kitchen without any need for conscious thought. When I sit down to meditate, however, I set a conscious intention to follow my breath and ignore all distractions. In so doing, that deliberate intention swims upstream against the habit of my attention to get caught by, and follow every chaotic and unconscious movement of my mind.

Meditators quickly discover that we're not the ones thinking. Just as your heart is beating by itself, your brain is alive and functioning outside your conscious control. That three-pound network of neurons excites itself and, by doing so, produces habitual patterns of thought and feeling that you recognize as "you." All that brain activity takes place by itself, requiring no effort on your part whatsoever.

When you learn to meditate skillfully, with objectivity and dispassion, it becomes evident that thoughts and feelings show up by themselves. That said, they do so chaotically. You can never be sure what mental object will pop up next. But consciously setting intentions plants a seed in your subconscious, which make thoughts *related* to that intention more likely to arise. That's the way intentions work—they incline an otherwise chaotic stream to flow in a more intentional direction.

An example of this deliberate seed-planting is when I set a conscious intention to keep my emotions in check when my daughter, Alana, struggles with self-control. That conscious attunement helps me manage my reflexive responses. When I get it right, I am able to guide her in healthier ways than my parents did me. If I don't set a conscious intention ahead of time, however, I run the risk of shifting into "autopilot." At those times, I'm much more inclined to unconsciously repeat ingrained patterns of parenting I'd rather extinguish.

Conscious intentions adeptly steer the ship of feeling and behavior through the storm of life as the future unfolds. When it comes to unconscious, ingrained, and habitual intentions, however, we are all mostly functioning on autopilot. Conscious, wholesome intentions enable you to take hold of the wheel yourself and guide your life in a deliberate way.

Karma and systems science show that everything we do unintentionally, we do out of habit. Change requires setting a conscious intention to alter the course of that habit stream while remaining vigilant and effortful. For the whole change process to gain energy and momentum, you also need to remember to keep reconnecting with your conscious intention. Time will pass, and as it does, stay mindful of your healthy intention. It's work, but this particular work is the price of freedom.

Siddhartha's meticulous mindfulness revealed that the actions that mattered weren't the atonements touted by the Brahmin in the Vedas. Instead, setting conscious intentions to act virtuously and increase the three transcendental values is the key to maximizing well-being. It was chiefly because of his rigorous self-inquiry that Siddhartha came to redefine karma as *intention*.[23]

Intentions incline the mind toward similar objects—positive to positive and negative to negative. What you relate to gives rise to future "actions" of thinking, speech, and behavior. Siddhartha was exactly correct that conscious intentions exist in the ethical realm. That is the very domain occupied by the values of beauty, goodness, and truth as they rise toward subjective well-being.

The moral sphere is also the abode of greed, aversion, and ignorance, which descend toward misery.

By his redefinition, karma becomes the sum of all one's past moral actions. There's a feedforward aspect to it, too. What you did in the past puts metaphysical pressure on your present, inclining you to enact a better or worse version of yourself. It's best to think of karma as creating a *cloud of probability* in your life. This cloud of likelihood never *determines* how you think, speak, and act. Instead, it predisposes you to think, speak, and act in patterned ways. Those patterns, wholesome or not, then influence your next thoughts, emotions, and reactions. Then it all repeats. The way you feel *always* emerges out of your probability cloud. You're the only one inside that mind-body of yours. You must, therefore, experience the effects of your past actions as they impinge on this present moment. Everything else will come and go, but your karma will forever be your closest companion.

Energy, information, and matter interact according to the laws of nature. As physical forces and chemical elements interact, life *self*-organizes into patterns that repeat and perpetuate. In other words, on both a micro and macro level, pattern-making is a fundamental characteristic of reality. The universe has been creating repetitious patterns since the beginning of time. Systemic and recursive feedback causes forms to emerge, which then drive the next series of actions, which then make new patterns.

You are a part of that flow. It follows then that infinite effauses and caufects co-create all the patterns in the universe, which include those contained within your subjective experience. Self-organization is both the beating heart of living systems theory and a primary principle of karma.

Keep in mind that all of this systemic activity is automatic. That's the chief reason why changing and healing are so difficult. Try as you might, changing habits of thinking and behavior can feel like trying to push infinity with a feather. The reality of the situation in which we live is paradoxical, which makes both of the following statements true: Because the universe makes itself, we have very little, if any, free will. And yet, it is also true that we can learn something new, effect change, and heal. So how do we square that circle?

Let's begin by clarifying terms, starting with your agency. Gratefully, you still have it. That said, your will is not, and can never be, *free*. It is instead conditioned by forces and patterns beyond your control. You don't control gravity or beat your heart. Instead, immeasurable universal interactions control you. Therefore, the hair's breadth of agency you have is utterly and completely *conditioned*.

These are the facts: life is chaotic and your will is conditioned. Therefore, should you desire healthful change, you must to learn to coax the meager current of energy, information, and matter flowing in your tiny corner of the universe in a more favorable direction. Not knowing how to consciously direct that current is the main reason most people stay stuck. It follows that ignorance of the way the system works is a primary cause of suffering.

For this reason, Siddhartha did not dispute that people cycle in their suffering. It was samsara then, and it is samsara now. Instead, he boldly redefined who's in charge. He took that power away from Brahman (God) and gave it back to the people. Siddhartha's philosophy was a creed of radical responsibility. Teaching people that they play the primary role in *co-creating* their experience forcefully upended the belief in a fatalistic universe.

Likewise, this philosophy challenged people to hold themselves accountable for the arc of their lives. Siddhartha taught that rather than Brahman capriciously throwing a person from one lifetime to the next, one's intentional actions were consequential in how their life unfolds. It's not God but the raw and reliable fact of interdependent karmic actions that either frees a person or keeps them stuck.

Siddhartha's revelatory redefinition of karma brought it down from the heavens. Finally, it was grounded in the practical domain of personal responsibility. There is the law of cause and effect, but operating within that law is the force of individual intentionality, the spiritual "energy" of which emerges from the moral spheres of beauty or ugliness, goodness or depravity, and truth or ignorance. Although most aspects of life are out of a person's immediate control, this fact does not ultimately determine the pitch of one's suffering. One's intentional actions do.

Years back when I worked in an inpatient psychiatric hospital, a young woman came into my office and sat with her body turned away from me, legs and arms crossed, head down. I felt the intensity of her agitation. The blankness of her stare suggested that her attention was wedged tightly into a very dark corner of her mind. I attuned to her and inquired, "How can I help you?" She told me how being "locked up" in a rehab hospital was "causing" her depression and anxiety to intensify. Even worse, she said her doctor, therapist, and parents were all conspiring to extend her stay by two weeks.

Who could blame them? From their perspective, it didn't seem that the young woman's condition was improving. Turning toward me, staring me straight in the face, she pounded my desk for emphasis. "This is why I'm depressed and anxious—because I'm stuck here!" Slumping back in her chair, she whimpered almost inaudibly, "I just want to go home."

Two weeks later, I had another session with the same young lady the evening before her flight home. You might imagine, given her earlier eagerness to go home, that her imminent departure would be reason for celebration. It wasn't. Instead, she sat in my office lamenting not having "gotten it." Now she was afraid to return home. The triggers that necessitated admission to residential treatment were still going to be there when she got back. This poor girl had traveled far to spend six weeks in rehab in the Arizona desert, hoping to learn something and return home a changed person. Unfortunately, although her body had traveled across the country, her mind had stayed cycling in samsara.

What she didn't "get" was the practical understanding that our mind-body is a recording-feedback device—it automatically and reliably repeats the patterns we enact. That's the *karma* of it. If we transmit anxiety, the mind-body grows increasingly anxious. We imprint ourselves through our actions—that is how current conditions determine future conditions. The way out of this trap is to open yourself up to new information, gain new skills and perspectives, put effort into setting conscious intentions directed toward amplifying beauty, goodness and truth, and remain mindful during times of stress. Then repeat. And repeat. And endlessly repeat. These are the effauses and caufects of healthful change.

What Siddhartha taught was accurate, practical, and beneficial. He certainly did not intend to create an orthodoxy based on a set of beliefs. On the contrary, his objective was to teach his followers an *orthopraxis*—a recovery model based on moral action. He led his students to wake up to the distortions of their perceptions. Further, he encouraged them to be mindful of their motivations and behaviors. That's how the profound principle of interdependence became his rationale for ethics and kindness.

Everything is interconnected. Personal actions don't just affect the actor's quality of life—they spread out and affect the quality of life of others, society, and the world. For that reason, Siddhartha actively made a case for an ethically based karma. Because all things are connected, exercising your sliver of autonomy by setting conscious wholesome intentions will eventually spread well-being throughout the system.

If I've succeeded in convincing you of the significance of setting conscious, virtuous intentions, you may now wonder, *How do I start, and which specific conscious intentions should I set?* Thankfully, Siddhartha didn't leave us hanging on this point. Being a systems thinker himself, in contemplating the big problem of karma he figured the best way to solve it was to take it apart. Siddhartha reckoned that voluntary activities arise from only three domains: the mind, speech, and the body. After much deliberation, he came up with a list of ten virtuous actions that thoroughly cover most human activities. The list includes three conscious intentions related to thinking, four linked to speech, and three concerning the actions of the body. Working on cultivating the following ten virtues will begin to blow your karmic cloud of probability into fairer skies.

THE THREE VIRTUES OF MIND

1. Correct understanding is knowing for sure that what you think, say, and do matters. Living this virtue means wholeheartedly believing that your intentional actions make a difference to your health and happiness. Also, what you think, say, and do matters to the health and happiness of others as well. The wisdom of this view underpins the remaining nine virtues.
2. Sympathetic joy is endeavoring to amplify your joy in response to the happiness, health, gifts, and successes of others. In other words, be happy for others when something good happens to them. On the flip side, sympathetic joy catches and lets go of greed, jealousy, and envy when those negative emotions arise in you.
3. Well-wishing is coming to the profound realization that wanting others to be well and happy is a primary cause of your happiness. It is appreciating the fact that holding on to resentments infects your mind and heart first. Therefore, the best way forward, for yourself and everyone involved, is to wish others well.

FOUR VIRTUES OF SPEECH

1. Honesty is consciously striving always to speak the truth and to be transparently straightforward in your

dealings. This virtue requires some skill and tact at times. As you practice honesty, hold the intention to speak kindly and gently so as not to harm others with your candid views. The virtue of honesty also includes being as frank and honest as possible when in dialogue with yourself.

2. Supportive speech is always intending to bring people together with your words. Gossip always tears relationships apart. Speaking divisively about others harms three people. First, it hurts you, because practicing divisive speech negatively influences your immediate feeling tone and inclines you to speak divisively in the future. Second, divisive speech injures the listener by bringing them into your cloud of negativity and encouraging them to engage in similar negative behavior. Last, divisive language harms the person about whom you are speaking. Help all three people by only speaking supportively of others. If you don't have anything good to say, remain silent.

3. Kind and gentle speech is earnestly striving to communicate so that your words land lightly on the ears of others. When you speak, the tone of your voice and your word choices should conjure a sense of safety, acceptance, and comfort in your listeners. This virtue is especially challenging to maintain in close, intimate, and familial relationships—the volatile mixture of intimacy and irritability can quickly intensify one's particular habits of harshness. Therefore, set the inten-

tion to practice kind and gentle speech, especially at work and at home.
4. Meaningful speech is about paying close attention to the listener and endeavoring to speak only about topics that are appropriate and relevant to the context. No one likes to be cornered by someone who drones on and on about issues that are not appropriate or relevant to the situation. Be on guard against choosing topics that would needlessly offend, put off, or otherwise agitate your listener. This virtue is the basis for the admonition not to talk about religion or politics in polite company. The best topics are those that augment beauty, goodness, and truth.

THREE VIRTUES OF BODY

1. Protecting and honoring life means recognizing the precious rarity of all life. With this in mind, we work to build relationships with all other beings based on care and stewardship. This relationship acknowledges that there is no Planet B, so we have to take care of this one. The long-term effects of your actions, even in seemingly little things like how long you shower, what you have for lunch, or which car you drive, add up. But remember, too, that you live in the context of a massive living system, the intricate workings of which are beyond your immediate control. It's impossible not to cause harm. So, no shame, blame or guilt;

just do your best. Because of fathomless interdependence, this virtue asks you to raise your awareness of the whole of which you are but one small part.

2. Respecting property starts with not taking anything that is not freely offered. Of course, this virtue precludes stealing, but it also involves caring for the property of others, including public spaces. The right way to embody this virtue is to consider yourself a steward for the greater good of all. You may find yourself picking up trash on your local playground because you take spiritual ownership of the park. Care in this regard turns you into a conscious steward of *everything* you see.

3. Sexual integrity is finally getting the attention it deserves. The #MeToo movement highlights the harm we perpetrate on each other when we don't exercise control over our sexual urges. Most immediately, this virtue asks you to avoid causing harm with your sexuality. That includes not respecting another's boundaries and disrupting other people's relationships. Obviously, it applies to anyone in a committed relationship as well. Full recognition of this virtue means maintaining a watchful eye over your attention whenever you feel the pull of attraction to someone other than your committed partner.

In elucidating these ten virtues, in no way do I want to imply that I'm a paragon of virtue and integrity. I am still a work in progress. That said, it is because I consciously wrestle with guilt and shame over past actions that I learn to better control my destructive shadow. That powerful, selfish, unconscious energy lives in all of us. But by setting conscious intentions, a person can learn to wake up to these primal drives and redirect the flow of their karma.

Practicing these ten virtues will definitely help in that regard. I'm particularly grateful to this practice for helping me recalibrate myself. We are, as yet, unfinished works of spiritual art. Every one of us is in process. We're all seeking to actualize the positive potential latent within us. So give grace, be kind, and keep practicing. The more we practice setting conscious, wholesome intentions, the more they suffuse our being, becoming habitual, and eventually, second nature.

I encourage you to visit this webpage (www.drmarkpirtle.com/virtues-log/) to access a Virtues Log that will help you track the 10 Virtues as well as other aspects of your daily spiritual practice.

CHAPTER 4

Bewegungsmuster

> *"We are but whirlpools in a river of ever-flowing water. We are not stuff that abides, but patterns that perpetuate."*
>
> Norbert Wiener

"Sally" did everything right, as she always had. She was the eldest daughter of immigrant parents who expected that she not only earn good grades in order to attend college but also care for her three younger siblings while her parents worked. Life was difficult, but Sally understood that her parents were trying to improve their lot and she had to do her part. Decades later, despite having a full-time job and a family of her own, her brothers left the care of her aging parents to her, too. Sally stoically handled it all.

As the years passed, the one indulgence she allowed herself was to dream of retirement. That was finally going to be her time, and happily, that time was approaching fast. Although she and her husband never had loads of money, they were thrifty and good savers. The government jobs they both had would also provide sufficient pensions to allow them to spend years exploring America in a motor home.

Within what seemed like the blink of an eye, their three children graduated from college. After their kids all had jobs and were settled into their lives, she and her husband decided now was the time and gleefully submitted their resignations. *I'm only sixty*, Sally thought. *I've got years ahead of me.* The decades of hard work and sacrifice now seemed worth it. She felt so grateful. Her husband was healthy, and their relationship was closer than ever. They had already spent a few years researching which motor home to buy, so pulling the trigger on that big purchase didn't faze them. After selling the house and wrapping up loose ends, they'd be ready to hit the road. They took out a calendar and set a departure date for ninety days hence. As an expression of love and gratitude, their children were even going to throw them a bon voyage party.

Then, out of the blue, Sally started feeling bloated, with occasional sharp pains in her abdomen. She hadn't changed her diet, so the symptoms didn't make sense. Conditioned to be tough, she tried to ignore the pain, but it got worse. Out of an abundance of caution, she decided to see her doctor for a checkup and dutifully acquiesced to undergo a barrage of tests. When the results were in, Sally went back for a follow-up visit.

The solemn expression on her doctor's face caused her chest to tighten. She braced for bad news. The doctor told her that she had Stage IV pancreatic cancer. At that point, there was little that could be done. Sally was dead five days before she and her husband were to depart on their retirement adventure.

Life can be so unfair. Hearing a story like Sally's makes me wonder about fate and destiny. I can't imagine some outside force, like God, playing such a cruel trick on a person like Sally. But if no entity is in control, can anything happen?

If I haven't made you aware of it already, Buddhists talk a lot about suffering. So much so that Buddhism has acquired the taint of pessimism in some circles. That's not how I view the philosophy, however. Instead, I think it's prudent, even spiritually mature, to talk about the predicament in which we find ourselves. Which is why I feel inclined to share the Buddhist take on suffering with you now. It identifies three types.

The first type of suffering is the "suffering of suffering," also called "the pain of pain." Of the three types of suffering, this is the most obvious. Everyone understands this kind of suffering. It's physical pain, but also more than that. Painful conditions like poverty or violence, neglect or rejection, disappointments, and irritations of all kinds fall under this particular category of suffering. Broadly speaking, getting whatever you don't want or, alternately, not getting what you want is part and parcel of the suffering of suffering.

The second type of suffering is the "suffering of change." This form of suffering is subtler than the blatantly obvious pain of pain. Here, suffering arises because of the impermanent nature of reality—objects, conditions, and relationships all change. When life situations are great, wait a while. Inevitably, the winds of change will turn. On the micro level, the suffering of change is like a spiritual Second Law of Thermodynamics.[24] All conditions seem to degenerate from order to disorder or, in this case, from pleasant to unpleasant. For example, consider the excitement that comes with a new car. It's shiny and dent-free, runs great, and smells good. Just wait a few years and see how much happiness you feel when it needs an expensive repair. The honeymoon phase of a relationship will move in the direction of disillusionment unless a couple works to keep the spark of love alive. What initially seems like a genuine source of happiness somehow changes into its opposite.

The third form of suffering is the "suffering of conditioned existence," also referred to as the "fundamental suffering of vulnerability." This last form of suffering connects the first two types, the sufferings of pain and change. The suffering of conditioning accounts for the actual physical way in which we exist, with a body that is subject to aging, sickness, and death. The suffering of conditioned existence also accounts for the fact that we live in an unpredictable world, where circumstances are always changing. Suffering isn't a bug in the system that can be gotten rid of; it's a feature of the system. Sally's cancer is an example.

But despite the relative lack of control we have, our intentional actions do produce a meaningful *influence*. As mentioned before, intentions create a fuzzy boundary space in which people live and their experiences materialize. Flowing patterns of effauses and caufects all add together and an average "shape" of a person's life emerges. The overall system, more often than not, then begins to incline in one direction or another, toward betterment or not. Should you keep acting in ways that keep the momentum flowing in the same direction, the results begin to increase over time.

You'll recall that in Yellowstone, when the wolves were hunted to extinction, an ecosystem-disrupting downward spiral began.

Seventy years later, when the wolves were reintroduced, the downward spiral halted and an upward spiral began. After a short time, it gained momentum, and eventually the ecosystem rebalanced and healed itself. But note that the park's initial transformation was undertaken in the external objective world. In other words, the park changed in ways that could be *measured*. A countable number of wolves were reintroduced.

My point is, what happens on the "outside" always affects what goes on "inside." The outward transformation of the park, initiated by the reintroduction of the wolves, led to *internal* shifts in the people managing and using it. In contrast with objective measurable changes associated with the ecosystem's restoration, the internal changes I'm speaking of were *felt* by people. These immeasurable internal changes altered the way the people who managed and used the park related to it. The restored park was more admirable, more lovable. That essential qualitative difference has made all the difference to the long-term preservation of Yellowstone.

The example of Yellowstone is relevant to our purpose in this way, too: people had to act out of love and care for the park *before* any objective changes were made manifest. Thus, valuing something creates its own positive feedback. Doing good feels good, which inspires more of the same. Systems prove that if you keep that simple process going long enough, you can create a positive pattern, too. The qualities of health, happiness, love, purpose, connection, and contribution just need a little consistent and concerted action to constellate and gain momentum.

There's a part of you that intuitively knows this already. Your inner artist acts out of love and care, driven to express more of yourself. Your future experience will materialize in the same way a potter molds clay on a wheel. They start with only a lump of clay and an intention. Then they guide the *relationship* between their eyes, hands, the clay, and the wheel until a moving pattern takes shape. The more adept the potter's attention, know-how, and handling of the spinning clay, the more often they find the end result rewarding. A pattern flows from one shape into another, until finally the potter sees in the shape of the molded clay a semblance of their original intention.

Throwing a pot is always a gamble, however. Every master potter knows that crafting a pot that pushes the edge of their skill is rife with complication and pitfalls. Moreover, every piece of clay has its unique shape and irregularities. So, staying present to, accepting, and working with the clay's inherent characteristics is part of the "right-relationship" game. Even then it's easy to make mistakes—the pot can crack in the kiln for no known reason—but consciously attuning to every moment of the flowing process generally leads to a welcome result or, if not, a lesson that leads to creative readjustment.

In that same way, your life is like throwing a pot. Setting your intentions, staying present, accepting and working with what comes, learning from your mistakes, and honing your skills is the best you can do. Despite the loftiest intentions and the skillfulness of your actions, you never know what form life will ultimately take. But setting and holding to a conscious intention is your best insurance against botched endings.

The current way you experience your relationship with yourself, others, and the world is more than a metaphor about clay, however. It's a reflection of the trajectory of your past intentions, thinking, and behavior. If you're in a distressed place right now, I'll repeat: you were never in *control* of most of what happened to you. Don't blame and shame yourself for poor past decisions and behavior. Cut yourself some slack. You weren't in control. Look at your life with compassion.

That said, you can't discount or deny your *influence* over where you find yourself now either. You, me, and everybody else are the ever-present center of gravity of a local system. That's the "karma" of living systems. Going forward, you have a choice to make: you can let the pot spin aimlessly into whatever shape is developing, or you can mold and shape your future into an authentic expression of who you want to become.

I'd like now to share a story with you, but before that, I'm going to borrow a German word to set it up. If you speak German, as I do (barely), you'll appreciate that Germans admire the accuracy of their language as much as the precision of their engineering. Similar to the exacting fit of a finely machined piston gliding smoothly within a cylinder, the German language is rife with well-crafted compound puzzle words that fit snuggly together. For example, instead of using six separate words to convey the concept "insurance companies that provide legal protection," Germans, ever parsimonious, link all those words together into one exacting term that stands for the same thing, *Rechtsschutzversicherungsgesellschaften*. How about this one: *Donaudampfschifftahrtsgesellschaftskapitan*. To Germans, wasting the three spaces between the words *Danube steamship company captain* is a needless extravagance. Constructing sentences to express utterances such as "That's Karsten—he's the Danube steamship company captain" is too great an effort. Far more efficient to stick a bunch of nouns together.

Mark Twain, while endeavoring to teach himself German, expressed a similar sentiment: "Some German words are so long that they have perspective." You'll probably feel a sense of relief when I tell you that the German word I intend to introduce to you is only fifteen letters long. "Short" as it is, *Bewegungsmuster* is still a perfect example of a quirky Teutonic-type of puzzle word.

Bewegung has various meanings. *"Movement"* is the most common, and *"motion," "exercise,"* and *"agitation"* are less common. *Muster*, standing alone, means *"pattern," "design,"* or *"example."* Placed together, these words can imply a relational pattern that moves through time and space and can reveal itself in a variety of guises, be they physical, biological, mental, emotional, or spiritual. For instance, imagine a rogue wave traveling across the empty expanse of ocean. All along its crossing, that one wave intersects and passes through the undulating crests and troughs of millions of other waves. They add to it and subtract from it, yet our wave maintains itself as a distinct moving pattern until it crashes onto a distant shore.

Likewise, basic, instinctive, and reflexive movement patterns are essential to every aspect of athletic proficiency. These also fit within the definition of *Bewegungsmuster*. Watch a pitcher and a batter face off during a baseball game and you'll witness a dance of ingrained and well-choreographed dirt-kicking, sideways glancing, chew-spitting, and cup-adjusting. Neither player is necessarily thinking; bodies are merely moving in a patterned flow, in perfect response to the moment.

Indeed, such entangled movement patterns are everywhere you care to look. On a personal level, the developmental path that culminates in your adult personality arises out of recursive interactions between inborn traits and lived experience. The interplay between nature and nurture is what "writes the software" of your self-sense and, further, your worldview, reflexive thoughts, speech, and behavior. All of which mold your outward expression of character.

Well-established patterns of personality can remain relatively consistent for years. No one will argue that in the sometimes-hot mess of family interactions, learning new ways of relating to each other is difficult. Moving patterns of personality and combustion exist within the family system and sustain themselves through their interactions. In other words, individual characters and family dynamics are themselves a *Bewegungsmuster*.

The stubbornness of chronic stress illness is yet another type of moving pattern. Insomnia, depression, addictions, and anxieties, each with their distinctive patterns of activating triggers, thoughts, and sensations, can last for decades.

Moving patterns are observable on every level of scale, from the smallest atoms to the most massive galactic clusters, and across every possible contextual frame—quantum, inorganic, microscopic, biological, psychological, interpersonal, cultural, political, societal, environmental, planetary, and cosmic. *Bewegungsmuster* is the way the universe creates and maintains itself.

It's easy to see a correspondence between *bewegungsmuster* and Siddhartha's conception of karma. Intentions self-organize into repetitious and related effauses and caufects—for both good and ill.

You've lived long enough to evolve many moving patterns throughout your life. These moving patterns were born out of a full spectrum of moral activities. On one end, there were principled, praiseworthy, and pleasing actions. On the other side, there were dishonorable, shameful, and painful ones. What a person feels largely depends on the "rightness" of their intentional actions.

With that in mind, consider the way a persistent pattern of spiritual energy passed through multiple human hosts to eventually show up in my life. To show how this inexorable karmic process has revealed itself, I'll share a shocking anecdote—the story of how someone came to write me a check for a million dollars. Well, to be accurate, it wasn't exactly one check—it was a whole bunch of smaller checks written over six-plus years that totaled more than a million dollars. And, importantly, the money didn't go directly to me. Instead, it funded the documentary that shares the same title as this book. I will tell you the story, but don't expect to learn the secrets of a get-rich-quick scheme. It wasn't like that at all. Instead, the inspired benefactor who funded the documentary was himself a happy consequence, immersed and flowing within the moving pattern of goodness.

I don't want to give the impression that arriving at such a threshold of positive potential was simple or easy. So indulge me as I provide a bit of context. First, I'll fill in some critical details from my childhood. Hopefully, that'll add perspective to the collapse of my business and personal life, with which you're already familiar. Then, from that low point, I'll detail how I made small, seemingly insignificant adjustments in my mind, heart, and relationships. These adjustments eventually conjured a field of goodness that helped me to recover my lost health and happiness and finally inspired a generous person to invest in me.

Growing up as a young adult, I was a perfect product of my family, generation, and culture. My early years were a fantasyland, literally. I grew up in Anaheim, California, in the 1960s, in a house only eight blocks from Disneyland. Both my parents worked at another nearby amusement park, Knott's Berry Farm. I was born on the first full day of the Kennedy administration. Years before the tumult of the civil rights and Vietnam War protests, the early '60s represented the dawning of the Age of Aquarius, Camelot, and the golden age of TV. Because no one told me, I assumed that everyone else lived like this, too, in a modern world on the cutting edge of discovery. This mostly idyllic backdrop of my childhood hinted at an existence without limits. America just put a man on the moon, and the art and music of the time were out of this world, too.

I was speaking in full sentences by the time I was one and a half years old. This early loquacity earned me lots of attention and implanted and reinforced the notion that I was a kid to match the time—in other words, special. My paternal grandmother further strengthened this view by telling me on many occasions, "You can grow up to become the president." I swallowed that grandiose idea hook and all. Later, that internalized sense of uniqueness morphed into a core conviction that I knew better than everyone else.

The circumstances of my upbringing, although rich with valuable learning experiences, were also a breeding ground for narcissistic tendencies. A sense of specialness and arrogance was beginning to infect my budding personality. I vividly recall my mother once asking me to clean my room. Picturing myself a perfect Little Lord Fauntleroy, I responded disapprovingly. "When I grow up, I'm going to be rich so I can pay someone to clean up after me." The inflated sense of superiority I radiated was just one of many distasteful moving patterns that began to take shape in my psyche.

Not only was I a smart little guy, but I was also a smart aleck. That choice combination of attributes put me on the receiving end of lots of bullying. Few bullies are born with the conscious desire to cause harm, but what a child experiences at home usually gets repeated elsewhere. Experiencing boundary-violating abusive behavior with regularity can begin to feel normal. When it does, and once a child internalizes it, that angry and powerless victim often turns to bullying to reclaim their lost power.

So starts a cycle of violence and reprisal. What keeps this dyad bound together are the fixating adhesives of loss and anger. Being on the receiving end of bullying put a chip on my shoulder. I wasn't always strong enough to defend myself, so I unconsciously resolved to reclaim my lost pride by winning at another game. The resentment I held fueled an "I'll show you" attitude that stayed with me for decades.

My parents married young. Jack and Susie were only twenty-three and twenty-two when I arrived on the scene. Patty, my older sister, was just eleven months ahead of me. There my parents were, two young sexy kids with two kids of their own in the freewheeling Southern California culture of the '60s. No wonder they couldn't hold it together—too much centripetal force was being channeled through the foundations of their relationship.

My dad was, and still is, one of the greatest loves of my life. He also was, hands down, the best, most fun father a kid could have. He was a slapstick specialist. No comedian before or since, not even Jim Carrey—and I *love* Jim Carrey—was his better. While Patty and I sat in the tub, he would play-act brushing his teeth, then absently jab the toothbrush into his eye, slam his fingers in the medicine cabinet, slip on the bath mat, and pull down the towel rack. To squeals of laughter, he would do all that and more in perfect rhythm; we honestly believed Jack Pirtle was that clumsy. When my parents split and my dad wasn't living in the house with us anymore, it left a mark.

I remember walking home from kindergarten one day when he drove by in his new red 1966 MG roadster. "Hey, Marky boy," he called out, and seeing him filled me with joy and excitement. After asking my mom if it was okay, he took me to Orange Julius for lunch. The next day on the way home from school, no dad. I still vividly remember making my way home with an intense ache in my belly, tears spilling from my eyes. For months I walked past that same spot on Katella Avenue, hoping my dad would drive by again. He never did.

I don't doubt that the pain of that early and significant loss left a lasting imprint on me. For most of my life I would characterize myself as being overly sensitive, but I never understood why. All I knew was that I had to work inordinately hard at controlling my emotions as a young adult. How much of my later impulsiveness, lack of social filter, addictive behaviors, emotionality, and shadow aggression had to do with that early trauma, I'll never know for certain.

Post-divorce, I lived in a blended family in which anger was the emotion that received full-throated ventilation. My mom was born in Berlin at the beginning of World War II. After she divorced my dad, it made sense she'd feel a resonance with her birth culture and remarry a German man. My stepfather, Joe, was an altogether different man from my father. He was at times severe and unplayful, strict and prone to unpredictable outbursts of rage. I learned later that he medicated his emotions by drinking and taking pills. We lived in America, after all, the quick-fix culture. He had unregulated emotions, ergo he managed them by drinking beer and topping himself off with a prescription for Valium.

Today I understand how trauma affects the brain. Couple that with my now more mature adult perspective and I can look back and have compassion for my stepfather. Decades later, after my mom divorced him, she told me how brutally hard his childhood was. In his youth he was traumatized beyond comprehension, with no chance to learn emotional self-regulation. Born in Germany in 1936, his formative experiences involved his family's navigating the labyrinthine chaos of World War II: carpet-bombing, displacement, famine, and other horrors. Near the war's end, at only nine years old, he was conscripted into the Hitler Youth, preparing to fight the advancing American army.

As a child, I had no understanding or context for these severe and violent conditions that left permanent emotional scars on Joe. To little Mark, he appeared as a monster at times. Once when I was seven years old, he and I were tuning up his new 1968 VW beetle, and my involvement amounted to obediently watching him fiddle with the engine and fetching tools when he demanded them. His tools all hung on a pegboard on which he'd drawn a permanent marker outline for where each belonged. "A place for everything and everything in its place" was an axiom by which Joe lived. I was just tall enough for my little chin to stick above the workbench, and when I scanned the pegboard for a wrench, all I saw was its vacant outline. When I returned empty-handed, he grabbed me by the arm and dragged me over to the workbench. His height gave him a perspective I did not have. He could see the wrench, which was lying right on the edge of the workbench in the spot where my chin had poked over. Then he came unglued. In an instant, he shoved my face hard into the workbench. The bottom row of my front teeth tore through my lower lip.

Unfortunately for me, I often stood in as the surrogate focal point for Joe's unregulated explosions. This is how his rage got mapped into me. Indeed, this is always the way the abuser and the abused become entangled. The intergenerational moving pattern of abuse finds another host to keep it alive. With shame and remorse, I shudder to think that I've sustained and perpetuated that revolting energy by raging on others myself. Another moving pattern made its way forward and into the future through me.

But now, let me balance the scales a bit. I need to make it clear that my childhood wasn't characterized only by abuse. Far from it. I grew up in a First World country where privileged kids like me start out well ahead of the vast majority of children in the developing world. All my basic needs were met. I had grandparents and parents who loved and cared for me (yes, even Joe did most of the time). Just as I experienced trauma growing up, so did I experience exceedingly enriching conditions.

For example, my paternal grandfather, Farris Pirtle, loved me unerringly. He cared for me in a way that personified the pinnacle of a moral and ethical standard. His foundational guidance became the spiritual floor I stood back up on after making such a mess of my life years later. I credit his example with helping me turn things around after I bottomed out. Additionally, my mother has always been there when I've needed her. Her loving generosity sustains me to this day. My stepmother, Klaire, has been a light in my life, exposing me to enriching social, emotional, and educational experiences that helped to expand my worldview.

It's also imperative to mention I grew up with many advantages and privileges that go with being a white male in this society. So, despite the intermittent abuse detailed above, there was a tremendous amount of good there, too. All of it taken together formed an amalgamation of moving patterns that shaped my character. Both the good and the bad blended to help or hinder my relationships as I grew into an adult. Your upbringing could probably be described as this same sort of mixed cocktail of experiences.

Before the feather woke me up on that run twenty years ago, I blamed my business failure on my former partners, and my relationship difficulties on other people. I couldn't see how the unconscious moving patterns of negative personality traits that lived in me were the real culprit. But there was also a big part of me that always wanted to help others, which is why health care interested me so much. Empathy and compassion live inside me in large quantities, too. And yet, right alongside that "service to others" orientation exists a selfish and greedy part. These disparate impulses live together inside me—light and shadow—like they do in everyone. Another part of me has always been courteous and polite, but up until beauty, goodness, and truth became prime motivators, I was the guy who forgot a person's name right after I met them. At times, I spoke harshly and divisively about others, too. That mixed way of relating and speaking produced consistently mixed results.

All those conflicting patterns of personality living inside me resulted in an unpredictable temperament and chaotic relationships. Those ingredients created a balancing type of feedback where my life was always two steps forward and two steps back. I should also mention that during that time I intermittently abused drugs and, woefully, other people as well. No one writes a million-dollar check to the kind of a person I was in my twenties and thirties.

Reorienting toward beauty, goodness, and truth has been a developmental process for me. It probably will be for you, too. Chenrezig was where I first learned about ethically based karma, but although the teachings of "doing good to feel good" resonated with me, I was far from a living embodiment of them. So even though it all made sense, the tangible experience of feeling better as a result of living more virtuously seemed abstract and far off. Not yet possessing an indwelling, lived sense of the significance of what I was learning, I didn't realize the power of the training I was receiving. But I did have faith. So I took my practice home with me, as directed, and started consistently enacting it. It took me five years, spiritually traversing this uneven road of trials, until I attuned *well enough* to myself, others, and situations, to create positive results that began to gain momentum.

I got my doctorate during that early awakening period. Since I was still battling with chronic pain myself, I focused my studies on it. Doctor, heal thyself! Chronic pain is easy to understand. It's an amplified signal. What's hard to see is that it's a person's habits of thought and emotion that do the amplifying. While meditating, I could see this amplification process working inside of me. Happily, when you start to watch the process unfolding, you're in an excellent position to begin doing something about it.

As I worked my way out of chronic pain, I was inspired to create programming to help others do the same. My next break came when I contracted with a Southern California inpatient rehab facility to provide pain programming. The owners of the center flew me back and forth from Tucson to San Diego each week to work with their patients. Finally, I was working again!

While at that center, I met their program director, Dr. Shari Stillman-Corbitt. Within a few months, however, she left to take another job, coincidentally in Tucson. Because of the close relationship Shari and I had, she lobbied for me to start a pain program at the rehab hospital outside Tucson. It was there where I would launch my career, creating content for people suffering from stress-related illnesses.

The status of that job led Miraval Resort—at the time, one of Oprah's "ten favorite things"—to hire me as its *stress-illness specialist*. Within the year, I was also asked to start teaching for the prestigious Andrew Weil Center for Integrative Medicine Fellowship program, at the University of Arizona. More was beginning to get more. All during this time, I continued to practice the effauses and caufects of healthful change. Finally, it came to pass that the ethics and attunement I was practicing began amplifying a decidedly strong and positive signal. I *bewegungsmustered* my way back to health and happiness!

Reclaiming my life helped me not only to empathize with others but to understand their pain as well. All of a sudden, I found myself in an enviable position professionally. The big problem of chronic stress-related illness needed fixing, and I was among the few well-equipped to solve it. My studies and experience enabled me to design a curriculum that empowered people with knowledge and solutions. Creating value for others was the primary reason for the reversal of fortune I began to experience.

By now, you must surely be wondering how all this eventually led to a fully funded movie. First, there had to be the faithful and inspiring voice that woke me: "Make a documentary!" Then I had to take action. Singer-songwriter Neil Young attributes his success to one thing: when the muse hits, he drops everything to follow it. That's what I did that night. When I heard those words of inspiration, I shot out of bed and began working on a business plan.

Then what? Rudimentary business plan in hand, I contacted a friend and movie producer, Brian McLaughlin. Brian is a beauty-goodness-and-truth guy himself, and with his help, we kept the synchronistic wheels of the universe turning. Brian was between projects, so he had time to look over the business plan. Let's just say he recommended a few edits. Then Brian suggested I meet director Frances Causey, who coincidentally lives in nearby Tubac, Arizona. Frances is a two-time Emmy Award winner, so she's always busy. Which is why I was surprised and heartened when she agreed to hear my pitch.

I'd never pitched a film idea before and assumed the chances that Frances would be interested were slim. But when we sat down together, the two of us connected like old friends. During our long conversation, she offered that her family also carried a history of stress-related illnesses. She had a genuine interest in the topic. As I sat with Frances, I felt a gentle tailwind pushing the project.

The next day, I called Frances and summoned the courage to ask her directly if she would work with us on the film. She laughed. "What? I was going to call you today to find out when we can start," she said. "Let's take a look at that business plan. It needs a little work."

With Frances onboard, we reworked the business plan and created a Kickstarter campaign. Meanwhile, I taught SkillfullyAware classes in my home community. The twelve-week course teaches mindfulness-based attunement skills for people suffering from stress-related conditions. Upon hearing we needed money to shoot a Kickstarter video, one of my former students pulled out his wallet and wrote us a check for $13,000 to pay for it! What?! Within two months, the crowdfunding video was shot and edited. We were ready to launch our campaign.

The crowdfunding plan went forward as I worked other jobs. One of them was a weekly speaking gig where I'd get up on stage in front of fifty to eighty people and talk about the causes and remedies of stress illness. The week we finished the Kickstarter video, I got on stage and introduced myself as a "filmmaker." Why not? I had a credible business plan, an award-winning director on my team, and a professionally produced Kickstarter video. Unbeknownst to me, there was an executive producer in the audience that day, and in less than a month he flew Frances and me out to Nashville to storyboard the film, work up a budget, and sign a contract to make the film! That's how it happened. I effaused and caufected all way to getting my film fully funded by one generous person.

The reason I tell you this story is to show how intending to amplify beauty, goodness, and truth creates a cloud of probability that can lead to extraordinary circumstance. It's also vitally important to note that all products of this particular effause-and-caufect stream emerged from countless contributions of many other people and over many years. My intentional actions were far from the singular and most significant contributions. What finally happened was a result of an interdependent web of virtuous activity that was not planned, predicted, or quantified ahead of time. It was a trophic cascade.

Additionally, I want to use this story to express a fundamental insight that will assist you in your journey of self-discovery. There are always patterns churning and emerging out of the chaos of life. Much like the moral view of karma we explored in the last chapter, this will be a story of how moving, probabilistic patterns play through an infinite field of energy and information. Every *now* moment is an effause-and-caufect stream that is an ending and a beginning at the same time.

Physics says the energy of a given system is always conserved, neither created nor destroyed. But that law holds true only when examining the interactions of objects in the physical world. Switch the context to the spiritual domain and that rule blows up. Spiritual energies of value and meaning cycle and recycle through a transcendental realm, beyond and outside the physical.

The inscrutable nature of spirit doesn't render its immediacy any less real, however. Spiritual energy enters into the physical world masquerading as your emotions. You feel an emotion as the gravitational push and pull of desire and aversion, which is as true, tangible, and consequential as the moon's gravity on the oceans. Within the foam of your being is where spirit operates. That energy is always on a journey to get somewhere. Although rarely by the shortest possible route, the spirit of emotion is always directing you toward betterment.

Longing for improvement as we do, our task is to increase our self-confidence as we navigate toward further unfolding. Applying this longing for growth with determination and skill generates an alchemical force that can and will feed back on itself, amplify, and produce the possibility for favorable outcomes beyond imagination. Apparently, some people do give a million dollars to strangers when the conditions are right.

We live in an incomprehensible universe where butterflies emerge out of cocooned caterpillars and the products of human emotion never quite equal the inputs. Merely uttering "I love you" or "I hate you" can rock your world.

Thoughts, speech, and behavior are mundane or spiritual, solely based on the intentions that lie behind them. If there's a ghost in the machine, intention is it. If you long for improvement, intend to increase the overall measure of goodness in your local system. Be kind to yourself, your family, and friends. Think of your good intentions and subsequent kind and skillful actions as the ultimate amplifier.

It is *meaning* that determines the emotion. Emotion is what creates the moving pattern. Through this process of attuning and intending to increase the overall well-being of the system, you set the spiritual tone for your life and eventually ensure a moving pattern of reciprocal goodness that invites collaboration. That is how a practice of setting virtuous intentions—that positively affects people on the inside and circumstances on the outside—makes your daily activities spiritual. That's also the way to start a *bewegungsmuster* that breaks all conventions. Once the momentum begins rolling, one plus one starts adding up to way more than two.

CHAPTER 5

The Mind System

"The mind is its own place, and in itself can make a Heaven of Hell and a Hell of Heaven."

John Milton

It was well into October, springtime in Australia, and this day was going to be a hot one. Chenrezig is in Eudlo, on the eastern coast—the sunshine coast. It falls just south of the Tropic of Capricorn in the Southern Hemisphere. Lush green semitropical eucalyptus forest that the locals call "the bush" surrounds the retreat center. The location is prime snake habitat. Temperatures in the winter rarely dip into the upper 40s (Fahrenheit), and now that the weather was warming, the many species of highly venomous snakes were stirring.

A day earlier, I was caught by surprise while typing at my desk as a slender tiger snake slithered through a hole in the screen door of my "motel" room. After jumping up the ladder to the safety of the top bunk, I watched it take a clockwise trip around the room. Its eyes and tongue resolutely inspected all the corners. Then, thankfully, finding no prey, it departed through the same hole in the screen it had entered moments before. It wasn't until its tail had vanished around the corner that I could breathe again.

By that time, I'd been retreating at Chenrezig for about six weeks. It was a proper monastery with more than forty full-time monks and nuns in residence. There were dozens of lay practitioners like me on retreat as well. I'd become especially close with two bright young men, Chad Foremen and Narayan Bastian. Chad was a local who was eager to take Narayan and me on a walkabout beyond the hilly cow paddock above the retreat center. Hiking into the hills would provide us a view to the idyllic shores of the southeastern Pacific Ocean. Walking to the top of the mountain would also put us in the neighborhood of a small town, only three kilometers away as the crow flies. Importantly, every small town in rural Australia sports a watering hole, and the view and the bar were reasons enough to strike out on that hot steamy October day.

Before we took more than three steps up the stone stairs leading to the upper boundary of Chenrezig, another tiger snake crossed our path. Seeing us, it raised its head, flattened its throat like a cobra, and released a chilling warning hiss, a devilish sound that pulled me back into myself. Then, without hesitation, it dived into a nearby bush.

Amazed by what I'd just seen and not fully appreciating the danger this snake posed, I stepped close to the shrub. Tentatively, I parted the branches into which the snake had disappeared. Less than a meter away, returning my gaze from within the plant, was a green tree snake. It sized me up, tasting the air with its red tongue. Luckily, these little guys aren't aggressive or venomous, but nevertheless I slowly let go of the branches and backed away. I wondered if seeing two snakes in the first thirty seconds of our walkabout might foreshadow what was to come.

Narayan was carrying a proper machete with him. Good thing, too—where we were going, it was needed. After crossing the cow paddock at the bitter end of Chenrezig's land, we ran into a mass of invasive lantana and took turns trying to hack our way through the tangled, sticky plants. In the back of my mind, I kept wondering when the next snake was going to surprise us. After thirty minutes of useless chopping gained us only about ten meters of ground, we quit.

Chad was still optimistic that we'd make it to the town, though. He reckoned that if we crossed back across the south side of the cow paddock, we'd find a road that would take us up the hill. So across the paddock we went again. Whereas the lantana grove had offered us full shade, the walk now was utterly free of protection from the blazing sun. We hadn't thought to bring water with us either, reasoning we'd arrive at the town after no more than a thirty-minute walk. How wrong we were wasn't yet apparent to us.

Salty sweat was pouring from my body, and fifteen minutes into the second pasture crossing, I started to feel the beating of my heart in my temples. The torrid heat and humidity were numbing my brain as well. I began to hear a monotonous type of mental sound, like a "wang, wang, wang, wang," droning on in the background of my mind. I was overheating and becoming dehydrated. When we finally reached the end of the rolling pasture, it turned upward. Here again, a thick grove of lantana blocked our ascent. Feeling like defeated warriors, none of us had the strength or determination to try to take that hill. Looking wearily into each other's red faces, we agreed to head back.

Carpeting the undulating paddock was a thick layer of green grass, nourished by the manure of multiple generations of cows deposited over many decades. Cutting through the middle was a deep and well-worn track, carved over time by thousands of heavy hooves. Mercifully, this gently swerving footpath made our crossing easier. But still, it was hot, and the "wang, wang, wang, wang" pulsing in my head had only grown louder. My weight shifted forward to help me keep pace. I felt as if I were shrinking, like a drying sponge.

Suddenly, so fast that I had no time to alter course, a two-meter-long snake dissected the footpath exactly where my left foot came down. I stepped on it and reflexively jumped into the air, as high as I could, anxiously focused on my bare ankles, waiting for the agonizing bite I expected would come. In the moment I hung above it, I could see it writhing and twisting to make itself right. Chad's and Narayan's screams only added to my panic.

I came down out of the air and landed on top of its thick thrashing body once again. More haunting screams, then another anxious leap. Tangled in knots below me, the menacing creature worked feverishly to free itself from the tight groove of the track.

One last time I fell onto it, and as I desperately kicked myself up again, my heel thrust lifted it into the air. The meaty snake landed halfway onto the grass and finally was able to free itself from the track and slip away.

In the immediate aftermath we all stood as statues, stone-still and silent. Within an instant, the dilation of time reset itself and my ears went back to picking up ambient sounds. Finally,

Chad's wide eyes caught mine. "That was a red-bellied black!" he said dazedly. I assumed he meant I'd just cheated death. Later, I found out that, although rarely deadly, a bite from this sizable snake would have caused a blood-clotting disorder and muscle and nerve damage. At that moment, however, I was ignorant of the lot of it. From the far upper end of Chenrezig's acreage, we were at least an hour and a half away from the closest emergency medical care. The confounding realities of toxic venom and dehydration would have rendered even that best-case scenario well nigh impossible.

An odd question suddenly sprang to mind. "If the snake had bitten me, would I have been able to chop off my foot to save my life?" Nervous laughter and a shivering shake were all I could offer in defense of that petrifying thought.

Once safely back at Chenrezig's Big Love Café, I came back to my fully jubilant self. Being an avid teller of tales, I was more than eager to recount this freshly minted snake story. However, I soon learned that every Australian has a snake story and theirs is better than yours! Not two minutes into my account, Harry, the cook, interrupted me to inform those gathered that living just over our heads in the rafters of the café was a five-meter-long python. Having made a pet of it, Harry told us how he fed the enormous beast unlucky kitchen rats he captured in his catch-and-release trap.

Next, it was Chenrezig's general manager Colin's turn to interject. Unimpressed by my having trod three times on a red-bellied black, he stepped to center stage and began to tell the growing crowd about his carpenter friend whose girlfriend died, foaming at the mouth, only fifteen minutes after being bitten on the finger by an eastern brown snake. As horrific and heartbreaking as that anecdote was, we would soon learn that it was hardly the story's climax.

Colin told us that a year after the passing of his girlfriend, the carpenter was working in his shop when, unthinking, he reached blindly beneath his workbench, feeling for a piece of wood. Suddenly he felt an alarming stab in his right pointer finger. Without hesitation, the carpenter held his finger on the chopping block and, with one clean swing of his ax, cut it off! My mouth hung open as I stood wide-eyed and blinking.

Colin paused. What he said next in his thick Australian accent caused me to stiffen with fright and astonishment: "And it was only a splinter!"

It's a shocking story, I know. Let the profundity of it sink in for a moment. How in the world does something like that happen? The tale was even more startling when I asked myself if, had it been me, I would have done the same thing. Would you?

I retell this story with one purpose in mind: to provide you with a profound and potentially lifesaving lesson. We are always and forever imprinting ourselves. What we think, say, and do matters. Our actions, whatever they are, create imprints or memories in our minds. High emotion empowers these imprints with potency and potential to initiate future actions, which, as was apparent from the carpenter's story, can lead to horrific and unforeseen consequences. Your mind is a whole system. What you put into and let circulate through it changes it. Those changes have consequences.

Few people ever consider what *mind is*. If they did, it might appear as a singular medium through which they experience their lives. The reality is far more complicated than that. Many distinct and interconnected processes make up the mind. Putting aside the hard question of what the mind *is* for a moment, we can say what it does: it functions as a multidimensional process that regulates the flow of energy and information (triggers, thoughts, sensations). In other words, your mind helps you sense and make sense of information. The primary functions of this regulatory process are monitoring and modifying.

Despite Herculean efforts to do so, no philosopher or scientist has been able to ascertain how the brain connects to the mind or vice versa. It is apparent, though, that there is a definite correlation between the anatomy of the brain and the way the mind processes information. Globally, the anatomy of the brain divides down the middle into two hemispheres. The right hemisphere allows us to take a holistic view of ourselves and our world. This right-hemispheric holism takes a big-picture perspective on our concerns. In that way, we can mentally sort through possible courses of action while at the same time imagine the potential consequences of those actions on possible futures. The right hemisphere also combines the many threads of our past experiences to render a narrative tapestry of who we believe ourselves to be. Thus the primary job of the right hemisphere is to map this big-picture gestalt, derived from past experiences and future projections, onto whatever is happening in the present moment.

Alternatively, the left hemisphere is concerned with only the limited portion of reality that it judges most significant in the here and now. Its job is to discern and measure the details of objects, helping us separate what we like and want from what we don't and what is safe from what is not. Although great for making critical distinctions, the narrow scope of the left hemisphere can become problematic. Without the guidance of the right hemisphere, the left's limited view is handicapped. The left hemisphere can't and won't concern itself with the big picture. An overly active left hemisphere will cause a person to fixate and lose their ability to prioritize. The left hemisphere also provides the overlay of language, which further helps us "grasp" ideas. In performing its tasks, the left hemisphere re-*presents* its view of what's happening.

The right hemisphere takes the left hemisphere's "story" and balances it with big-picture data. This dual view is necessary for our survival. Like us, all vertebrate life forms have a divided brain. The left hemisphere of animals focuses attention on what's immediately present and salient, and like ours, their right hemisphere sees the big picture. Given direction by the right hemisphere to search out and find seeds, a chicken can focus its left hemisphere on the task well enough to discern and peck single seeds out of the dirt. It can hunt for seeds while remaining vigilant to potential predators because the chicken's right-hemisphere awareness maintains its view of the big picture. Such a divided task would be impossible without the simultaneous activity of both hemispheres.

This double view of the world works fantastically well when both right hemispheric global *awareness* and left hemispheric local *attention* remain in balance. But that isn't always the way it works. The left hemisphere, having only a limited view of the world, doesn't know what it doesn't know. The left hemisphere functions somewhat like a teenager who adamantly believes they know better than their right-hemispheric parent. The self-centered and blind ignorance of the left hemisphere can cause big problems. Indeed, quite often the left hemisphere ineptly takes control of the mind-system, as was the case in the sorry story of the carpenter chopping off his finger. After he felt the stab of the splinter, his left hemisphere took control, causing his attention to narrow and his awareness to dim. Lacking the big picture provided by the right hemisphere, the myopic left hemisphere led him to act on limited information and execute the unfortunate chop.

Immediately after our first encounter with poisonous snakes, both the carpenter's and my right hemisphere set to work on saving us in case we ever found ourselves in a similar situation. Indeed, everyone, not just him and me, possesses that same survival drive. That drive acts as an organizing principle, prompting automatic, contextualized problem-solving. In our case, a hypothetical threat to our survival arose—a potential bite from a highly venomous snake—and that threat simultaneously prompted both the carpenter and me to consider something otherwise outrageously unthinkable. "If I get bitten by a snake, I'll sacrifice my finger/foot to save my life." After the carpenter's girlfriend was bitten and died, he undoubtedly spent plenty of mental energy envisioning several scenarios in which he might get bitten and what he would then do to save himself.

Unbeknownst to him, his left hemisphere took over the problem. Instead of envisioning all possible scenarios, especially those where he maintained big-picture awareness long enough to check for splinters, his left hemisphere fixated on that single dramatic course of action that would leave him fingerless. His unconscious anxiety created an emotionally charged flow of energy and information through the system of his mind. That activity was the substantial cause of the imprint (memory) that *primed* him to take that fateful *future* action.

The flow of energy and information, imprints, and potentials for action were all organized and kept alive by the carpenter's drive to survive. In this way, that preoccupation became a *bewegungsmuster*, where he became the kind of person who would chop off a finger to save himself. Then, unfortunately for him, the right conditions *did* assemble themselves. When he blindly reached under his workbench and felt that horrifying stick, the latent motor program triggered itself.

That story is just another example of the truth of our living in a stream of effauses and caufects that produce patterns of thinking and behavior that influence our future. There's no escaping the fact that emotionally charged thoughts and feelings leave potent imprints on the mind system. It's also important to understand that fervid imprints like those described above not only affect your mind but also, once "deposited" there, remain, dormant just like seeds that lie on the ground. Should favorable conditions arise later, unconscious *intention-action* feedback loops in the mind will activate. The process of imprinting and amplifying feedback that compels the mind one way or another explains much, if not all, human behavior. How else does one explain how an otherwise careful carpenter amputates his finger?

Western scientists, psychiatrists, psychologists, and researchers have studied the mind and speculated about its nature for hundreds of years, and as yet there still is no universally agreed-upon definition for what is *mind*. *Thoughts* have become the most popular Western interpretation for the mind. That makes sense. Studying people's minds objectively, from the "outside," gave researchers the mistaken impression that mind is synonymous with thoughts. Which is why, until very recently, that outside-looking-in approach led most academics and clinicians in the West to restrict their research to studying brains and disturbances of thought.

Meditators in the East, however, have a long history of contemplating mind. Rather than observing a test subject or a brain in a lab, they took an insider's view. They used the "observation platform" of meditation to enable them to examine their "internal" experience. Meditation provided them with a first-person perspective on the qualities and operations of their minds. Over time, these meditators, primarily from the Buddhist tradition, came to a broad agreement about what they were observing. Their consensus view led to a thorough and exacting description of consciousness, or mind. The breadth and specificity of their findings fill a voluminous text, the Abhidhamma, which remains an essential reference for today's modern consciousness researchers.[25]

The scientific method assumes that the causal laws of nature are detectable through careful experimentation. That thesis inspires individual scientists to labor for their whole careers seeking to uncover what are called "third-person truths." A third-person truth is something that is—all things remaining equal—measurable by anyone else at any time. For example, let's say my daughter and I set up an experiment to measure the time it takes for a rock dropped from the height of two meters to hit the ground. Let's suppose we run dozens of trials in an attempt to calculate the average fall time. Science assumes that as long as the conditions in which we drop the rock remain relatively consistent, anyone else at any other time, past or future, who can match those conditions should get the same average result.

Ultimately, this experiment, like all other valid experiments, would narrow in on a third-person truth: an observable time, derived by investigation, that future scientists would agree on. In other words, a measurable *fact*. As previously stated, science is founded on the principle that facts are derivable by experimentation. Science enables humans to model the world of cause and effect. It allows them to make accurate predictions and engineer workable solutions to problems. Thus empowered, they gain the secondary ability to make technological advancements in every conceivable domain.

What science proves is that there is an objective universe, the evolution of which sets in motion a causal flow of mass, energy, and information. Putting aside the paradoxes of quantum physics, which follows its own set of causal laws, the manifest physical world is measurable by anyone who cares to set up the appropriate experiment.

There is nothing about the truth of objectivity that directly denies *subjectivity*, however. In my view, science in its examination of the universe has diminished the importance of inner subjectivity simply because it is impossible to measure. Yet there's no denying it. I would argue that our inner world is equally, if not more, worthy of scientific exploration. No one has a view of the "outside" world but from within their inner subjective experience. You *are* your experience, and the felt sense of that experience is the reference point from which you judge everything in your life. Further, the perspectives you hold determine your relationship with everything that exists. Discovering what determines those views can shine a light on the pathway of your personal choices and, ipso facto, your development. (Much more on perspectives and development in Chapters 11 through 13.)

Meditators of the East implicitly recognized this opportunity. Rather than gather their data from the objective world, they turned their attention inward, to the flow of inner causality illuminated in the subjective realm of the mind. Theirs was a noble enterprise, too. They were motivated not only to uncover how the mind works but also to perform that task in service of an exceedingly worthwhile goal, to learn the secrets of lessening personal suffering. First, Siddhartha Gautama set up the experimental parameters of stable attention and open, keen awareness. Later, meditators who reproduced this mental "setup" gained an unprecedented consensus on the qualities of mind and how the mind *system* works. To these countless meditators, the mind exposed itself as a multilayered and multifunctional entity. It also appeared paradoxically, as simultaneously having both ultimate (unchanging) and relative (changing) qualities. The ultimate qualities relate to the nature of the mind itself. The relative qualities relate more to how the mind system shapes and is shaped by the "objects" that pass through it.

Still, gaining an insight into the mind isn't as straightforward a task as gaining insight into the nature of an object that you might hold in your hands. Indeed, your attention is programmed to shine on and illuminate everyday objects, identify them, and discern their details and properties. All that information is immediately knowable through your senses. "Objects," as

I'm defining them here, would include anything you could see, hear, smell, taste, touch, or think about. Directing your attention back to your mind is different, however. The mind isn't an object. Instead, it's the *field of knowing* in which all knowable objects arise and pass. In that way, watching the mind is more like turning a flashlight back on itself, which is a tricky thing to do. But now, let's try.

Pay close attention to the *sight* of these next few sentences. Notice how easy it is for you to consciously point the flashlight of your attention *outward* onto the words you are reading. Now let's turn the flashlight of your attention back on itself. Read the next sentence very slowly, and as you do, stay aware of your *internal* experience. *Now, pay attention to the attention that is paying attention to the sight of this sentence.* Again, slowly: *Pay attention to the attention that is paying attention to the sight of this sentence.*

Not so simple, was it? Confusing perhaps? That simple attentional exercise demonstrates that focusing your attention on itself takes a bit of getting used to. Attention is not an object in the world but rather the conscious medium that *illuminates* the world. Not to worry, though—I will begin to familiarize you with your mind and its qualities as we venture further.

One of the fundamental and essential qualities of unchanging *ultimate mind* is that of *spaciousness*. Again, let me attempt to orient your mind in a way that might help reveal this quality. As you read this page or screen, begin to notice the *space* around you. Do it now. Don't necessarily look at the space directly, but rather, keep reading this sentence while becoming globally aware of "space." Notice the space between your nose and this page or screen, for example. Using your peripheral vision, notice the space of the room in which you are sitting. Be aware that the space of the room "contains" all the objects you see. Space, when you pay attention to it, has some impressive qualities. Notice that it doesn't have a shape or a size. In other words, space doesn't have a boundary. Walls and other structures divide space into sections, but space itself is boundaryless—no shape, no size, no edges. Remove the barriers, and space opens up to infinity.

Notice, too, that space is empty. The quality of emptiness is what allows objects to occupy the space around you. Emptiness is the quality that further enables those objects to pass through the space. The spacious quality of your mind is like the space of the room in which you are sitting. That's because it is empty and edgeless, too. The empty edgeless space of your mind allows all mental objects—the energy and the information of sights, sounds, smells, tastes, touches, feelings, and thoughts—to arise and pass through it.

Part 1 of this book endeavored to teach you to meditate. In that section, I pointed you to the spacious quality of your mind. Examine the space of your mind and you can discover for yourself that no matter how hard you try to discern the boundary of your consciousness, you'll never be able to locate it. Exploring the space of your mind is how you'll learn to monitor the arising and passing of mental "objects" and modify your reaction to them. Staying aware while monitoring and modifying your responses to the arising and passing of objects is the beating heart of skillful awareness.

Not only is mind spacious but it is also *merely clear*. Here, the word *mere* means that nothing is there—no objects, no information, nothing. It is the merely clear quality that allows every conceivable object you perceive to arise and pass through the mind. Mere clarity does all that without the ultimate mind's interfering with or being affected by the passing. For example, you can perceive the color red, but ultimate mind itself is "empty" of any trace of red. If the nature of ultimate mind were colored red, everything you perceive would carry a red "stain." The merely clear mind is also empty of sounds and allows you to hear sounds as they are, without any background interference. Similarly, you can feel warmth, but the mind itself is not warm. You can think thoughts, but the intrinsic nature of mind is without thought. Mere clarity means that the nature of mind itself is empty of any objectifiable quality. Because of mere clarity, ultimate mind, enabled by your senses, can come into contact with anything—sights, sounds, smells, tastes, touches, feelings, and thoughts—without itself or the objects it contacts interacting and changing each other.

Imagine passing infinite objects through the space of the room in which you are sitting. At the end of that infinity, when you stopped moving objects through that space, the space itself would remain, precisely as it was at the start, unchanged by the moving. The qualities of emptiness and mere clarity eternally endure in that thought experiment. Ultimate mind also functions like that; it remains eternally spacious, empty, and clear no matter what passes through it.

But to me and many other philosophers of mind, the most incomprehensible quality of mind is its *luminous* nature. Luminosity, in this context, means that mind can "know." The fact that we can have a conscious experience at all is confounding. Indeed, the question of why and how the luminous, aware quality of mind exists at all is termed the "hard problem of consciousness."[26] It's utterly baffling if you stop and think about it. Why and how are we conscious in the first place? What is consciousness? Until very recently, it was probably the hard problem of consciousness that dissuaded most Western scientists from tackling these questions. But just because we haven't been able to answer those perplexing questions shouldn't stop you from exploring the qualities of your mind. Indeed, we can discern the ultimate qualities—spaciousness, mere clarity, and luminosity—through meditation.

What, then, will you discover when you explore your mind? You will find a *merely clear field of knowing* that stretches endlessly in every direction. Everything that you know of as your "life" arises, abides, and passes through the entirely open, empty space of your mind. *Everything* you can experience and know happens in mind. Your life exists solely within that field. A lack of understanding and skill in influencing the subtle flows of energy and information circulating through the mind is the primary source of a person's suffering.

The first sentence of this book read, "Sometimes, doing one thing can magically change everything else for the better." The "one thing" I'm offering is mindful attunement: sensing into yourself, others, and contexts with acceptance and care and a wish for a higher good. Mindful attunement starts with a clear understanding of what mind is, how it functions, how to watch it, and, importantly, how to influence it.

My Tibetan meditation teacher, Geshe Tashi Tsering, was keen to point out to his Western students that every conceivable mental, emotional, and relational difficulty stems from a lack of education and training of the mind. He once told us, "If you do not study and train your mind, you will not know how to deal with your problems when they arise." He was right. Lacking that crucial and necessary understanding of mind condemns us to cycle in our issues and patterns. We can't develop higher perspectives that free us from our psycho-emotional entanglements without mental training. Einstein is famously credited with the aphorism "You can't solve a problem with the same thinking that created it." That's the message here. Without proactively raising your perspective on yourself and your issues, the *story* that cycles through your mind has the potential to make you sick.

So far, I've explained the ultimate qualities of mind that reveal its nature as a merely clear field of knowing. Now let's explore the functions of mind and the systematic way in which "objects" (sights, sounds, smells, tastes, touches, feelings, and thoughts) arise, pass through, and interact with consciousness. It is paradoxical, but the ultimate unchanging knowing space of consciousness is accompanied by changing "mental events," "mental factors," or "states of mind" (all synonyms). Paradoxically, these irreconcilable properties of mind—eternal and relative—exist simultaneously. No one can explain how this happens except to say that ultimate mind provides a space for the relative mental events to engage with each other. Thus, there's this unchanging "space" with "objects" flowing through it. The characteristic way the relative mental events flow through your mind creates the patterns of your personality—in other words, your karma, or a *bewegungsmuster.*

For example, say you establish a habit of intentionally amplifying beauty, goodness, and truth. That virtuous practice will predispose you to contact subsequent mental objects positively.

The relative mind, unlike the ultimate mind, absorbs and carries action potentials that correspond to *all* your habits of relating. The relative mind is the part of your mind that "learns" and carries the influence of the new learning forward. Value-based changes in relating *always* feed back into your mind system and prime your relative mind for more of the same. Importantly, this imprinting works in both directions of the value spectrum. Should you relate to the objects in a way that amplifies negativity, you'll incline your system of relative mental events to engage with similar objects with enhanced negativity. *More always gets more in the relative mind.* This accumulation process explains addictive behaviors of all kinds; indeed, it explains how anxiety and depression grow into entrenched patterns in a person's consciousness.

Buddhist meditators were the first group of people to identify and describe a similar type of amplifying feedback. Because the science of living systems was unknown to them twenty-five hundred years ago, they defined it as karma. But now we can look at and compare these two seemingly separate, value-based causal paradigms and appreciate how well they map on top of each other.

Buddhist philosophy postulates that all mental events exist on a continuum from positive to neutral to negative. In essence, there's a value gradient embedded in everything we engage with. Neuroscientist and philosopher Sam Harris echoed this principle when he said, "The concept of well-being captures everything we can care about in the moral sphere. Values are a certain kind of fact. They are facts about the wellbeing of conscious creatures. So, when we're talking about right and wrong, and good and evil, and about outcomes that matter, we are necessarily talking about actual or potential changes in (our) conscious experience."

Every stream of information entering your mind system is charged with the value-laden energy of emotion—liking and disliking on that continuum of positive, neutral, and negative. Here's the vital point for you to understand: where the information lands on this value spectrum—positive, neutral, or negative—will determine the composition and flow of matter (chemicals and proteins) through your brain and body, changing both in the process. What you perceive and how you relate to those perceptions changes you!

No one knows how, but the "internal" subjective mind connects with the external objective world. Your body lives in the middle of these domains. It seems like there is, but if you really check using your mind rather than your eyes, there's no dividing line between the outer and inner worlds. It's a completely open channel, an unbroken causal flow of information from the world to the body and to the mind. But there's also an opposite flow of causality, initiated in the mind, that flows back into the body and the world. The deep interconnectedness of the world-body-mind system means that intentionally working to positively influence the unfolding relative mental events in your mind will benefit your physical health and extended relationships.

Now let's explore these relative mental events in more depth. Tibetan Buddhist meditators identify five omnipresent mental events: contact, feeling, discrimination, attention, and intention. Before I go further, you must understand that these five mental factors don't arise singularly, one after the other. Instead, they are all present in every moment of mind. That's why they are called "omnipresent mental factors." These five factors all act in unison, allowing the ultimate mind to engage with the relative world. It is through your intentional engagement with objects, facilitated by these mental factors, that you condition yourself, creating patterns of character and personality. Let's look at these five in turn.

> 1. CONTACT is the mental factor that brings the relative mind into contact with objects. An object, as I'm defining the term here, includes all sights, sounds, smells, tastes, touches, feelings, and thoughts. Any bit of energy and information that contacts your consciousness becomes an object *in* your consciousness. Contact happens by itself. As my twelve-step readers know, the first step of the twelve-step process informs you of your powerlessness. I'm not a fan of that word, simply because you can unwittingly take its meaning too far, but I will concede that some aspect of powerlessness does exist. Namely, you are powerless over contact. Your sense "gates" are continuously open and receiving value-rich energy and information in every moment. Apart from falling into a deep, dreamless sleep or in any other way rendering yourself unconscious, there's nothing you can do to stop information from flowing into your consciousness. When you're conscious, there's contact. Contact implies a relationship between the sense of yourself, the subject, and, the object *in* your consciousness.
>
> 2. FEELING is the mental factor that "places" the contacted object somewhere on the value continuum of

pleasant, neutral, and unpleasant. Feeling is a gut-level, nonverbal, body-centric *energetic* knowing. The pleasance of an object has the effect of drawing you closer, coaxing your attention to further engage with it. A neutral object, if you become aware of it at all, will leave you unmoved. Who cares, right? Finally, the many objects that fall on the negative side of the spectrum will invite a fight, flight, or freeze response. Emotional pitch increases as you contact objects that sit farther out on the edges of the pleasant, neutral, unpleasant range. Contact with highly emotional objects magnetizes and fixates attention. Attentional fixation is the precursor to *all* stress-related conditions.

The way you feel is intimately associated with what you value. Alcoholics, for example, value alcohol. An alcoholic's feeling about alcohol won't change unless his values change. If and when they do, his feelings about it can't help but change. As a person develops their character, values very often do shift, which in turn modifies feelings arising in response to contact with related objects. For example, when I was in my late teens and early twenties, I was addicted to smoking pot. Seeing, smelling, thinking about it, or hearing someone else talking about marijuana always triggered a craving in me. At that time, I valued getting high, so contact with any object related to that experience caught and fixated my attention—both of which are requirements for any addiction. But as I grew up, my values changed. When I entered graduate school in my late twenties, maintaining a clear head became far more important to me. That new value-rich priority altered the system of my mind, lessening, and eventually wholly relieving me of my attachment to marijuana. Feelings are value-laden. When one changes, so does the other.

3. DISCRIMINATION is the mental factor that distinguishes the many characteristics, qualities, and features of an object. The processing of various types of information collected through our senses—sight, sound, smell, taste, touch, and discursive thought—is handled by different nodes in our brains. Each of these nodes further divides into smaller sub-nodes that process ever-smaller bits of related information. For example, within the nodes responsible for processing auditory information exists a collection of smaller nodes that sort through data related to differences in volume, pitch, tone, duration, and so on. The same "parts-divided-into-smaller-parts" arrangement is an overall characteristic of the whole mind system. That way, the smallest bits of information that eventually rise into your conscious awareness do so only after considerable unconscious analysis and interpretation.

The left hemisphere acts to clarify specific features of a particular object, while the right hemisphere sees where each part or feature fits into a larger whole. Besides distinguishing particular characteristics of objects, the mental factor of discrimination is also tightly bound into the left hemisphere's narrating function. Once basic features of objects are clarified, the narrating mind performs an even higher level of information processing. That last step of taking already highly processed information and overlaying narrative distinctions takes a lot of mental energy. Consequently, any increase in activation of the narrating mind results in a loss of perception of the subtlest sense data. We can, and often do, get lost in our stories. Unconscious overactivity of the narrating mind is one of the reasons for it. Getting lost in our story happens when what we perceive is the mere projected construction of our unconscious narrating mind. What we miss, then, is the real, rich, and raw data that arrives through our senses.

Most of us don't see how the mind constructs reality, because it happens so fast. To an untrained mind, what arises in consciousness seems like the raw truth. It's not. Unless you're an adept meditator, trained to see your mind construct reality, the whole hyper-quick constructive process will happen below your level of awareness.[27]

To my knowledge, adept meditators are the only people who see, and thus recover, all that lost perceptual detail.[28]

When I first started meditating, I was instructed to pay attention to the changing sensations of breath at the tip of my nose. I practiced this activity for two years before I realized that what I had been paying attention to wasn't actual breath sensations. Instead, I inadvertently focused on the mental commentary related to the breath sensations. In untrained humans, that layer of projected analysis covers over every bit of raw sense data, altering their perception of it, even before they are conscious of it. Without mind training, people are doomed to re-experience the repetitious patterns of personality and emotion constructed by the mental factor of discrimination. In other words, it's nearly impossible to change moving patterns of thinking and feeling without first developing the perceptual acuity required to see the construction and then influence one's response to it.

4. ATTENTION focuses the relative mind on an object and keeps it there. Attention is the mental factor that brings the mind into contact with, and sustains focus on, a particular object. It is through your attention that you develop relationships with objects. Attention functions much like a flashlight: in the same way the beam of a flashlight isolates and illuminates objects, attention selectively extracts bits of information out of your larger field of conscious awareness. Just as the scope of a flashlight's beam is limited, so is the scope of attention. Attention is only able to highlight a few bits of information out of all potential stimuli within a person's internal and external field of awareness. The benefit of that narrow view is that it helps a person identify, connect with, and relate to objects of *intention*.

You may recall that earlier I used a chicken analogy. It is the chicken's left hemispheric attention that allows it to peck out seeds from the dirt. The chicken's attention, oriented by its intention and facilitated by discrimination, can isolate every single seed. It does this even though the seeds are lying on the ground mixed with similarly shaped but inedible pebbles. Therefore, the discrete beam of attention isolates and, through the mental function of discrimination, assists in identifying, categorizing, analyzing, and assessing the *value* of objects.

Like the mental factors of feeling, discrimination, and intention, attention develops habits. Imprints are left on your mind by the specific way you use your attention. Which objects you pay attention to and the intensity of the emotion that inspires your focus create the habits. Those latent imprints then incline your attention to re-create the same subject-object relationships in the future.

Why are people addicted to things? Because their awareness is programmed to repeatedly bring their attention back to particular objects. After contact, their attention fixates, forcing them—the subject—to relate with the object of their addiction in a habitual way. In the case of addiction, that "relationship" becomes distorted because, through attentional fixation, feeling, and discrimination, the significance or value of the object amplifies. The narrating portion of the mental factor of discrimination is where the value-laden story gets layered onto and distorts the object. All the pleasant qualities of a particular substance or behavior get exaggerated, while the negative aspects are ignored or diminished. Since focusing attention is mostly a left-hemisphere activity, an attentionally fixated person loses touch with their big-picture values. Ethical and moral agreements fly out the window. They remain unaware of the long-term consequences of their actions. That's why attentionally fixated people are much more prone to self-centered, unskillful, and sometimes destructive behavior.

Habits of a person's mind develop as a direct result of

their attention coming into contact with objects. Feeling and then discrimination amplify and distort a person's relationship with those objects. The cyclic and repetitious activity of attention, feeling, and discrimination act to prime a person's *intention* to solidify their relationship with particular objects and mental states. The more-gets-more system behavior of the mind is the moving pattern-maker.

5. INTENTION is the mental function that inclines the relative mind to enact behaviors that cause you to come into contact with specific objects.

You are a complex system and, as such, have a history. You carry your past with you. Through the five mental factors set in motion by intention, you evolve into the future—the flow of energy, information, and matter through the system continually modifies your parts and patterns. This flow determines the development of the physical parts of your brain and body and various psychological and emotional patterns of your personality. Your past, whatever it may be, is co-responsible for your present behavior. It is through your present moment relating to the world through the five mental factors that your living system "self-organizes."

Habits of intention, which drive contact, feeling, discrimination, and attention, create states of mind that we all recognize, like irritable, pessimistic, anxious, cheerful, generous, trustworthy, and all the rest. Global patterns, like stress-related illnesses (depression, anxiety, addictions), are all examples of larger, more "solid" imprinted patterns moving through and coloring the relative mind. As mentioned before, there are multiple streams of causality: physical and chemical, biological, psychological, intentional, and collective. You don't have control over any of them. The one slight exception is that you can *influence* your intentional or "karmic" causality. How much influence your intention has on the other streams is impossible to say, but there is some bleed-over.

Siddhartha Gautama was the first to connect karma with intention. Intentional or karmic causality means doing right and being kind. It is through the small window of your intention that you can exercise your autonomy, initiative, and follow-through to engage in new value-based actions that modify your life.

We live in an infinitely nested universe of living systems. Of that greater whole, you are but a minuscule part. The whole thing, top to bottom, is organizing itself. All the universal energy, information, and matter is moving, and will move on, and evolve, no matter what you do. That said, you have a tiny bit of influence. You can set intentions to monitor and modify your focus of attention. In doing so, you can and will shift your value-infused relationship with some of the objects in your world. Changing those relationships alters the way your living system organizes itself. Over time, you may significantly alter them such that your evaluation of particular objects changes. That may not seem like a significant shift, but such small shifts can and do amplify into patterns that make considerable differences in how *you* perceive yourself and your world.

As I mentioned, I no longer value smoking pot. I got to the point where I attuned better to my ambivalence and stopped smoking it. In that way, my system, in the act of self-*re*organization, revalued my relationship with pot. That shift in value was initiated by intention, which, with the help of the other four mental factors, constructed a new relationship. The benefits I enjoy as a result of that relational shift are immeasurable. Everything I hold dear now is traceable back to small shifts I made. I've worked hard to shift my relationship to many other things besides pot—for example, an unhealthy attachment to unwholesome thoughts and feelings. I'm still in process—development never ends—but having made the effort, I rarely allow myself to fixedly engage in stories of resentment, which formerly used to occupy much of my mental space. The result is that I no longer experience the rage and various stress illnesses that sprang from the rage-generated stress chemicals my body marinated in. These and many more changes I made were subtle but significant. As a result, I'm no longer the person I used to be. Conflict and suffering no longer dominate my inner life.

If a person who knew me in my twenties saw me at the grocery store today, they'd only see the minor surface changes of my body, such as gray hair and wrinkles. Unless they had a conversation with me, the massive internal upshifts in my perspective, which help me relate to myself and the world with more wisdom and compassion, would remain hidden. Nevertheless, those internal, spiritual changes have made all the difference to me and my life.

The five mental factors detailed above determine what you experience. *All* experiences are psychodynamic, which means everything you experience changes you. Therefore, if you want to change your experience, the first, best, and only place to start is by becoming more consciously intentional.

I'll conclude this chapter with this reminder. Your ultimate mind, the merely clear space of consciousness, is perfectly clear and empty by nature. It remains unaffected by the relative flow of energy and information that passes through it. As a result, the potential *always* exists for you to become more intentional. If you are reading this book because you happen to carry the pattern of amplifying suffering, know that it's not too late to alter the negative conditioned patterns flowing through your *relative* mind. Through practice, you can learn to recognize, nurture, and develop the effauses of health and happiness and refrain from the caufects that bring suffering and illness. In other words, you can *recondition your conditioning* and create more stable patterns of health and joyfulness moving into the future.

CHAPTER 6

Disrupted Development

"If you are going through hell, keep going."
Winston Churchill

Trauma has a tendency to create distortions of perception. Perception *is reality* for most people, which is why early childhood trauma can affect how a person feels about themselves, others, and the world for the rest of their lifetime. Suffering trauma as a child is one of the primary reasons why a person's story makes them sick as an adult.

Consider the case of "Sophie." At thirty years old, she was just beginning to accept herself and had mostly resolved the worst aspects of her anxious and obsessive thinking. The usual range of suffering through which Sophie's thoughts still conducted her was, by now, psychic terrain she knew well. Nevertheless, the lifelong habit of berating and second-guessing herself and an on-again-off-again eating disorder, depression, anxiety, and panic left her emotionally scarred and vulnerable.

Sophie had survived an intensely traumatic childhood. She initially sought my help to teach her how to objectify her thoughts, feelings, and perceptions. She'd lived too long with a distorted lens on herself and the world; she needed help getting clear. Despite having lifelong emotional challenges, a part of her knew that she had the potential to manage her inner world more capably. She desperately wanted to learn how to better exercise more influence over the activities of her mind. My job was to empower her by teaching her mindful attunement skills that would help bring that intuited self-efficacy forward. Sensing, accepting, and making subtle but significant shifts in her perspective was the *SkillfullyAware* game I was trying to teach her to play.

Human consciousness develops, step by step, up through an ascending level of stages, or perspectives.[29] One of the most mature and liberating of these viewpoints arises when a person acquires the ability to observe their thoughts and feelings dispassionately and with clarity. That perception is achieved by cultivating and intending to maintain a "witnessing" awareness. We refer to this well-known cognitive ability as *mindfulness*. But it doesn't take much stress to cause a person's growing light of awareness to dim. It happens all the time that some trigger will prompt the shadow of a lower perspective to descend and cover over the newly developing higher one. I'm sure this has happened to you—you go over to your parents' house, your mom or dad says something that triggers you, and—bang—you're behaving like a teenager again. This cycle of rising and falling perspectives is part of the process of cognitive development. It was this intermittent, state-type mindfulness that Sophie was beginning to experience.

Notwithstanding popping in and out of mindfulness, Sophie knew well how to use the attunement techniques I'd taught her.

Having worked together for about five years, we'd picked all the low-hanging growth-related fruit available for her to harvest in the early stages of our engagement. What she needed most now was not more coaching from me but everyday life experiences that would help her integrate those practices into her adult personality.

Sophie's parents live in Europe for a portion of the year and she had a trip planned to visit them in the first part of October. As the day approached, she began experiencing intrusive anxiety-laden thoughts. Alarm bells went off in her mind when, awakening from a fixation, she found herself staring judgingly at her naked body in the bathroom mirror. Sophie had not fallen into unconscious and savage bouts of body-shaming like that in years. Not surprising, that same day her stomach started hurting as well. And the nervous habit of picking at her hair also resurfaced.

Intense inner turmoil had the effect of derailing her well-established self-care routine, which included morning meditation and exercise. The mounting agitation was not only disrupting her meditation practice but became an impediment to it. Stress is a primary reason why people lose their mindfulness. When one lacks stable mindfulness, the practice of meditation itself can inadvertently magnify their anxieties.

Racing thoughts began to disrupt her sleep, and if there was anything that triggered her, it was not sleeping. Sophie had been under the care of a psychiatrist for decades, and she had a ready supply of medicines available to help her level the jagged edges of her emotions, although she had not taken any of them for nearly a year. Everyone knows this, but it's worth restating: it's not advisable to start back on medicines you've successfully weaned yourself off of, especially without the guidance of a doctor. Unfortunately, that's precisely what she did.

By mid-September, less than two weeks after our last session and two weeks before she was due to visit her parents, she languished in bed well past noon, numbed out on meds. Now, paradoxically, sleeping too much began to initiate a graver problem, as gloomier, more depressive-type thoughts began to take her over. The dark vortex of Sophie's downward spiral slowly began to turn.

Every child's brain develops in relation to an environment. The relative "health" of that environment is consequential as to whether it fosters healthy emotional development in the child or instead is disruptive to it. Factors like safety, security, soothing, care, nourishment, validation, and enriching opportunities to explore, learn, and individuate all add up to determine whether a particular environment supports or hinders a child's emotional development.

Emotions are central to how humans live and relate. Emotions inform us about everything we care about and value. In that way, emotions are context-dependent, springing from energy and information flowing into us from the world and cycling through our bodies and minds. Since emotions are context-dependent, they also depend on a conscious or unconscious story circulating through the *whole* system. Processing emotions and working through one's story requires *integration*.

One of the definitions of integration is the linking of distinct or distant parts. We integrate metaphorically, through our self-stories, connecting one event with another in order to make sense of our lives as a whole. Integration is a natural process. When not disrupted, integration occurs during development, as we grow from infant to child to adolescent to adult. For us to feel and be well, our neural networks must connect and integrate. When they don't, big problems arise.

Trauma, which comes in many forms, disrupts healthy brain development and, with it, emotional development. Kaiser Permanente, a large California health maintenance organization (HMO), conducted a landmark study of adverse childhood experiences (ACEs) and found a direct link between childhood trauma and stress-related illnesses later in life.[30] Children who experience more trauma had higher rates of disease later in life than non-traumatized children. The ACEs study proves that experiences are psychoactive; they change you.

Trauma disrupts the brain and nervous system's natural integration process. That, in turn, restricts the person's emotional balance and increases the likelihood that they will develop a stress-related condition during their lifetime. The lack of full and healthy integration, caused by trauma, prevents a person's brain and nervous system from accurately perceiving signals coming from all value fields—beauty (intrasubjective), goodness (intersubjective), and truth (objective).

Sophie's family was wealthy, and theirs was old money, the kind that can make some people feel superior. As a blameless child, Sophie grew up in a household where both parents aimed double barrels of haughty superiority right at her. Being perfect wasn't ever good enough for young Sophie.

For many wealthy children, the doors of opportunity are wide open, and sometimes it becomes clear to the more astute of these kids that without the grace bestowed on them by their privilege, their opportunities would be far fewer in number and significance. Should these children judge the effect of their privilege to outweigh the influence of their industriousness, it can cause a debilitating insecurity to develop in them.

Insecurity is an attractor. An attractor is a feature of living systems akin to a self-fulfilling prophecy. When a person believes they are incapable of winning or achieving in some domain, they often quit. Then the shame and inertia associated with giving up further deepens their insecurity and self-recrimination. Every one of us is susceptible to distortion and insecurity, and wealth is certainly no buffer against it. When facing the stiff headwinds of life's developmental storms, well-off children often have a choice their less fortunate peers don't. Namely, to forge ahead through their own initiative and grit or give it all a pass.

In some cases, should life circumstances appear too challenging, many wealthy children do choose to take the more leisurely track. Please, I'm not judging. Indeed, there have been innumerable times in my life when, had I been better-situated financially, I would have certainly chosen a path of lesser resistance. But when a person cuts themself slack too often, they may unintentionally develop an intolerance for difficulties and distress.[31] Sophie's life story smacked of many flavors of this incapacitating type of justification.

To be clear, Sophie wasn't lazy, a dummy, or an academic slouch. On the contrary, when she held a more realistic opinion of herself, as she often did, she functioned at a high level. Indeed, Sophie put in the effort, earned the grades, and, by her hard work and initiative, got accepted to one of the most prestigious business schools in the United States. But tragically, plagued by her cellular-level insecurity, she never enrolled. She desperately wanted to attend graduate school, but the thought of more years of struggle and all those other smart students who might earn better grades than her activated her handicapping self-doubt. Not having enough faith in her abilities smothered her youthful drive to take self-directed action. After that once-in-a-lifetime opportunity passed her by, she never got over the shame that its loss evoked, and when her family got together, Sophie's parents never failed to pick at that weeping scab.

In hindsight, it makes sense that the fast-approaching trip to visit her parents would intensify her emotions. They had high expectations for their daughter. When she was in their presence, Sophie had to be on her game. When they inevitably asked her about her life, she had to be ready to spin a yarn detailing suitable career and romantic prospects. All that fabrication took a lot of emotional energy that she did not possess. At that particular time, Sophie was running on empty. Insecurity was breeding more insecurity, her depression was depressing her, and not having energy was exhausting. The walls of the anxious vortex were closing in as her downward spiral accelerated.

In her degrading emotional state, contemplating visiting her parents became almost unbearable to Sophie, especially when she thought of how well she'd been doing just a few weeks earlier. Finally, when the day came for her trip home, she woke from a medicated sleep in a dense fog. Her memory of the Uber ride to the airport and passing through security is equally hazy. The last thing she recalls is sitting at the gate and curling into a ball as her mind spun out of control.

Every emotional experience is based on a conscious or unconscious story circulating through a system. Intense emotions like those Sophie was feeling are no different. To a traumatized person, one without a well-integrated nervous system, such intense feelings often activate unconscious, threat-based, self-protective reactions. Caught between the hard rocks of panic and ignorance, a traumatized person often has no choice but to "check out." That's exactly what happened to Sophie while waiting at the gate in the airport.

In the past few decades, extraordinary progress has been made in the treatment of trauma. A groundbreaking piece of work referred to as the theory of structural dissociation[32] postulates that trauma disrupts the natural integration processes of the body, brain, and nervous system. It further posits that each type of trauma-related coping response is driven by innate animal defenses to fight, flee, ask for help, or feign death (freeze).

The structural dissociation theory takes a systemic neurobiological perspective. It hypothesizes that the brain and body are inherently adaptive. This new view helpfully suggests that the crippling aftereffects of trauma reflect an attempt at adaptation rather than a confirmation that something is "wrong" with the survivor. To clinicians holding this more compassionate perspective, the distressing symptoms and disordered behavioral manifestations are simply best attempts by their patients to adapt and cope in a world they perceive as dangerous.

When we are young, our primary caregivers have almost total control over our inner lives. They create the environmental conditions that evoke both pleasurable and painful emotions in us. They also establish the ground rules for how relationships function. The first chapters of a child's lifelong self-story begin encoding themselves onto their budding nervous system during this time. A child's initial conception of self and worth emerges directly out of their relationship with their primary caregivers. Parents who neglect or, worse, abuse their children plant self-defeating narratives in their children's minds that challenge how they relate to themselves, others, and the world from that point forward.

Children are also born with innate drives to attach, explore, play, and develop social skills.[33] But should it become necessary, a child will enact their instinctive defenses to ensure their safety. How a particular child organizes themself to enact any one of these defenses (fight, flight, flee, ask for help, or freeze) is distinctly different in each case. Should a child grow up in a home where their primary caregiver is the source of both love and fear, the ability to rapidly shift from state to state to deal with different threats may become a necessity. At times it might serve the child to flee and hide from an enraged caregiver. Other times, the child may exhibit a defensive lightheartedness to pacify their parent's volatility.

To pull this off, a child must deftly shift from one ego state (sense of self) to another. Trauma expert and author Dr. Janina Fisher thinks of these adaptive responses as trauma-related procedural memory.[34] In other words, when *this* trigger arises, so does *that* behavior. In such cases, the dysfunctional behavioral adaptations and emotional dysregulation observed on the outside leave corresponding evidence of brain disconnection and disintegration on the inside. Strictly speaking, the child's brain displays the same dissociation among its various parts.

Sophie's ensuing panic attack and paranoid ramblings caught the attention of airport security. The two large men who approached and questioned her panicked her all the more. In her terrified state, she resisted their every attempt to move her to a more secure location. Finally, they chose to forcibly detain Sophie and call the paramedics.

Unfortunately, it's not yet the norm that a patient who admits to a psychiatric hospital also receives a soft, "trauma-informed" landing on their way into such an austere and unfamiliar environment. When not stressed out, Sophie was a friendly, polite, and cooperative person. In that paranoid state, however, she was anything but. She arrived at the hospital kicking and screaming. After transferring her from the ambulance, the hospital staff strapped Sophie to a gurney and put her in isolation. Now that she was fully restrained and all alone, her paranoia peaked.

As mentioned in Chapter 5, our brain's two hemispheres are structurally distinct and specialized, and each brings a unique worldview forward. The right hemisphere takes a holistic view of the self and the world. It also holds the "gestalt" of our nonverbal implicit memories in the form of body feelings. The left hemisphere, on the other hand, is task-oriented, concerning itself with the limited portion of reality judged most relevant here and now.

Since our two hemispheres prioritize different aspects of experience, they need to develop in relative isolation. Indeed, it takes until the age of twelve for these two distinct brain regions to fully integrate and communicate with each other.[35] That early childhood "fault line"[36] sets the stage for trauma to disrupt the natural integration process and create a *structural dissociation* that can last into adulthood.

A traumatized person who develops such a split brain is susceptible to having their "here and now" left hemisphere disabled by a highly emotional situation or a simple trigger. This can also potentiate their right-hemispheric, nonverbal, holistic, trauma programming. If you've had trauma yourself, you may identify with "being one person one moment and another the next." Neuroscience explains why this happens.

Fortunately, the systems view of mental health is that vanishingly few of us have irreparably broken brains. Instead, a truer and more compassionate perspective sees mental illness in the context of past experience, present support, and relative education and empowerment of the people who suffer. While biology is an indispensably important aspect of a systems perspective of medicine, from a systems view, biology is only one part of a much bigger whole. A systems outlook is far more comprehensive. It understands that the *emergent property*, in this case Sophie's psychosis, resulted from an entangled effause-and-caufect stream that stretches far back in time. In other words, her psychosis was the result of a combination of the immediate context's effect on her biology and psychology and the indwelling imprints she carried forward from her many emotional wounds and traumas, which adversely affected the development of her body and mind. All of it added up to co-create her psychosis.

Long before Sophie was born, her parents struggled with significant emotional issues of their own. Sophie's mother was battle-scarred and bloody from having fought on the front lines of the women's liberation movement through the '60s and '70s. Dauntless in her struggle, she was successful in ascending to the E-Suite of a *Fortune* 100 marketing firm in Manhattan. Having climbed so high up the corporate ladder, she wasn't ready to let go of the spoils of those hard-won career victories when Sophie came into the world.

For his part, Sophie's father endured life-changing traumas in childhood. Born into the British upper classes, his parents shipped him off to boarding school as a young boy. The shock of the abandonment was made worse by the emotional abuse and repeated sexual assaults he suffered while there. Later, after Sophie was born, the normal and natural responsibilities associated with caring for an infant frequently triggered his sensitivities, leading to explosive emotional outbursts.

Further back in time, both sets of Sophie's grandparents raised her mother and father by following the "strict father"[37] model of child-rearing, which was the dominant parenting style in many parts of the developed world during the first half of the twentieth century. According to the strict-father model, playing with a child before six months old was highly discouraged.

Furthermore, mothers were encouraged to wean their children off the breast in favor of infant formula at the earliest opportunity. The aim of restricting mother-and-child skin-to-skin contact was to encourage an earlier and stronger sense of independence in children. Sophie's parents didn't think twice about applying the same methods when raising her. Many were the nights tiny Sophie cried herself to sleep while her parents watched TV at the other end of the house, secure in the notion they were teaching baby Sophie to self-soothe. Conveniently, that firm approach to child-rearing fit hand-in-glove with Sophie's parents' neurotic self-absorption. It enabled them to guiltlessly detach from the stress, burdens, and 24/7 commitments of raising an emotionally needy infant.

But rather than instilling more healthy self-reliance in Sophie, the authoritarian approach caused deeply ingrained anxiety to develop in her. Lacking consistent parental attunement, she grew up not knowing whether she could trust her primary caregivers to meet her basic needs of warmth, safety, and love. Such an emotionally impoverished environment is profoundly disturbing to a developing child.

All children are programmed to relate. They learn about themselves only through the reflective feedback they receive from others. When children are not well-attuned to their parents, they will often develop what's called an "attachment disorder," which itself is a type of trauma. Sophie's lifelong habits of self-criticism, second-guessing herself, and, later, depression, anxiety, her eating disorder, and trichotillomania were symptoms of it.[38]

Attachment parenting[39] is a model of parenting that grew out of the late twentieth century work of John Bowlby and Mary Ainsworth on *attachment theory*.[40] Attachment parenting sees child-rearing through a completely different lens from the strict-father approach. As its name implies, attachment parenting encourages various ways of stimulating the healthy attachment of children to their parents and vice versa. The central premise of this method is that parents who embody an attuned empathy and responsiveness create the conditions for their child to develop a sense of safety that encourages exploration and autonomy, which eventually leads the child to a healthy relationship with themselves, others, and the world. The establishment of a secure parent-child attachment is the declared and pivotal goal of attachment *parenting*.[41]

The principle aim of attachment *theory* is to categorize the different ways children adapt to their primary caregivers' responsiveness to their needs for protection and emotional support. When a parent meets a child's needs for connection, attunement, and comfort, that child develops "secure attachment." In its mind, a securely attached child develops a beneficial working model of themself in relation to the world. Central to that healthy ideation is the belief that they can trust their primary caregiver(s) to meet their needs. The mere presence of just one person who provides a child with that security, referred to as a "safe base," empowers the child to safely explore and interact with the world.

Thus, securely attached children carry with them an indwelling sense of worthiness, and further, they come to believe that they live in a mostly trustable world. When gifted with such a nourishing perspective, securely attached people tap their highest potentials as they grow. A child like Sophie, who did not have her basic need for nurturance met, will develop a distorted style of relating to themself and others.

Attachment theory and the subsequent attachment parenting approach are both predicated on the fundamental truth that healthy human development rests on the edifice of *attuned* connection with another person. Establishing that healthy, secure attachment allows the bourgeoning emotional centers in a child's brain to grow and connect in ways that foster emotional self-regulation, resilience, and physical and mental health later in life. In the absence of this loving, attuned connection with a caregiver, a child's brain won't develop healthy, integrated connections. People who missed that crucial emotional support early in life are far more likely to develop attention problems, depression, anxiety, addictions, and other stress-related conditions later in life.[42]

Unhealthy attachment styles become the thematic backdrop for these children's self-stories. In their eyes, *unlovable* and *unworthy* describe who they are. In the absence of intensive therapy later in life, the story that constellates in a person's childhood becomes the tie that binds them to their traumatic past.

Beyond the need for attachment, though, humans also live with an innate requirement for authenticity. Authenticity, in this context, relates to a person's feeling secure enough to express their needs, emotions, and drives—to live their truth, in other words. Insecurely attached children face an unsolvable conflict. They've grown up in a household where their parents don't attune to them or meet their attachment needs. Unconsciously, the child concludes that authentically expressing their needs and emotions might further threaten the tenuous attachment they have to their parents. Since a child's life depends on attaching to a parental figure, they can't safely choose authenticity over attachment. Therefore, the need for authenticity often gets repressed. These children, faced with that no-win choice, grow into adulthood detached from their innate body awareness and confused about their feelings and often give themselves away in codependent relationships. This pattern of self-betrayal then leads to heightened stress, emotional conflicts, behavioral health issues, and chronic physical diseases.

As you can see, growing up with primary caregivers who are unreliable sources of comfort and care produces attachment trauma. I don't want to suggest that Sophie's parents didn't love her—I'm sure they did, and they probably did their best—but the everyday stress that her parents lived with—her mother's work pressure and long hours and her father's anxiety—held them in a state of chronic activated emotional dysregulation. Overloaded in this way, they couldn't control their own emotions, much less attune to the unpredictable feelings of a newborn baby. Then in their parenting role, they unconsciously acted out their attachment wounds and traumas and thoughtlessly disciplined Sophie for expressing her real and valid need for attunement and emotional nourishment.

Although the attachment wounds Sophie experienced early in life didn't determine her later psychotic break, they greatly increased her chances of having one. Indeed, we can rightly attribute all the stress-related conditions for which Sophie sought medical help—her depression, anxiety, eating disorder, and obsessive hair-pulling—to her early life traumas. Sophie wasn't born with a broken brain, but because of all her childhood stress, she developed one.

I did not receive her characteristic timely reply when I e-mailed Sophie to confirm our October session. Then, more unusually, our regular session time came and went without a word from her. After two more weeks of e-mailing and not hearing back, I became concerned and contacted her parents. They let me know she was convalescing with them after having spent a few days in a psychiatric hospital in New York. I expressed my condolences and offer of assistance. They informed me that Sophie was under the care of her psychiatrist now and that they would contact me when she felt better.

I remember a sense of foreboding rising in me. Given our siloed behavioral health-care system, it's a roll of the dice how a psychologically vulnerable person like Sophie is going to fare as she passes through it. Imagine my surprise when I opened my e-mail more than a year later to see a message from Sophie, who was back in New York and attempting to live an independent life again. But she let me know she was still not fully recovered from the psychotic break. In that short e-mail, she shared a few of her many fears with me, the principal one being that she was now questioning whether she would be able to adjust to living independently again, given her numerous psychiatric diagnoses: manic depression, generalized anxiety, panic disorder, comorbid insomnia, and trichotillomania. Carrying the spiritual burden of all those pathologic labels, she just didn't trust herself. The message she'd gotten from her doctors seemed clear: the diagnoses she had were *real*, and she had to learn to manage them.

Soon after I received her e-mail, we set up a reintroductory video call. I was shocked when I saw her again. The courageous mask of energetic optimism Sophie usually put on for me was missing; instead, this time she showed me her real face, which revealed a defeated, highly medicated, scared young woman. More unnerving, never before had she let me see her without a sheer layer of astutely applied makeup. In every meeting before this one, she had presented to me as if she were about to sit for a high-stakes job interview. But on this occasion she looked as if she'd just rolled out of bed, with bleary eyes and disheveled hair.

After a few minutes of convivial conversation to get reacquainted with each other, she began to open up about the nightmarish year she'd just had. I spent the rest of our session seamlessly attuned, listening and occasionally mirroring back key words and paraphrasing. I wanted her to know I was actively *with* her. Over the course of that fifty-minute call, Sophie gave me an earful. More than anything, she was confused about what was next for her. Only a year earlier, before her psychotic break, she was coming into her own. Despite the devastating setback of not following her dream of attending grad school, she had still found the courage to cut the cord to her parents, move to the United States, and explore other opportunities. It took some real creativity and guts on Sophie's part, but with great effort she had been able to establish a nonprofit organization with the stated mission of supporting disadvantaged women and children in rural America. But after her nervous breakdown, all the momentum she had gained after years of hard work had faded. Her most promising fundraising leads dried up, and the many colleagues who supported her work had moved on to other opportunities. Just one year later, her life was desperately off track.

More confusing for her, the advice she was getting from her parents and doctors didn't fit for what she wanted for herself. She craved more independence, but given the stark warnings she was receiving, she couldn't help but worry that her mental health diagnoses might flare up at any time. It was as if she were living with a ticking time bomb inside her brain that could explode with the slightest bit of jostling.

Throughout that year, she established a regular daily routine of prescription medications and frequent doctor's visits. Although now deemed psychologically "stable," she wasn't feeling even close to her old self. The burden of self-doubt she carried after the breakdown took the form of a more robust expression of her childhood attachment traumas. She didn't know which choice was best: to approach or to avoid her caregivers. She craved healthy autonomy, but her indwelling anxiety kept her from trusting that impulse. She also expressed an interest in reconnecting with me to see if she could rediscover her self-confidence. But even that desire stirred anxiety in her.

Before her breakdown, I had always given full-throated support to the notion that there was nothing wrong with her that she couldn't work through. Sure, she'd had trauma, and it had changed her in ways that sensitized her to particular triggers, thoughts, and sensations, but her brain could still take in new information, make connections, rewire itself, and integrate. Furthermore, there was nothing preventing her from acquiring higher, healthier perspectives again. She could still learn to make sense of her past and integrate her traumas and experiences into a new self-story that would then inspire and strengthen her mental and physical well-being.

All that was still true, but now she couldn't rid herself of the crippling fear of relapse. The perspective I was offering must have felt too risky to her, because soon after our reconnection call, communication from her ceased.

The Sophie who spoke to me over Zoom that day was mired in a more severe encumbrance than even the one she was admitted to the psychiatric hospital with the year before. She wasn't acutely psychotic anymore, but now she embodied the unshakable fear of relapsing, pressed into her by an orthodox medical theory of disease that conflated her with her diagnoses. Having for over a year been immersed in a system of beliefs that sees the brain as the beginning and end of mental health had convinced Sophie she *was* depressed, anxious, and all the rest. It was as if she had *become* her diagnoses. Over that year of convalescence, a disempowering brain-centric orthodoxy tainted her mind. That enfeebling view conflicted with and undermined the foundational faith she had in her innate sanity. She still remembered being the person who could dispassionately observe and work with her triggers, thoughts, and sensations, but now she didn't entirely trust that mindfulness was a safe option anymore. The long-standing habit of self-doubt that arose from her attachment wounds, amplified by the trials of the past year, snuffed out all that remained of her self-confidence. When a person doesn't believe they can get better, they're often right.

The amplifying feedback that took Sophie down began with her childhood traumas. As she grew up, she developed a disconnected nervous system. It came to pass that merely making arrangements to visit her parents activated a traumatic stress response in her. Her subconscious mind-body then cast up mental imagery and implicit feelings that flooded her with intense and confusing emotions. Isolated as she was, without the proper grounding support of a wise and kind person, those frightening thoughts and feelings intensified as the trip drew closer. All that unrecognized psychological distress destabilized her capacity to cope and her abilities to recognize what was happening, use her mindfulness tools, and reframe the experience in a more emotionally balanced way.

There are countless others like Sophie, spread over the globe, who suffer similar aftereffects of their trauma. The vast majority of these many millions will experience a mental health-related challenge, condition, or crisis at some point in their lives. Most of them will receive a diagnostic label and then a prescription for their pain.

The new approach to behavioral health and trauma treatment seeks to reintegrate a disintegrated brain and nervous system through education, compassion, and attunement. Childhood attachment wounds can heal through formative experiences and relationships. The result of such experiences is the establishment of a sense of secure attachment in the heretofore-traumatized person. Outside of the health-care system, becoming a loving parent or bonding with an attuned intimate partner are other reliable ways to recapture lost security and heal past traumas.

If you're suffering from the effects of childhood trauma, there's nothing innately wrong with you. Happily, there's far more you can do to change and heal than take a pill. The human brain never loses its capacity to take on new information, make new connections and meanings, and reprocess and recapitulate old narratives. Anyone can learn to be curious about their feelings instead of afraid of them, to accept them, and to inquire into their triggers and subsequent reactions. Curiosity and courage will build confidence and commitment to a self-care practice.

"Earned security"[43] is possible when traumatized people do the necessary spiritual work to make sense of and integrate the whole of their life's story, both good and bad. The work takes wise and kind guidance, discipline, courage, creativity, and self-awareness. Becoming a new person through active engagement with life will devalue the negativities in your past and amplify pleasure in the beauty, goodness, and truth value fields here and now. Imagination is a human superpower. Use it to inspire yourself to take self-directed action that feels resonant with who you want to become. The challenge is not believing the negative scripts from the past that may still be pulling on your soul.

In the next chapter, I'll tell you the story of Jim, who was born with a predisposition to be ultra-sensitive. You'll learn how he used his curiosity, creativity, courage, and compassion to build his confidence and make a meaningful life despite his ongoing mental and physical challenges.

CHAPTER 7

Is Your Story Making You Sick?

> *"You do not need to know precisely what is happening, or exactly where it is all going. What you need is to recognize the possibilities and challenges offered by the present moment, and to embrace them with courage, faith and hope. In such an event, courage is the authentic form taken by love."*
>
> Thomas Merton

We all grow up through the progressive maturation of our senses. Babies are born into bodies they don't know how to operate. They can't roll over, sit up, control their bowels, none of it. I remember my daughter, Alana, at just a year old walking naked around our back patio. Suddenly and unexpectedly, she began to urinate. The surprise and chagrin that flashed across her face caught my attention. She was definitely baffled by warm urine squirting out of her. Additionally, she was completely unaware of how to stop it. I watched as she ran frantically around the patio in a zigzag fashion as if she were trying to flee from the stream.

That story is an amusing reminder that we need lots of experience, informed by our senses and emotions, to learn how to operate our bodies. Over time, the feedback we receive helps our senses mature. To newborns, all the incoming information is initially fuzzy, unfamiliar, and incomprehensible, but as they grow their nervous systems get better at decoding it and making finer and finer distinctions.

That's what I mean when I say we grow up through our senses. As information flows in through your senses, your nervous system gathers, associates, reworks, organizes, and makes sense of it. All that brain processing produces a "model" of you and your relationships. To say it another way, we come to understand how we fit with the rest of the world. That model then carries within it all your habits and imprints, and that imprinted code feeds forward to influence how you react to future circumstances. All that information runs along your brain's fast and slow pathways, and it is through these massive parallel coding systems that your mind and brain make meaning. For all the reasons stated, emotionally significant experiences, including stressors, are inherently meaningful.

Considering how often we use the word, one would imagine there would be a tidy definition of *stress* that researchers could all agree on. That's not the case, but we know stress when we feel it. Stressful events are emotionally demanding, sometimes even threatening. Under such duress, we often wonder whether we have the resources to cope with and overcome the challenge. The conclusion we come to is consequential. There is an emerging view in medicine that disease is less the result of errant genes or an attack by an external pathogen than the result of a vulnerable person, lightly resourced, who concludes that they're not coping well or, worse, that they can't cope. If that's true, it must also be true that finding and expressing one's courage, grit, and creativity can do the opposite and spawn healing.

Jim is an HSP. If you're reading this book, there's a fair chance you're one, too. If the term HSP is new to you, it stands for "*highly sensitive person.*"[44]

About one in five people meet the criteria for this personality trait. Interestingly, it seems that 20 percent of all animal species are highly sensitive as well. That proportional similarity running up and down the phylogenetic tree suggests that instead of being a disorder or diagnosis, heightened sensitivity might be an evolutionary survival strategy that confers coping advantages in some situations. I say *some* situations because being highly sensitive doesn't always feel like an advantage to Jim. When they arise, his big feelings beg for an explanation, which pushes him into compulsive overdrive to make sense of them. All that "word processing" can make Jim feel like a story machine.

HSPs process information differently from most people. First, they take in more sense data than does the average person. Like a sponge, an HSP's nervous system soaks up many more and varied incoming signals and lets them pass through their less dense filters on the way to higher brain centers.[45] Taking in all that information often leads to significant "arousal," a term used to describe body feelings that come with emotional experiences, like tightness in the chest, queasy stomach, or a pounding heart. The experience of a particular emotion is in part produced by the intensity of the arousal a person feels.[46] Because HSPs feel their feelings more intensely, the sheer mass of raw sense data that HSPs process often overstimulates them.

You could liken an HSP to a supertaster, but with an HSP, their heightened perception generalizes not just to tastes but to everything happening in their world, body, and mind. For example, subtle noises easily perturb Jim. Here's a story that's weird but true. Years back, while Jim was visiting a friend, he was awoken by a battery-powered alarm clock ringing in a garbage can more than a block from where he was sleeping. That faint noise penetrated his consciousness and persisted until he could think of nothing else. After a long internal debate, he summoned the energy to get out of bed in the middle of the night and find the clock in that back alley and shut it off.

For Jim and other HSPs, the absolute requirement that they soothe their inner turmoil prompts them at times to undertake surprisingly tenacious action. Which is why HSPs are well-known for inflexibly managing their environment. For years Jim has worked hard at assembling the perfect conditions for sleeping. Alas, all that effort has had the reverse effect. Instead of aiding him in sleeping better, his persistent and perfectionistic attempt to eliminate every conceivable disturbance is an ever-present impediment to his getting a good night's sleep.

When not distracted or overwhelmed with sense data, HSPs can be very sensitive observers. This was certainly true for Jim as he grew up with an unusual degree of interest in the natural world around him. In a sort of figure-ground reversal, however, he is oversensitive to being observed. Growing up, Jim never developed an adequate social persona or "mask" to help him lubricate the more regular and superficial interactions with people, and thus as an adult he often feels intense anxiety in everyday social situations. His anxiety in turn becomes its own stress, which further triggers his HSP tendencies.

As you well know by now, the mind-body is an interdependently linked living system. It makes sense then that Jim, because of his excessive nervousness, would also manifest an assortment of minor chronic bodily aches and pains. In a self-deriding way, his keen observational skills turned against him. As he grew older, he developed into an ever more sensitive observer of his own maladies.

Jim grew up in an eighteenth-century farmhouse in rural Massachusetts, near the town of Concord. His family home was surrounded by fields, swamps, woods, and old trails, where Jim spent long days walking and observing. He was only in first grade when he subscribed to a newsletter published by the Massachusetts Audubon Society called *The Curious Naturalist*. But Jim's fascination for the natural world extended well beyond observation and facts. Indeed, his curiosity for nature was finely tuned toward beauty and wonder. Dwelling in the sublime overjoyed him. He can still vividly recall his solitary explorations from that time. Once, he found a snake's skin, crinkled and translucent, pressed into the soft brown mud of a stream bank. He also remembers losing himself and becoming transfixed by the fractal patterns of ice crystals along the frozen edge of a brook. Another time he forgot himself while tracing with his probing finger the wriggling tracks of a boring beetle under the bark of a fallen pine tree bough. To Jim, there was a language beyond words rising out of the mysterious patterns he found all around him in nature.

When he was eight, Jim's physician father moved the family to the crowded urban center of Baltimore. Leaving the quiet of his rural home, the plants and animals that he loved, and the endless forests he explored for a city he found "alien and awful" had a disorienting and depressing effect on Jim's young spirit. His brothers and sisters seemed to take the move in stride, but Jim couldn't. He describes his experience in Baltimore as one of never feeling at home, unable to stave off the advancing clouds of dark thoughts that ushered in unhealthy habits of isolation and avoidance.

His parents, siblings, and classmates had no idea how bad he felt. The crush of the big city was discomforting and, ironically, isolating. Even before the move, he had occasionally found himself troubled by deep and unmanageable questions about the meaning and purpose of life. The move to Baltimore shifted into a higher gear this habit of cycling in self-reinforcing negative thoughts and sometimes paralyzing indecision.

Happily, though, a little more than a year after moving to Baltimore, his family moved again, this time to Tucson. Although relocating to the Sonoran Desert was initially shocking, its unique beauty and rugged landscape were also enthralling. Tucson quickly started to feel like his new home. On a more personal level, Jim made what turned out to be some of the closest friendships of his life. But barely more than two years had passed when his father again took a new position, this time back in the northeast, in Rochester, New York. The move away from Tucson was hard for the whole family, but again, because of Jim's sensitivities and penchant for rumination, it seemed to hurt him the most.

By this time Jim was close to entering high school. As we all know, the junior high-to-high school transition is rife with emotional stress. Kids are managing the conflicting requirements of establishing their autonomy while at the same time feeling the need to fit in with a peer group. Finding oneself while at the same time safely connecting to one's tribe is hard for anyone. But for a pubescent tween, it can feel like a life-and-death struggle. To Jim's credit, while living for those couple of years in Tucson, he'd successfully juggled those competing demands and recovered his emotional equilibrium. So it hurt all the more to leave his new friends and the desert that had felt like home.

All people, not just HSPs, experience four basic, or primary, emotions. These are anger/disgust, fear/surprise, happiness, and sadness.[47] We also experience what are called secondary emotions, but there isn't a short list that covers all the many and varied secondary emotions.[48] The countless ways individuals learn to interpret their personal experiences explain why secondary emotions are far more numerous and nuanced.

Our basic emotions are so hardwired into our brains as to make them virtually reflexive. Basic emotions allow us to make quick decisions—for example, if the driver you're following slams on their brakes, your foot will immediately do the same. Fear is a basic emotion, so no thinking is required on your part before your body takes corrective action to keep you safe. The terrifying image of rear-ending the car in front of you is enough to move the foot. By contrast, a lot of thinking accompanies secondary emotions. Do you eat the second chocolate cookie or not? Hmm, let me think about that. Because we process primary and secondary emotions so differently, the brain has developed distinct pathways for each set.[49]

The circuits that process the primary emotions are collectively called the "fast pathway." Evolutionarily speaking, the fast pathway is one of the older parts of the brain. On the whole, the emotional brain is referred to as the limbic system, which includes the amygdala, the hypothalamus, and the thalamus. The amygdala is the part of your brain that is always scanning for threats. When you sense a threat, the amygdala is active. The hypothalamus is small but a mighty part of your brain. It coordinates many body functions, like arousal, which explains how it helps to regulate emotions. The thalamus is the brain's relay station. All signals flowing in from your body and senses pass through your thalamus and are then rerouted to other parts of your brain for further processing. The short, direct connections between the amygdala, hypothalamus, and thalamus explain why we experience the primary emotions so quickly.

The circuits that process the secondary emotions are termed the "slow pathway." The reason it takes more time for emotionally significant information to pass through this pathway is that the thalamus routes those signals up to and through the cerebral cortex. The cerebral cortex is, evolutionarily speaking, the newest part of the brain. The cortex sits on top and covers the rest of the brain. It is responsible for our higher brain functions. Our cortex enables us to engage in rational thought, consciously influence the focus of our attention, regulate our emotions, learn from our mistakes, use language, connect with others, imagine the past and future, ponder the significance of our present moment choices, and much more.

It's no exaggeration to say that it's the cerebral cortex, specifically its frontal lobe, that makes us human. When you contemplate your thoughts or desires or how you feel about decisions you've made, especially regarding your relationships with others, the higher brain centers included in the slow pathway are evaluating that information, making associations, and integrating it with new learning and decisions. It takes much more time to route all that additional emotionally significant information through the far-flung areas of the brain.

In the case of HSPs, both the slow and fast pathways are on overdrive. In other words, an HSP's sense gates are more open to incoming signals while, at the same time, they more thoroughly process the lot of it. In HSPs, then, all that extra input often leads to bigger emotions, which lead to more dramatic internal dialogue, which is why someone like Jim often feels like an overaroused story machine.

So, it's paradoxical, but HSPs can be painstakingly persnickety and positively panoramic at the same time. When HSPs face challenges, they puzzle through all the seemingly trivial details and yet also weigh all the long-term consequences. This pattern of exaggerated conscientiousness involves issues in their personal life but also can include global systemic challenges facing humanity. Mundane concerns at home and work keep them up at night, but so do climate change, terrorism, and political polarization. For many HSPs, all these issues are in one way or another linked. Everything feels personal and consequential to them.

It didn't take long after the move to Rochester for Jim's mood to turn south again. He couldn't help mulling over his manifold concerns well past what was reasonable and healthy. His habit of ruminating was a lifelong pattern, but it wasn't until he moved to Rochester that his overthinking hit its stride. Intensified by teenage hormones, the negative mindsets that had previously been psychically contained through connection to nature and friends now began to expand and work themselves more pervasively into his everyday behavior. Worse still, that summer he read several books by the somber German author Hermann Hesse. Depressed as he already was, reading for weeks on end about struggle, strife, and dissociation pulled his fragile psyche into a pit.[50] In his own words, he became "disturbingly morose." This distressingly gloomy episode was long and deep enough to attract his parents' attention.

This period of his life coincided with a time when much of the country was undergoing a boom in suburban development. Just as with countless other areas, the rural outskirts of Rochester were being bulldozed into housing tracts at an alarming rate. Jim couldn't help notice this progressive and jarring transformation. On regular walks and runs, he'd explored many of the open spaces around his home, and he frequently made special trips to nearby woodlands to sketch. The tranquility of the yet-undeveloped fields felt similar to undisturbed desert spaces he'd visited near Tucson. They also reminded him of the woods and swamps he'd explored in Massachusetts as a child. In both places, he'd come to know the vegetation and the lay of the land personally. Relying on those connections for a sense of belonging and security, he was deeply distressed when even the smallest section of woods or farmland near Rochester was cleared for housing. To Jim the permanent destruction of nature in favor of mass-market construction that wouldn't last three generations was an abomination. As his awareness of the workings of the outside world grew, he found himself increasingly at odds with a culture he regarded as shallow, jarring, insensitive, and disconnected from anything he found meaningful.

Because of the complexity and ambiguity of his perceptions and feelings, Jim rarely had a definite opinion or clear way of expressing himself. Furthermore, all the ruminating made Jim increasingly self-conscious. At his new school in Rochester, Jim began to avoid speaking up in class or otherwise drawing attention to himself. Although he remained a good student and gradually acquired a new set of friends, Jim never felt quite at ease in school—except in art class, where drawing provided a pathway toward mastery and genuine expression.

During his childhood in Massachusetts, he had spent uncountable hours wandering through the pastures and nearby forests alone, often coming home to draw what he'd seen. Art was attractive to him—as an HSP with refined senses, he possessed a natural talent for it, and art allowed him to share and connect more deeply and intimately with others without putting himself on the spot.

Labeled an "artist" by his classmates, Jim developed a reputation for being eccentric and unconventional. Jim's innate observational talents and obsession with beauty, along with his HSP tendency for precision, yielded an artist of the highest quality.[51] Open as he is to both the external world and his internal feelings, Jim possesses a preternatural ability to render the mundane beautiful. Now, as an adult who lives with anxiety and depression, he still turns to his art as a refuge from a world he views as tumultuous and often stressful.

It should be abundantly clear by now that Jim and other HSPs carry more emotional baggage than do most people. For them, the weight of it is heavier, but it must be noted that their weightier emotions aren't something HSPs *did* to themselves. In other words, being born an HSP isn't the result of their stories' making them sick. Genetic predisposition plays a big role in the construction of personality traits. Even so, Jim's tendency for carping analysis is an aspect of his personality over which he *could* become more self-aware and influence more intentionally should he make the effort. So on the one hand, sensitivity can be an advantage, as when it serves Jim's exquisite artistic expression, but on the other hand, *reactive* sensitivity that fuels overthinking is problematic if it turns into a stress-related pattern. Jim's lifelong anxiety is a manifestation of the latter circumstance.

In the language of modern emotion researchers, "appraisal" refers to the *meaning* that your mind-body system makes as you experience a stressful or otherwise emotionally significant event. The meaning I'm speaking of is synonymous with your most immediate thoughts and feelings upon contact with the stressor. In other words, *stress appraisals* represent the immediate thoughts, feelings, and judgments that issue *from* you as you meet a present moment stressor.

Figuratively speaking, stress appraisals can be likened to the immediate recording of emotionally significant details in the "diary" of your self-story. Life is a series of unfolding events, and right along with these events, your mind-body system makes appraisals. Every appraisal adds meaning, and feeling tone, to your ever-expanding self-story. That is how the story of you writes itself. Think of appraisals, then, as the "themes" of the story circulating through your mind-body network.

Appraisals will determine the emotions you feel. The three negative primary emotions of sadness, fear, and anger arise out of circumstances in which you experience a loss, a threat, or an injustice, respectively. A loss appraisal occurs when you experience the loss of something precious, like the death of someone close to you. Sadness is the emotion that automatically springs from a loss appraisal. For example, one time just days before her fifth birthday, Alana asked me, "Are you going to miss the four-year-old me?" Before I could answer, I burst into tears. Why? Because it hit me: I am going to lose the precious four-year-old and there's nothing I can do to hold on to her. Therefore, if you're feeling sad about anything, your mind-body has made a loss appraisal.

Fear arises in response to threats. Expect to feel afraid if you lose your job, step too close to a cliff edge, or receive a cancer diagnosis. Fear is nature telling you, in the form of emotion, that something nearby is threatening. Fear is the emotion that will always and forever arise in connection to *any* perceived threat.

Anger and its associated secondary emotions emerge out of situations you regard as unjust. How do you feel when a person cuts you off in traffic and then has the nerve to flip you off? Pissed off, right? That's an injustice appraisal.

Each moment of contact with a value-loaded context or object is, by definition, meaningful. Which explains how appraisals—or the themes of your self-narrative—lead directly to emotions, and then to the further development of your story.

The two types of emotions—primary and secondary—link directly to primary and secondary appraisals. Your brain's fast-track circuits process the primary emotions of sadness, fear, and anger. The primary emotions and appraisals are sparked by anything you perceive as harmful to you, your loved ones, or your stuff. The slow-track circuits process all the more nuanced emotions that arise as you reflect on your circumstances.

Jim's story can help us better understand the connections between primary and secondary emotions and appraisals. Jim felt immediate primary emotions of sadness and anger as he watched the fields near his Rochester home bulldozed to make room for tract homes. Witnessing that destruction generated primary appraisals of loss and injustice in him. His looping negative appraisals and coincident sadness later morphed into the secondary emotions of despair and a sense of powerlessness. As he continued to ruminate about the injustice of it all, his anger evolved into the secondary emotions of bitterness and a sense of personal violation. Jim's persistent perseveration amplified and distorted both his sadness and anger. That intensification *is* the distressing downward spiral produced by the energy and information flowing through his world-body-mind system.

It is accurate and helpful to think of stress as a consequential aspect of your world-body-mind system. Indeed, stress researchers evaluate the impact of stress on a person through this type of lens. They view stress as a "transaction" among the many parts of a person, including their mental, physical, emotional domains, and how these aspects interact with the ever-evolving environment.[52] The final effects—physical, mental, and spiritual—are therefore the natural results of a system processing energy and information.

Any time you find yourself in a stressful situation, appraisals will come from you, too. The primary appraisals and emotions, as reflexive as they are, will make themselves. You won't be able to alter primary appraisals and emotions, as they arise too quickly for you to stop or alter them. But if you're mindful, you can watch yourself process the secondary appraisals and emotions in real time.

The secondary "projections" that will come from you travel over the slow pathway. For that reason, you'll have a hair's breadth of time in which to influence the flow of the narrative and emotions through attunement. If you're able to dispassionately watch the way you relate to your secondary appraisals, emotions, and projections, you may discover crucial insights into your unconscious and reactive programming.

In that way, stress is great for revealing the already well-established beliefs you hold about yourself, others, and the world. Your self-concept, whatever it is, will correspond to how you've handled past challenges. If you remain aware the next time you're under stress, you'll see a parade of thoughts and feelings march into existence.

Recall the first three of the omnipresent mental factors: contact, feeling, and discrimination. These ever-present mental factors are crucial to this process. All the cycling feeling and discrimination is meaning making itself inside you. Those karmic projections issuing from your mind-body further evolve your system of beliefs. In other words, upon contact with a stressor, your mind-body activates automatic thoughts and feelings that coincide or conflict with beliefs you already hold about yourself. Emotional processing like this will always either certify or deny judgments about how strong, creative, and capable you think you are. Based on your evolving self-assessment, you'll choose to cope with the situation in one of three ways.

Self-confident people, when facing life challenges, mostly adopt a "solution-focused" coping strategy. If you're already a relatively self-confident person, it's in part because your life experience validates that confidence. Possessing indwelling self-assurance can help you through present challenges. A person with a solution-focused style proactively looks for ways to minimize the distress in their life. For example, a solution-focused person who struggles with an abusive colleague at work might take a class on nonviolent communication.[53] Self-confident people look for ways to better manage emotionally challenging circumstances, which lessens their stress. Their foundational belief in their self-efficacy allows them to enact the positive changes that improve their life.

On the other hand, if you're an HSP or were otherwise traumatized in the past, you may have grown to doubt yourself. So, when facing challenges now, you might instead adopt a disempowering "avoidance-oriented" or "emotionally focused" coping strategy. Coping with stress by denying it, as in the avoidance-oriented style, is no solution. Letting stress spark bigger emotions, as with the emotionally focused response, is equally ineffective. These latter two types of coping may also be seen as "pain behaviors." Pain behaviors are typically associated with chronic-pain patients, but other people who feel helpless can exhibit them as well. Chronic stress of any kind can bring pain behaviors to the fore.

Pain behaviors are defined as verbal and nonverbal actions that communicate emotional overwhelm, impatience, displeasure, or distress. Overt examples of pain behaviors include loud sighing, exaggerated grimacing, catastrophizing, hypervigilance, OCD-type preoccupations, persistent complaining and blaming, and addictive acting out. The point is not whether the person is in pain or not—they are—but that the person exhibiting the pain behavior is inadvertently focused on and amplifies their discomforts and difficulties and therefore distorts them.

Some people exhibit pain behaviors to relieve distress or gain understanding, empathy, or emotional support. Other times people use pain behaviors as a form of defense or manipulation. Whatever the reason, when a person repeatedly displays pain behaviors, they become habitual and therefore hard to discontinue. Pain behaviors then become just another *bewegungsmuster* in the unfolding of a person's personality.

By definition, pain behaviors involve negative emotions. Since emotions are contagious, the people living with someone who's fallen into the habit of this type of dysfunctional coping will also suffer. Consequently, people who routinely exhibit pain behaviors often find themselves unintentionally pushing away their closest relations. Then, sensing a rift between them and their relations, they often, in a bungling attempt to keep them close, increase the intensity and frequency of their pain behaviors. This, of course, only makes matters worse. This misguided reaction is yet another woeful example of amplifying systemic feedback.

It's important to remember that each coping style says less about you and more about what you've experienced in the past. Who you are now emerges out of a whole system that's been running for a long time. The mental factors of feeling and discrimination are carrying your self-story forward. Remember: contact, feeling, and discrimination also cycle with attention and intention. It's through these last two, attention and intention, that you become bound to your story.

The connection among a context, the appraisals you make in response, and the subsequent emotions you feel should now be clear. What may not be clear, however, is *how* your particular story can make you sick. Remember, your mind (where the story resides) connects to a physical brain. Because of this intimate relationship, the activity of your brain in an immediate and tangible way determines the nature of your emotional experience. For example, when your amygdala—the part of your brain that scans for threats—activates, you *will* feel fear. Not only does your brain activity determine the tenor and intensity of your emotions, but it also acts as a central processor for the rest of your body.

Should you find yourself in a threatening context, the activation of your amygdala will set off an instant chain reaction of physiological events. Automatic fight, flight, or freeze protective responses will kick into high gear. Nerves will transmit threat messages to every cell in your body. Stress hormones will start flowing through your bloodstream and tissues. Your pupils will dilate, your heart will race, digestion will halt, your palms might sweat, and a myriad of other biological reactions might take place, all organized by your brain for the purpose of keeping you safe.

Repeated stress reactions like the one described above automatically fixate a person's attention. Through accelerating feedback and by the physiological mechanisms I've mentioned, living with a chronically fixated attention inevitably exhausts and harms the body. Muscles tend to tense up when people are under stress. Unconscious holding patterns like neck tension and raised shoulders can cause upper back pain and headaches. Stressed people sometimes clench their teeth at night, which can lead to TMJ or other types of facial pain. If you've ever hurt your back, stress can activate that old pain.

Chronic stress also affects your heart and lungs. People under stress often hold their breath, which diminishes their circulating oxygen levels and leads to a whole host of other problems. Anxious mouth breathers can cause air passages in their lungs to constrict, which can lead to or worsen asthma. Couple mouth breathing with hyperventilation and a person can inadvertently precipitate a panic attack.

Naturally, hearts beat faster and blood pressure rises under stress. The gut is infused with hundreds of millions of nerve cells that are in constant communication with your brain. Stress disturbs those communication pathways and can lead to bowel motility problems like diarrhea and constipation or even diseases like Crohn's or colitis. The delicate ecology of gut bacteria is also thrown off by stress, which can have the further effect of altering a person's mood. Chronic stress will eventually disrupt the delicate coordination between your immune and endocrine systems as well. Because these two systems affect the functioning of every cell in your body, lack of coordination between them can lead to the development of many physical and mental health conditions and even autoimmune diseases, cancer,[54] and psychosis. Indeed, it's variously reported that symptoms attributable to stress trigger between 75 and 90 percent of all doctors' visits.[55]

Stress affects HSPs like Jim even more than the rest of us. Their system's naturally heightened arousal leads them to feel more. Their intense feelings become the wellspring of more dramatic self-stories, which magnetize and fixate their attention all the more, sustaining the effause stream that keeps a chronic affliction going. That said, you don't have to be born an HSP to be hypersensitive and develop a stress-related condition or illness. A history of trauma, persistent and ongoing current distress, a habit of displaying pain behaviors, or a maladaptive coping style will sensitize your nervous system just as readily. But the good news is that your potential to change and grow past entrenched negative patterns never wanes. Each one of us, no matter how diminished, has indwelling strength and resources we can call upon.

It's taken us a long time to get here, but now we can recount the part of Jim's story where he enlists his warrior and artist to help himself heal. As mentioned before, being born an HSP is both a blessing and a curse. On the positive side, Jim's life is more immediately poignant to him. On the negative side, Jim can distort his self-stories, which can then culminate in chronic aches and pains, anxiety, and depression. Flip it again and he can use his innate curiosity, observational faculties, and creativity to cope with those negative states in a solution-focused way. Often when he feels horrible, he doesn't just stay in bed, curl up into a ball, and curse the world. Instead he activates himself, draws on his inner strength, and makes something happen. Indeed, this has been his healthy moving pattern since high school.

One example of this is how Jim has managed his artistic career. As we've noted, Jim sometimes feels disconnected from a culture at odds with his sense of meaning. Art has been a way for him to show and share what matters to him. But after art school, Jim found himself discouraged by the world of art itself. Galleries often seemed to cater to elitism; the focus on ego, money, and pretension was uncomfortable, and while museums and critics made grandiose claims about art, the general public seemed not to understand it or even to care.

After several years of ambivalent participation in the art scene, Jim came up with an alternative, something he calls the *Itinerant Artist Project* (IAP).[56] For about a month each year he travels across the United States, around the northeast, or even just around his hometown. On these adventures, he lives with volunteer hosts, paints scenes based on the surroundings, and gives a painting to each host in exchange for room and board. Trading art for hospitality is extremely rewarding. As he puts it, "My art becomes a meaningful part of other people's lives." Having a more or less supportive, interested audience to interact with on a daily basis has proved to be a welcome contrast to the usual routine to which most artists resign themselves: working in isolation and, maybe once a year, meeting a small crowd at an exhibition opening for a few hours.

Jim admits that the project is a real challenge, pushing him way outside his comfort zone. But it also creates what he finds most affirming: a social setting in which he can see himself as connected and contributing while doing what he does best.

I want to end this chapter with a story Jim told me that introduces and underscores another key point: sometimes the best coping strategy is to shift focus away from our own negative self-stories and simply focus on others, especially on helping others.

When Jim was in high school a number of his cross-country teammates decided to commemorate the first day of spring, and also Jim's brother's birthday, by breaking through the ice on a local pond and taking a plunge. Jumping into ice cold water became an annual tradition for the boys, but for Jim, this practice morphed into something more significant. He discovered that these swims offered more than exercise—they provided a way to connect to places he loves and immerse himself in the beauty of nature. Thus began Jim's regular practice of plunging into natural bodies of water wherever he could find them and at any time of year.

As I write this book, Jim is in his late fifties. He still lives with and manages his anxiety and depression. As with most people, Jim's anxiety and depression grow out of prolonged self-oriented preoccupation. A few years ago, Jim let his gloomy thoughts transfix him so completely that he lost all perspective. His morose story trapped him in a net depression for months. He told me once that at that time, getting through each day felt like "walking through tar."

We must remember that Jim also possesses a robust and decades-long habit of solution-focused coping. Even at the nadir of this round of depression, he was able to call on his inner reserves to care for himself. With great effort, Jim began ramping up his swimming routine. His intent was to blend the sense of spiritual connection he felt when jumping into a natural body of water with his need for activity. That double intention led to an incident and an insight that were completely unexpected.

One afternoon, while in the grip of obsessive, discouraging negative thinking, Jim drove himself out to his regular swimming hole, Round Pond, in upstate New York. It's about two hundred yards across, and it was Jim's habit to swim to the far shore and back. For these therapeutic swims, he prefers the breaststroke so he can look around.

On this particular day the sun was low, the sky blue, and the trees along the shore beautiful and bright. The water was a soft, still mirror. Normally all that natural beauty would make him very happy, but that day even the brilliant scenery could not break him out of his dark mood. Absently, Jim went through the motions, stripped to his bathing suit, and waded into the water. His initial crossing was uneventful, but on the way back, near the middle of the pond, Jim detected a small commotion on the surface of the water. He swam closer to get a better look. It was a honeybee trapped by the water's surface tension and unable to free itself.

As you're well aware by now, Jim is a tenderhearted man. He can't abide the suffering of even the smallest creature. Throughout his lifetime, he's rescued countless drowning beetles, wasps, bees, moths, and various other bugs from pools and ponds. But if the bug has a stinger, as this bee did, Jim usually prefers to use a stick to help the little guy out.

Jim paused as he considered swimming back to shore to find a stick, but he reckoned that if he did that, he would risk not being able to find the bee again. It seemed clear to him that if he did not take action now, the bee was doomed. Putting aside his fear of being stung, Jim brought himself alongside the struggling bee and, gently as he could, brought the back of his hand up under the bee and lifted it out of the water. Jim was hoping that with a quick buzz of its wings it would take flight, but that's not what happened. Instead, it crawled around on the back of his hand, flexed its wings only slightly, and then seemed to peter out. The bee must have been cold and waterlogged. It had energy enough only to accept the ride.

Jim had to swim with one arm out of the water all the way back to shore, an awkward and difficult task. While doing so, he was forced to both concentrate on balancing the bee and remain alert for any sign that it might shift into attack mode and sting him. The novelty of the task wore off quickly, but not his interest in saving the bee. When he finally made it to shallow water, the relatively firm mud under his feet was a welcome relief. He waded to shore and found an appropriate flowering bush to place the bee upon. Happily, it obliged and painlessly crawled onto a leaf.

Well, I saved the bee, Jim thought to himself. Then he looked around and noticed that something else had happened. He was in a good mood. The gloomy spell was broken. For the first time in weeks, he felt happy. He was also confident that this newly brightened emotional state would last. He had been altered by his own compassion. Compassion is the concern we feel for another being's welfare. Neuroscience demonstrates conclusively that feeling compassionate concern for another activates areas in the brain associated with positive emotions. Indeed, the compassion circuits are the same brain structures that light up when we experience the gratification of our personal desires. It is verifiably true that it makes us feel good when we alleviate the suffering of others.[57]

An amazing thing happens when compassionate people encounter others in distress or, in Jim's case, a bee in need of rescue. In such circumstances, we can't help but consider what the other being's experience feels like. The emotion of compassion causes us to imaginarily put ourselves in their shoes, which can compel us to act on their behalf. Taking the perspective of another is one of the great developmental leaps in consciousness and has led to far-ranging positive impacts, not only on evolving human societies but also on the mental health of individuals.

In the next chapter, I'll thoroughly explain the systems-based self-care method I developed to help you become your own best therapist. I call this method SkillfullyAware. You'll see how everything you've learned so far is integrated into this one approach to mindful attunement. When you start practicing the method, you'll begin to rewire your brain so you can do the work of rewriting your story.

CHAPTER 8

Becoming SkillfullyAware

"The self-replicating cycle continues automatically unless the observing mind can see the conditioning. This awareness allows one to interrupt the habit and do something else."

Kenneth Bausch

I'd tried psychedelics decades before, LSD twice and magic mushrooms half a dozen times, so I had a passing familiarity with hallucinogens. While tripping on hallucinogenic drugs holds no interest for me anymore, I certainly am interested in opening doors of perception wider, glimpsing psychic and spiritual realms I have yet to access, and further developing my consciousness. For those reasons, in February 2016 I partook in two ayahuasca ceremonies held on successive nights.

For those not familiar with it, ayahuasca is a psychoactive brew made from two plants that grow in the tropical rainforests of South America. One of the plants, *Psychotria viridis*, is the source of DMT (N,N-Dimethyltryptamine). This powerful hallucinogenic occurs naturally in many plants and animals. Our brains and bodies produce DMT as well, but only in small amounts. Enzymes in our bodies break the molecule down so quickly that we don't experience any hallucinogenic effects. The second plant, *Banisteriopsis caapi*, contains a substance that prevents those very enzymes from breaking down the DMT. Pounding those two plants into a pulp and brewing the mixture over an open flame for a couple of hours yields a tea that produces a wildly psychedelic experience that can last up to six hours.

Traditionally, indigenous peoples of the upper Amazon drank ayahuasca as part of spiritual healing ceremonies. These native peoples sometimes used the brew for divining the causes of an illness, for shamanic journeys to recover lost parts of their soul, or to expunge malevolent entities that might have taken up residence in their minds or bodies. But more often, indigenous peoples drank ayahuasca for the same reasons people all over the world now do: to open their sense gates wider for the purpose of gaining spiritual insights and promoting healing.

It took a bit of Internet research on my part to find and connect with a well-qualified ayahuasca *curandero*, but my persistence paid off. Serendipitously, I found a shaman who has a regular gig in Tucson, swinging through town at least once a year. As is common with this type of stateside ceremony, one of the participants offered up their home so that the whole group of us seekers could take up residence, day and night, for an entire weekend. Participants began arriving at our designated ceremonial location early Friday evening, and walking into the house, I found the entire living room completely empty of furniture. Our *curandero* gave each of us a warm greeting, then a polite instruction to spread our sleeping bags, blankets, and pillows out along the perimeter walls of the room. He asked that we organize ourselves into a *U* shape and be careful to leave space at the head of the room for the ceremonial altar, his assistant, and himself. I tried to feel out if there was a particular spot in the room that might be more conducive to sparking a positive spiritual experience. Eventually, I set up camp near one of the corners, which for me always seems the most comfortable location in any room.

Once we had all taken our places, we ate a light meal and spent the next few hours getting to know each other. There was a lot of earnest conversation surrounding hopes and intentions. Many of us were new to the experience and were able to ask questions, which was not only instructive but also helped to settle any lingering fears. Finally, well past midnight, the *curandero* invited each of us in turn to the altar, where he gave us about a cup's worth of ayahuasca. As he did, we voiced our intentions aloud and then drank the brew. Then we sat back down on our cushions.

I felt an anticipatory anxiousness sweep over me, something I was expecting given what I was about to experience. As I attuned to myself, I also became aware of the significant physical and mental tiredness I felt. I was recovering from a long-lasting, intense chest cold. It would have been preferable to experiment with ayahuasca in a healthier state, but the timing was what it was. Given the delicate state in which I found myself, it was important to get my head straight as I waited for the plant medicine to kick in. Accordingly, I began to meditate.

Within about forty-five minutes the visual and sensorial effects of the ayahuasca began to unfold. Earlier, while standing at the altar, I'd made a request of the plant medicine to help me see more clearly into the self-making nature of the universe, and when the ayahuasca kicked in, that's exactly what the visual hallucinations began to reveal. My view of the room underwent a drastic transformation. The regularly seamless visual field began to break apart and the room took on the appearance of a mosaic. In other words, the whole perceptual field seemed made of individual parts. These innumerable bits of reality fit together like tiny jigsaw puzzle pieces, but each piece was the same size and shape. They all looked like flowing paisleys, reminiscent of a type of fractal [58] called a Julia set.[59] Just like a fractal video you can find on YouTube,[60] each paisley was alive and flowing with color and form.

En masse, the paisleys displayed a cooperative coordination. If you've ever seen an octopus instantaneously change the color of its skin to perfectly blend with its surroundings, the paisleys behaved just like that, except that they were *producing* the surroundings. I had no idea where the colors and form came from or where they went back to, but one thing was apparent: the emergence of color and form sprang from and flowed back into the same well.

In 1985, I'd read *The Tao of Physics*, by Fritjof Capra, in which Capra explores the parallels between subatomic physics and Eastern mysticism, and it blew my mind. I've since read many other books on the nature of existence, and to better explain the perplexing and paradoxical reality of the quantum realm, some theories of physics now postulate that the universe arises out of consciousness, not matter.[61] I find theories like that highly intriguing. Is the universe alive? My inclination is to believe that is so. When I combine my intuition and meditation insights with the real scientific possibility that there's more to the universe than dead matter banging against itself, it's plausible to imagine the existence of a sort of cosmic consciousness. But before that ayahuasca ceremony, I had remained agnostic. I just didn't know. Now, the plant medicine seemed to confirm my bias. Everything I could sense was in flow, existent one moment and gone the next. The inescapable conclusion I came to was that the only thing that appears to actually *exist* in the universe is flowing information. Somehow, all the apparently solid, tangible matter that makes us and the world is nothing but energetic and perpetually rolling information.

Later I discovered I wasn't the first to posit this hypothesis and its implications.[62, 63] A universe made of information will exhibit specific qualities. One qualitative example is that no real boundaries exist in an informational universe. Ask yourself: In a rainbow, where does red end and orange begin? Where does cold stop being cold and start being warm? Even more confounding, in an information universe, it's a false view to believe there's any sort of dividing line between the external world and the inner workings of the body and mind. The boundary of your skin is a mere illusion. A helpful way to visualize it might be the streaming code in the blockbuster film *The Matrix*. In such a world, there are no boundaries. Instead, it's all just informational soup.

Because I am who I am, the poignancy of what I was seeing got me thinking about the nature of stress-related illnesses. Truly, a significant part of my trip was taken up with contemplating how stories make a person sick. It's one thing to acknowledge that your story can make you sick and quite another to fully grasp you *are* your story. A further leap to a higher, more specific, and confounding perspective is to realize you are *a* story. Why? Because there's nothing *but* story.

The ayahuasca was vividly showing me that story and biology are informational analogues of each other. In the way living systems always build more complex phenomena, information (story) eventually morphs into biology. Each is an expression of the other, entangled and co-creative. Yes, there are many flows of causality, physical and chemical, biological and psychological, karmic, and collective, but if one can distill the whole flow down to information, then in a very real sense story and biology are part of a larger system process where biology emerges as an epiphenomenon of story. This psychedelic trip was showing me both the inner workings of karma and living systems in the form of flowing paisleys parading before my eyes.

If that shocking insight was all I had taken from the weekend, it would have been worth the price of admission. But I still had one night to go. I did my best to sleep and rest during the long hours of the day before the second ceremony. But despite provisioning myself with ample pillows and cushions, the makeshift sleeping arrangements were uncomfortable, as if I were camping. My lingering cough didn't help matters either. By nightfall, my exhaustion was peaking.

Despite how poorly I felt, the evening unfolded in a fashion similar to the night before. The group of us shared a light meal and conversed for a few hours. Our shaman and his assistant played entrancing indigenous music using various drums, flutes, singing bowls, and didgeridoos. Appropriately prepped for the experience, after midnight we made a single-file line in front of the altar again, declared our intentions, and drank a second dose of ayahuasca.

Blech! What a foul brew. I was quick to register the intense displeasure that came with the realization that I had drunk more of it than I had the night before. Hmm—was I in for a more tumultuous ride tonight?

The answer came quickly. The medicine hit me hard and fast. The fractal psychedelics were overwhelmingly intense right from the start. The physical tiredness from my drawn-out bronchitis and lack of sleep made it extremely hard for me to maintain my mindfulness. I kept having to remind myself that I was just experiencing a drug-induced altered state, nothing more. Even so, I was aware of a rising fear in me. Because of how physically unwell I was already feeling, I wasn't up for a bad trip. I found it a significant challenge to keep up the mental energy to stay present and work with my fears. I found the marching fractals exasperatingly relentless.

For the first hour of the second trip, I bargained with the plant medicine. Kindly, and repeatedly, I invited the ayahuasca to partner with me. "Please reveal insights that would benefit my spiritual development, but do it gently, like last night." Apparently, my entreaties fell on deaf ears; it seemed the "spirit" of the plant had different ideas. In contrast with the gracefulness of the previous night's experience, this night's trip began to verge on feeling like abuse. The plant had taken hold of my consciousness and was dragging it somewhere I didn't want to go. And to hell with how I felt about it.

As a survivor of trauma, I'm deeply aware that mental health is built on a foundation of emotional security and resourcefulness. For that reason alone, I was resolute: I was not going to let this plant erode mine. I redoubled my efforts to stabilize my attention while maintaining full awareness.

Earlier in the day, there was some talk about the need to "let go of control" and "surrender" to the plant medicine. I get it; I understand the balance a person must strike to allow themself to open fully to potentially transformative experiences like this. Pushing one's edge is vital for growth and development. But at the same time, there is a point where an experience can become too overwhelming. A heightened state of overwhelm is not conducive to clear insight. And anyone who suggests you let go of your intrinsic sanity is giving you bad advice.

Circumstances that feel too unsafe can set a person back spiritually and emotionally. Feeling already sapped of strength, I wasn't up for crossing too far over that line where I would capitulate and relinquish all measure of healthy discretion. So, after much unsuccessful bargaining with the plant medicine, I finally got to the point where I said, *If you're not going to play nice, I'm out.*

Right then and there, through an act of will, I shut down the psychedelics. Don't ask me how I did it exactly. But whatever I did had the effect of ripping down the curtain of marching fractals and reestablishing my mental footing on the solid ground of full, open, and unperturbed awareness. Intense body waves continued for another four hours, but the hallucinations disappeared completely. In the immediate aftermath, I sat still, meditating in the peace and satisfaction of my victory over the inexhaustible fractals.

Putting a stop to the hallucinations with my mind was an outcome I had not expected. Both surprisingly and astonishingly, shutting down the fractals easily won the award for the best insight of the weekend. In retrospect, I regard that event as one of the foremost spiritual teachings of my life. I was witness to a critical truth: that a strong intention and skillful awareness are a formidable combination! The ability to maintain mental clarity and objectivity while under the influence of such a powerfully mind-altering substance was clear evidence of the effectiveness and potency of the meditation techniques I'd been practicing.

Imagine how good it would feel if you could exert such influence over whatever plagues your mind. I submit that if I was able to maintain perspective while tripping on ayahuasca, you can resource yourself and eventually learn to maintain emotional balance through all manner of physical and psychological challenges as well. Physical and mental well-being are alike in this manner: both improve with exercise.

SKILLFULLYAWARE

One of my first meditation teachers, Shinzen Young,[64] said to me once, "If you're only as enlightened as your meditation teacher, then you're only half as enlightened." He was implying that to keep the Dharma alive and relevant, students need to bring something of themselves to it. His statement stuck with me.

Although, my interest in self-development has not waned and I've kept up a consistent meditation practice for nearly twenty years, I don't claim any of those profound realizations that bring with them thorough and instantaneous enlightenment that one sometimes hears about, although such cases do happen. Eckhart

Tolle is a well-known spiritual teacher and best-selling author who exemplifies that sort of fast track to awakening.[65] Alas, that has not been my experience. To this day, I'm still a work in progress. That said, all the studying and meditating I've done have enabled me to add something to the Dharma. What I do is simply let systems science inform my meditation and mindfulness practice so that the process becomes intentionally therapeutic. I add to that an ethical scaffolding that accounts for our collective interdependence, and the result is an evidence-based method that helps people work through and heal all manner of stress-related conditions. I practice and teach this method, which I call SkillfullyAware, because I want the same for everyone: that we become our own best therapists.

SkillfullyAware holds these three system axioms to be true:

- The more you know about the flowing effauses and caufects of living systems, the better you'll be able to manage and improve your condition.
- Your mind "constructs" your world. Therefore, to consciously change and heal, you must understand and learn how to train your mind.
- We're all embedded in a larger, morally consequential informational system. Therefore, what you think, say, and do matters.

Each of us exists interdependently within a larger system. Although self-care is paramount, self-care alone will never replace the loving support we receive from countless wise and kind others. In this way, the health and happiness of us all collectively is dependent on each of us individually. We all have our part to play. A fully fleshed-out network of attuned relationships is the end goal of practicing skillful awareness.

Becoming SkillfullyAware starts with setting a conscious intention to attune. Attunement has many subtle qualities to bring forth, so let's take a look at our definition of it. "Sense into yourself, others, and circumstances with acceptance, care, and a wish for a higher good." Now let's examine the meaning of the second half of the definition first, the "acceptance, care and a wish for a higher good" part.

ACCEPTANCE

This may come as a surprise, but fully and completely accepting your present circumstances is the key to attunement and, more important, to your recovery. Whatever your issues may be, acceptance is such a big part of resolving them that whole books are written about the subject.[66] Indeed, acceptance is a better predictor of both wellness and psychopathology (in the absence of acceptance) than emotional competence, emotion regulation, or mindfulness.[67] On the other hand, when a person's relationship to themself, others, and the world is characterized by avoidance and resistance, the more emotionally unwell they report to be.[68] You can choose to accept conditions as they are and work through them or to avoid them and resist, but you must understand that what you resist will persist.

Twenty years ago, one of my clients did so much drinking and drugging that he almost died of an overdose twice. That shock trauma left an imprint on his nervous system. Ever since the overdoses, he's been afraid to leave the house. He said he felt that "the stimulation of the world was too much." And so early on he chose to avoid going out.

Do you think those years of hiding out in his house made him feel better? They absolutely and unquestionably did not. Now, twenty years later, he's a father who needs to work to support himself and his family. But because of that early pattern of avoidance, every day he leaves the house now he has to battle a gripping fear. I implore you, don't make that same mistake. Don't start avoiding your issues as a way to cope with them. Fully accepting the way things are is warrior's work. By all means, emotionally resource yourself first and get support, but you must also make the hard choice to accept the burdens of your present coding while you learn to work with and deconstruct it.

You may rightfully ask, "How do you expect me to accept what is if it's objectively bad?" It's fair to assume that you wouldn't be reading this book if you were completely happy and content with your life. Where else can you start to reclaim your life but from the exact spot you find yourself? There's no other way forward than through.

Thankfully, there are a couple of reality-bending tricks you can employ to help you. One way to achieve acceptance is through an extreme practice that may seem a bit unreasonable at first, but be warned—it's difficult to pull off, but if you stick with it, it does work. Sometimes, the best and only way to reverse a downward spiral is to turn a blind eye to it and start pretending that things are better than they are. If someone asks how you're doing, stand up straight, put a smile on your face, and say, "Great!" This truth-twisting acceptance practice harks back to a popular aphorism that circulates widely through twelve-step recovery communities: "Fake it till you make it."

We all know people who argue for their pain and limitations, keeping meticulous score of every real and potential negativity. They take no account of anything positive. In the final tally, their balance sheet is full of debits and no credits. After such asymmetrical accounting, with a waft of masochistic flair they're almost giddy to report to someone, anyone, how pitiable their situation is. That's pain behavior!

If that's even partially true for you, please do your best to resist the impulse. The habit of broadcasting your troubles to yourself and others is *the* way people inflate, multiply, and perpetuate negative conditions. Getting ego strokes from playing the victim victimizes you all the more. It takes daily intentions and consistent effort to quit complaining. Activating your warrior and artist can turn things around. In the pages that follow, I'll teach you techniques that can break you out of victim mode by amplifying the positive. But for now, one way to shift yourself is to start broadcasting that you feel better than you actually do.

Faking it means conditioning yourself through pretense and practice to tolerate negative emotions despite very real feelings and circumstances that tell you otherwise. There are many ways to fake it before you make it. The easiest way to start is through the body. Sit and stand with a straight posture and put a smile on your face.[69, 70] Anyone can muster the energy to do at least that. Remember, everything you do lights up your brain. It happens that brain areas that fire together begin to associate with each other.[71] In other words, neural networks form and connect related areas. Later, when one area lights up, the other area will light up as well. Activating your postural and facial muscles when you stand up straight and smile, for example, initiates activity in motor control areas of your brain. Those same motor control areas associate with brain areas responsible for emotions. You, like everyone else, associate positive feelings with smiling and a strong and erect posture. For that reason, when you stand up straight and smile, areas in your brain responsible for happiness, vigor, and self-confidence also light up.

Take advantage of this reinforcing feedback. Give yourself a dopamine hit; it really does feel better to act as if you feel better. [72] As hard as it might be in the beginning, faking it till you make it can initiate an upward spiral.

Another reality-altering acceptance practice involves taking a spiritual leap. If you're open to the idea of life between lives, this technique can work for you. This practice involves you seeing your present difficulty as a spiritual test that you consciously chose before your present incarnation. In other words, a soul challenge you chose for your development. I've used this practice myself and it works.

Instead of resisting and resenting some grievance or negative situation, I transform it by mining it for its developmental gems. I open myself up to the spiritual lesson by asking, *If I chose this challenge, what was the lesson I was hoping to learn?* That simple shift in perspective is a far better way to relate to your troubles than going to war with them. There's always a lesson in the pain. Consider your current situation—what can it teach you? Your soul wants you to evolve. How will working through this struggle fulfill your soul's aspirations?

Last, don't forget that you're the one who gets to decide how you're going to frame your situation. I know a man who thought he was in a forever marriage right up until the day his wife asked him for a divorce. The shock threw him into the most painful grief of his life. A month later he got another gut punch when he accidentally discovered his soon-to-be-ex-wife also had been engaged in a secret affair. It would have been easy for him to fall into a story of injustice, which, as you know now, would have kindled the fires of anger and potentially rage. But he realized this was *his* story to tell and he could tell it in a way that served his growth and happiness. After all she had done, it was still true that he loved his wife unconditionally. So he decided to frame it this way: if divorce was what her soul needed, then he must let her go, and he would even provide her support in her transition. The last thing he wanted was to make an enemy out of the woman he loved. They also had a child together, and he desperately wanted to limit the harm that the infidelity and divorce would cause his daughter. So it was even more important for him to hold on to his ennobling story for the sake of their child. Choosing his story wasn't easy, nor did it change his circumstances—his wife was divorcing him, and she did cheat on him—but his consciously ennobling narrative provided the support he needed to make the best possible transition. It also kept him from getting sick.

Remember, the heart of practice is *radical* acceptance. Accept everything. You'll never hate your way out of your pain. It will take time, but keep at it. "Making it" means that you stay in the practice long enough to begin to feel ever-increasing confidence, energy, and distress tolerance. More positivity will bring more, so stay with it. Like everything you practice, these skillful actions will begin to create a self-reinforcing moving pattern.

Faking it till you make it won't just make you feel better in the moment. Like Yellowstone, it will also initiate subsequent system-wide benefits that will continue well into the future.[73] If the universe is one big bowl of information soup, then pretending it tastes better will actually make it more appetizing.

CARE

Now let's explore what care means when we speak of attunement. The embodiment of care in this context is dual. First, we should set the intention to be *careful*. In other words, with everything, earnestly try to do your best. An implied quality of mindfulness is carefulness, such that a person intends to act with care in all situations. Of course, this means being careful about what's happening on the outside—we should drive with care, parent with care, prepare food with care—but attuning with care also includes what's happening on the inside. Be careful to acknowledge what you're feeling and thinking; reach for higher and more optimistic and compassionate perspectives.[74] That's caring, too, for yourself and others.

With this in mind, intend to be present and carefully attend to everything. As the old adage goes, how you do one thing is how you do everything. Picture Soto Zen monks carefully raking a white sand garden or meticulously arranging flowers in a vase. That Zen attitude is what you're going for, simultaneously infusing both your outer and inner experience with care.

The second quality of care is taking care to do what's right. Care in this sense implies the moral impact of actions—i.e., consciously trying to lessen the harm that comes *from* you. First, let me state the obvious: it's impossible to not cause harm. That's not to say people don't try. Jainism is an ancient Eastern religion for which the principle of non-harm is the fundamental tenant. The purest and most devoted Jain adherents sometimes conclude that the only way to stop causing harm is to sweep off a spot on the ground, sit down, and refuse food and drink until they die. One could argue that killing oneself to prevent causing harm, though noble in intent, is still causing harm. So, in the case of lessening the harm you cause, we're always speaking in relative terms. You are going to cause inadvertent harm. That said, do your best to try to limit the willful and unskillful harm you cause to yourself, others, and the planet.

Both qualities of care are important to SkillfullyAware practice. Why emphasize these qualities of "care" in the practice? Because the opposite of carefulness are actions that spring from fixation, mindlessness, and carelessness. Obviously, those are mental states that create effause-and-caufect streams opposite to the one you're trying to generate. You don't have to look far to see the woeful effects of unskillful actions on our many interdependent systems, individual and collective. So be careful!

A WISH FOR A HIGHER GOOD

A *bodhisattva* is a person who takes a vow to hold off their own enlightenment, however long it might take, to help all other living beings reach that goal, too. Through their spiritual practice, a bodhisattva works on perfecting six qualities of character known as the Six Perfections.[75] The first of these transcendent perfections is generosity.

Generosity, in the case of a bodhisattva, starts with a wish for the happiness of all others. Bodhisattvas are happy to extend themselves to provide others with what they require, whether it be time or material needs, information, skills, or support. Intrinsic to this practice is a willingness to give with joy, free of resentment or any expectation of reward in return.

Generosity is seen as a primary value and devotional driver for adherents of all three great Abrahamic religions as well. Judaism teaches that the act of giving benefits the benefactor as much or more than the receiver of the gift. Though the recipient receives some material benefit, the donor obtains something far greater: spiritual merit.[76] The most poignant examples of charity in Christianity come, of course, from the life and teachings of Jesus. "He who sows bountifully will also reap bountifully … for God loves a cheerful giver."[77] Generosity is one of the highest expressions of God's love made manifest through the unselfish acts of men. Generosity, unsurprisingly, is a leading virtue for Muslims as well. The prophet Muhammad said, "A generous person is closer to Allah, to the people, and to heaven."[78]

When you're generous, you become the first and most immediate recipient of your charity. Research proves that generous people are happier.[79] People who wish others well (loving-kindness) experience lower anxiety, greater happiness, and empathy. They also receive more reciprocal love and care than do those who do not practice loving-kindness.[80, 81]

Generosity is a value we can all approve of and get behind, a place where sectarian and secular worldviews can finally bridge the wide and long-lasting cultural divide and agree. Both science and religion endorse it, so set the intention to attune, to sense into yourself, others, and situations with acceptance and care and a wish for a higher good.

Now let's explore how the practice of skillful awareness increases your influence over present-moment circumstances by consciously monitoring and modifying the scope of your awareness and the focus of your attention.

BECOMING SKILLFULLYAWARE

Think of a time when anger had you completely in its grip—when you snapped and yelled at someone you love, fired off a harsh e-mail, or threw something against a wall. Most of us have been there. At times like that, the anger *had* you instead of you having it. If you'd had a higher perspective at that time, you'd have been able to hold the anger in the larger space of your awareness. I'm sure you've had the experience, too, of being able to remain aware, keep your cool, and manage your thoughts and feelings without losing control. There's no getting around it—to respond skillfully in the face of stressful circumstances and intense emotions, you must stay aware. Awareness is necessary for experiential deconstruction.

Deconstructing experience means breaking down something potentially overwhelming into workable parts. That's what I did on that second ayahuasca trip. Deconstructing that experience required that I manage the *scope* of my awareness and the *focus* of my attention. As you well know by now, stress fixates attention. While I was battling the marching fractals, I had to consciously oppose that tendency to fixate by keeping my awareness open. I had to hold in reserve a part of my awareness that was *above* the experience, a part of me that knew that everything I was experiencing was just part of a hallucinogenic trip. Psychologists call that higher awareness "metacognitive awareness." Skillfully-Aware teaches practitioners to establish metacognitive awareness as part of attunement. Think of metacognitive awareness as your internal therapist supporting you through difficult situations.

Becoming metacognitively aware is easy: just become aware that you're aware. It's really as simple as that. Holding metacognitive awareness in the face of stress, however, is the hard part. I'll explain how to do that later in this chapter. For now, let's break down the basics of SkillfullyAware theory and practice.

ATTENTION AND AWARENESS

Recall that in Chapter 5, I had you imagine attention as the "flashlight" of your consciousness. Just like a flashlight, attention illuminates particular objects one at a time. You're always more conscious of whatever object you direct your attention toward. Awareness, on the other hand, is more like sunlight, which shines radially on everything, without preference. Awareness illuminates the whole space of your consciousness: all of the sights and sounds in the world, all of the sensations in your body, and all of the thoughts in your mind. Awareness and attention work together as a conscious system.

Remember how the chicken from Chapter 5 used its attention to peck for seeds and its peripheral awareness to remain alert for predators at the same time? For the chicken, and for us, achieving that balance between global awareness and local attention is the healthier way to relate to the world. That optimal balance of attention and awareness is mindfulness.[82]

THREE DOMAINS OF AWARENESS: WORLD, BODY, MIND

Everything that arises in your experience arises in one of three domains of your awareness: in either the world, the body, or the mind. Truly, there are no other places you can become aware of an object. That's the theory—now test the truth for yourself.

Keep reading this sentence, but use your eyes and ears to become more aware of the world around you. Don't look around. Instead, use your peripheral vision to become more aware of where you are. Be aware of what you see right, left, up, and down all at the same time. After becoming more aware of the space of sights, open your ears. Listen 360 degrees. Sense the whole space of sounds, as if you're sitting in a sphere of sound. Notice what it's like to be more aware of the whole space of sights and sounds. We'll call this space the "world." Acknowledge that you are consciously placing your attention on an object (the words on this page) while staying aware of the whole space of the world.

Next, become aware of all the sensations in your body. Use your feeling senses to scan your whole body, from the tips of your toes to the top of your head. Miss nothing. Feel all the sensations, in and out. Don't look at your body, just feel. The space where you feel sensations we'll call the "body." Now pause. Consciously place your attention on a specific object—breath sensations at the tip of your nose—while at the same time staying aware of the whole space of your body. Really pause and do that. Focus on breath sensations at the tip of your nose while remaining aware of the whole space of your body.

Now, finally, let me guide you to become more aware of your mind. Start by imagining where your brain is. It's right behind your eyes. But notice that try as you might you can't perceive your brain. What do you perceive there, immediately behind your eyes? You perceive an awake space, looking through your eyes. Can you sense that wakefulness? That's your mind. In SkillfullyAware practice, we refer to that as the space of the "mind."

Can you become aware of anything that does not arise either in the world, body, or mind? No—the universe of things comes and goes through those three spaces of awareness. The world is full of sights and sounds. The body feels the external world but also can turn inward and feel its interior. The mind is the domain of thoughts and mental feelings. Everything you've ever experienced comes and goes through one of these three spaces: world, body, or mind.

IN TRUTH, THERE IS ONLY ONE WHOLE SPACE OF AWARENESS

Conventionally, people agree we can partition objective and subjective experience into exterior and interior domains, respectively. The objective world of sights and sounds is on the outside, and the subjective world of thoughts and feelings is on the inside. But as you become more skillfully aware, the conventional boundaries that demarcate outer from inner begin to blur and eventually dissolve completely.

Your body seems to sit in the middle, between the external objective world and your internal subjective mind. Your body can feel the objective world outside, as when it feels the heat of the sun. But it can also feel your interior, as when you have a headache or feel anxious. Your body can attune both outwardly and inwardly. It can pick up the external objective sights and sounds of two people arguing, but it can also feel your internal emotional reaction to that same argument.

Yes, the body feels sensations, but do you feel a body? Without thinking, most of you will automatically say "yes." If I may, let me pop that bubble of self-assurance and posit that no one actually feels a *body*. What you feel are *sensations*. Sensations are a type of edgeless energetic information. Remember, there are no boundaries in an informational universe. It's subjectively true that energy and information don't communicate shapes or sizes. Test this out for yourself. Do you feel your edges? You've been conditioned to think you do, but let's use the sensation of warmth to test our hypothesis. Close your eyes, concentrate, and see if you can discern where your warmth starts and stops. Really, try to feel all the way to the end of your warmth. Confirm for yourself that you can't feel the precise *end* of warmth. I know you can *imagine* the edges of your body, but notice you don't actually *feel* the edges. You feel *sensations*, which are edgeless. If you're not convinced, spend some time meditating on it. This paradox may finally dawn on you: the clearer and truer your perception of your body, the less you will feel its edges.

The mind exhibits this same spacious quality. Just as you can't feel the edges of your body, notice that you can't sense any boundary surrounding your mind. You know you have a skull, but notice your mind seems unconstrained by a skull. The mind reaches as freely into the body and world as it does into itself. As you did with the body meditation, see if you can discern where your mind starts and stops. Close your eyes again. Is there a discernable limit to the expansiveness of your mind? Take a moment and appreciate the spacious quality of your mind.

When you practice becoming SkillfullyAware, the conventional sense of a boundary between the interior experience of body and mind and that of the exterior world begins to dissolve. That experiential "fact" is discernable because, in truth, there's just one whole space of awareness. Now that you're able to open your awareness into each of these three domains—world, body, mind—try to become aware of all three at once.

Do it sequentially. Start by focusing out, on the space of the world. See and hear peripherally. Next, become immediately aware of the whole space of body. Focus in both directions, outwardly and inwardly, using your body. Turn your body into a space. Last, go behind your eyes and become instantaneously aware of the whole space of mind. Now try to stay aware of all three at once. As you do, confirm this fact: you can't discern a boundary that separates any of these three domains. Outside and inside merge when you're fully aware.

Stop reading for a moment, pause with your awareness fully open, and take that in. Everything, both in and out, exists in just one whole space of awareness. Don't just read these words. Experience it for yourself. Pause and prove for yourself that awareness has no edges. Awareness is spacious.

- If you were not able to realize the boundarylessness of awareness by yourself, follow this link: www.skillfullyaware.com/boundarylessness-of-awareness-mediation/. Let me guide you on a meditation that will give you the experience at which I'm pointing.

SIX OBJECTS OF ATTENTION

I assume you took the time to confirm for yourself the truth of the experiences I was pointing you toward. Now let's get back to deconstructing your experience and why that's so important.

There is a lot happening on the inside and outside in each moment. To accurately catch more of what's going on and then to grow, change, and eventually heal, a person must learn to monitor and modify the activity of attention. We've covered the three domains of awareness—world, body, mind—but to optimally stabilize your attention for the purpose of self-change and healing, you need to take an additional step of consciously placing your attention on an "attentional target." To make it easy, I've divided the universe of things into just six categories of objects.[83] Each space of awareness—world, body, mind—contains two attentional targets.

Let's start with the space of the world. As you did before, become peripherally aware of the world again, using your eyes and ears. Realize that you are free to place your attention on either of two distinct categories of objects: sights and sounds. Again, prove this fact to yourself. Stay aware of the world, and alternatively, consciously, move your attention from a sight to a sound and then back. Notice paying more attention to a sight— for example, the words on this page. Now pay more attention to sounds. Notice the subtle shift of your attention. Make sure you genuinely sense the shifting of your attention back and forth between sights and sounds.

As we've previously discussed, you are not in control of most of what's happening. That said, you can influence the placement of your attention. You can alternatively choose to shift attention from a sight to a sound and back again. For the purposes of the SkillfullyAware method, we'll refer to these external attentional targets as "Sight" and "Sound." When you are consciously attending to sights, you are focusing outwardly, into "Sight Space." Likewise, when you are consciously focusing your attention on sounds, you are focusing outwardly into "Sound Space."

Moving on, your body feels sensations, and you can easily discern two separate streams of sensorial energy and information that circulate through the space of your body. One category of sensations you feel are physical in nature. Warmth, coolness, tingling, pressure, itches, pain, comforts, discomforts, joint position sense—all these give you information about your physical body. But you can also feel emotional-type sensations in your body. For example, if you're sad you might feel a lump in your throat. That sensation isn't telling you about a body part like your trachea. No, it's telling you about the emotion of sadness. Every emotion you have will arise with a simultaneous and corresponding body sensation.

The SkillfullyAware method refers to all physical-type sensations as "Touch" sensations. This method calls all emotional-type sensations "Feel" sensations. When you direct your attention toward Touch sensations you are monitoring "Touch Space." When you direct your attention toward Feel sensations you are monitoring "Feel Space." Feel into your body right now. Discern each of the two distinct categories of body sensations, physical and emotional, Touch and Feel. (Note that if you're *not* feeling any discernable emotional-type Feel sensations at present, their absence will feel like peace on the inside.)

Last, the mind contains two attentional targets as well, in the form of sound-like and picture-like thoughts. We all experience these two types of thought. Do you often lose yourself, "listening" to yourself think? Sure, we all do. Having a song stuck in your head happens to everyone as well. When either of those two scenarios happen, you're paying attention to sound-like thoughts. SkillfullyAware refers to all sound-like thoughts as "Talk." When you use your mind's ear to listen to sound-like thoughts, you're directing your attention toward "Talk Space."

But what about picture-like thoughts? What happens when your read the words *Eiffel Tower* or *Golden Gate Bridge*? What just flashed through your mind were two distinct picture-like thoughts. SkillfullyAware refers to all picture-like thoughts as "Image." When you get lost in your head, focusing your mind's eye on mental imagery, your attention is in "Image Space."

SKILLFULLYAWARE SPACES AND OBJECTS

To become SkillfullyAware, you must use your awareness and attention to break your experience into these aforementioned parts. To recap: There are three spaces of awareness, and each space of awareness contains two objects or attentional targets.

SPACE OF THE WORLD
- Object: Sight—all the sights you see in the external world. When your attention is on an object of Sight, you are focusing in Sight Space.
- Object: Sound—all the sounds you hear in the external world. When your attention is on an object of Sound, you are focusing in Sound Space.

SPACE OF THE BODY
- Object: Touch—all physical-type sensations that tell you about your body and its parts. When you are focused on a physical-type sensation, you are focused in Touch Space.

- Object: Feel—all emotional-type body sensations that tell you about your emotional states. When you are focused on a physical-type sensation, you are focused in Feel Space.

SPACE OF THE MIND
- Object: Talk—all sound-like thoughts that arise and pass through the space of your mind. When you are using your mind's ear to listen to yourself think, your attention is focusing in Talk Space.
- Object: Image—all picture-like thoughts that arise and pass through the space of your mind. When you are using your mind's eye to imagine something, your attention is focusing in Image Space.

Now let's make use of this new way of deconstructing the world-body-mind system.

THE SKILLFULLYAWARE INSTRUCTIONS

1. Set a conscious intention to attune.
2. Focus your attention on an object—one of the six attentional targets: Sight, Sound, Touch, Feel, Talk, Image.
3. Open your awareness sequentially—world, body, mind.
4. Be mindful—maintain the balance of a stable attention and a fully open awareness.

THE SKILLFULLY AWARE® HEALING SYSTEM

The Skillfully Aware Instructions

1. Place your attention
2. Become aware of the whole space–world, body, mind
3. Be Mindful: balance your awareness and attention. *Meaning, monitor, and modify*
   a. Be clear
   b. Concentrate
   c. Stay calm

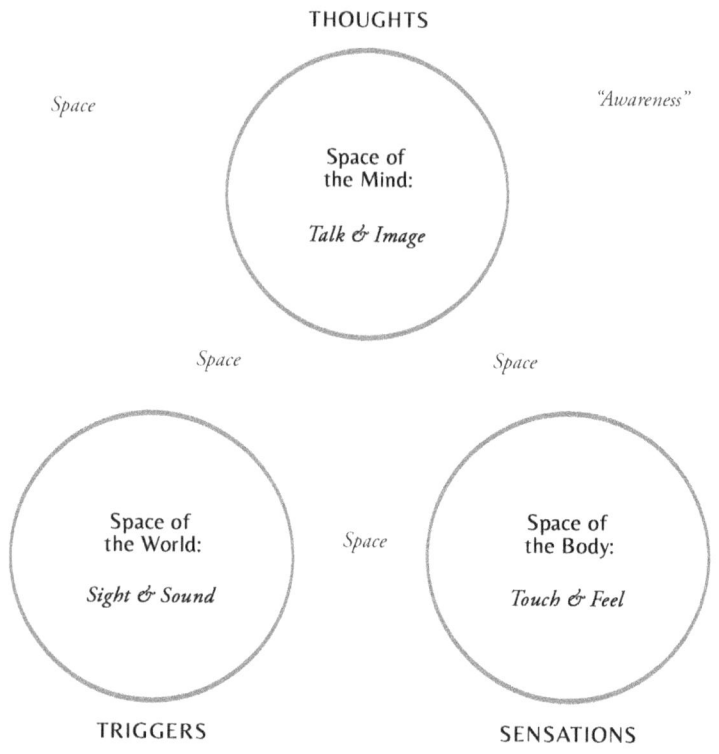

As mentioned in Chapter 5, attention and awareness form habits. Those habits construct our moods, temperaments, and personalities. If you have a habit of attending to and amplifying negative self-narratives, with time your distorted story may morph into a stress illness. You don't want that, which is why knowing your particular patterns of fixation is a necessity. To change or heal, you have to recognize where the triggers are, the space of either world, body, or mind, and upon which of the six objects (Sight, Sound, Touch, Feel, Talk, Image) your attention habitually fixates.

You *can* exert influence over the placement of your attention. Yes, it does takes practice—lots of intention-setting, attuning, monitoring, and modifying—but that's the price of change and healing. Placing your attention and opening your awareness and then working to maintain that mental balance is what it means to be SkillfullyAware.

FIVE FUNDAMENTAL TECHNIQUES OF BECOMING SKILLFULLYAWARE

Everyone learns to relate to *concrete* objects—things we all regard as solid and real. Indeed, the objective world of concrete objects is the ground of all our relationships. Most adults evolve yet further and learn to relate to *subtle* objects like thoughts, feelings, ideas, plans, and agreements. Few people, however, develop their consciousness to the point where they can relate to ultra-subtle objects like attention and awareness.

The reason I took time to explain attention and awareness so exhaustively is that I want to help you begin to relate to those most subtle aspects of your experience. Why is that important? Because raising the "window" of your perspective will offer you more potential peace.

The following five techniques are designed to help you augment your understanding of attention and awareness and help you reframe your story while amplifying beauty, goodness, and truth.

1. Focus on Positive

What you focus on expands, which is why so much of this book is dedicated to amplifying beauty, goodness, and truth. I credit one of my meditation teachers, Shinzen Young, with first teaching me this transformative technique. But depending on who you talk to, there are various versions of *focus on positive*. My colleague, Howard Glasser, originator of the Nurtured Heart Approach®, calls his version "see and name what's great." Positive psychologists often call their conception of the practice "savoring."[84] There is even an ancient Buddhist meditation technique commonly referred to as loving-kindness, or metta practice, that emphasizes amplifying the positive feeling states of love, compassion, sympathetic joy, and equanimity. No matter what you call it or how you practice it, setting the intention to amplify positive feeling states will reorient you toward more beauty, goodness, and truth. But to get traction with this technique, you must employ it so often that it becomes second nature.

You can start right now. Consciously notice whatever is pleasurable in your immediate experience, whether it be something you see, hear, think, or feel. Once you identify a pleasurable target, appreciate it, amplify your appreciation, and finally sustain your appreciation. That's focusing on positive. All you have to do now is set intentions to keep it up. You might consider putting reminders in your phone.

2. Prime Ahead of Time

You must remember to remember to be mindful. So *prime ahead of time.* This is my aphorism for remembering to always set wholesome, conscious intentions. Without setting wholesome intentions it's easy to get off track. The act of parenting has proved this to me time and again. At the end of a long hard day of exhausting work, the last task that parents need to accomplish is getting through the nighttime routine of putting their children to bed. That responsibility might sound like a simple one for readers not yet initiated into the fellowship, but it's anything but. I have only one child, and it's my fate that Alana invents and enacts every conceivable distraction to interfere with the execution of that nightly obligation.

If I don't prime ahead of time, I may end up losing my cool and raising my voice. Then I have penance to pay when I lie down to sleep, recall my day, and feel the shameful gap between my behavior and my principles. Maybe you don't have a habit of losing your cool, but if you are like most people, you will encounter particular people, substances, behaviors, or contexts that can and do push your buttons. This prime-ahead-of-time technique suggests that you make a habit of identifying all such triggering circumstances. What that means is reminding yourself of your wholesome intention and aligning with it before some emotional trigger overtakes you. After you experience success in maintaining your center through a challenging circumstance, a clear conscience and a good night's sleep will be your reward.

3. Name It to Tame It

Think of the first two positive priming techniques as sowing seeds of emotional resilience in your garden. Yes, there will be weeds that you'll have to root out, but your soul's nourishment will come from cultivating positive emotional states. That said, despite priming and positive focus, there will be many challenging and triggering circumstances ahead. When those conditions arise, employ our next technique, *name it to tame it* (NITTI). In the literature, researchers refer to NITTI as emotional or affect labeling.[85] I share this technique because there is solid neuroscience that backs it up.[86] When people give a name to their emotions, like saying "anger" or "fear," they report feeling less emotional. Amazingly, just saying, "Wow, I'm stressed," lowers your stress.

NITTI is so easy and effective that it is the first stratagem I employ in times of stress. I use it as soon as I become aware of any emerging strong emotion, urge, or habit of self-sabotage. When you're feeling stressed, I encourage you to do the same. Become aware that you're aware, and then start talking yourself down. Name the emotion; name the saboteur.[87] You can also add something that your inner warrior might say, like "I got this." I have a client who interrupts threat-laden self-talk twenty or more times a day by saying, "Thanks for trying to keep me safe, but I can take it from here." Just this one simple technique has quelled her penchant for fixated rumination and subsequent anxiety.

4. Shift Open Stay

Immediately after NITTI, *shift* your attention to one of the six SkillfullyAware attentional targets: Sight, Sound, Touch, Feel, Talk, or Image. Really open the sense channel to that object. See it, hear it, feel it, be aware of it. Then, after shifting your attention to a neutral object, *open* your awareness—world, body, mind (in that order). Last, *stay*, means maintaining a balanced, mindfully attuned state—stable attention, open awareness, and moment-to-moment monitoring and modifying. That's SOS. This practice is mindfulness in action in daily life. Do it often and you'll boost your positive intelligence, guaranteed.

5. Zooming

Zooming is an extension of the "stay" part of SOS. The monitoring and modifying I refer to when you're "staying" is, in fact, zooming.

Let me explain. Zooming refers to both narrowing attention and opening awareness. You have the ability to consciously monitor and modify how your consciousness functions. You can both place your attention and open your awareness. Zooming goes in both directions. You can zoom in and focus on details of your chosen object, concentrate, and make distinctions, and you can also zoom out and maintain a big-picture view. In that respect, zooming raises attunement to the level of an art form. Indeed, zooming is what renders awareness skillful.

Zooming *in* to focus on what's important is what enables mastery in any endeavor. Zooming *out* to reach higher perspectives is precisely what happens when people grow and mature. It's not an exaggeration to say that no other technique will help you develop as fast or as assuredly. In fact, zooming is so vital to the process of self-change and healing that it is implicit within the four SkillfullyAware instructions. By making the implicit explicit here, I hope to accelerate your progress.

Very simply, zooming is the technique that deconstructs your experience. In other words, it breaks your whole experience into its parts. You accomplish that mind trick by alternately zooming out and in. Zooming in with your attention gives your left hemisphere a job, to concentrate on a non-triggering object. Zooming out with your awareness gives you a right-brain, big-picture, wise-and-kind view of a situation.

When I'm tired and hungry at the end of the day and Alana is resisting brushing her teeth, if I zoom out and appreciate the big picture, I can better regulate my emotions. Alternatively, when you zoom in you can examine the finer details of a particular aspect of your experience. For example, when I narrow the scope of my attention on breath sensations while meditating, I can consciously increase the strength of my concentration.

Zooming in both directions at the same time is how to deconstruct and work through stressful situations. On the odd night when I don't sleep well, I zoom out and remain consciously unattached while zooming in on the "light show" behind my closed eyes. That's just one of a million practical uses for this technique.

SKILLFULLYAWARE IN ACTION

Now let's put all these five techniques together so you can better understand how they synergize with each other. The following is a hypothetical but real-world example. In this case, I will not only describe the use of the five SkillfullyAware techniques but also reveal how the five omnipresent mental events from Chapter 5—contact, feeling, discrimination, attention, and intention—fit into the process as well.

Okay, let's say a man has the habit of using alcohol to numb his feelings. He's mostly overcome this habit, but when he feels overwhelmed by stress, he still sometimes gets a strong urge to drink. In the past, that habit caused damage to his relationships with his wife and child. They both still feel significant distress should they see him take a drink. So, for his sake and the sake of his family, he had to learn to manage his stress and urges in healthier ways. One of the ways he chose to cope with his stress was by starting a gratitude list. He discovered that tracking his blessings really did make himself feel better. The result of that practice is that he feels less on edge. That gratitude list is a way of *focusing on positive*.

Now imagine that an economic downturn makes it likely that layoffs will be coming at our guy's company. Needless to say, that situation causes him to feel some major stress. Still, he's feeling somewhat emotionally resilient because he's keeping up with his gratitude list.

At the end of each workday, his route home takes him by a liquor store. Knowing that he's already on shaky emotional ground because of the work stress, before he drives home he sets an intention to remain mindful. That's him *priming ahead of time*.

Additionally, he *zooms out* to take in the big picture. "These are stressful times," he says out loud to himself. He even zooms out further and reminds himself that whatever happens, he can and will accept the outcome. "I have faith in my strength (warrior) and creativity (artist) even in the face of this uncertain future" (NITTI). Then his warrior says, "I got this" (NITTI).

Then, as always, on the drive home he does indeed pass the liquor store without stopping.

This is the process that unfolded in his world-body-mind system:

- CONTACT: Sight of the liquor store

    In the next moment, he's aware of an immediate squeezing in his solar plexus.

- FEELING: Feel sensation in his gut

    But he stays aware, *zooms in*, and *names it to tame it*. He says "Trigger!" out loud to myself. (NITTI)

- DISCRIMINATION: Talk arises in his mind. "Here we go," it says.

    He *zooms out* and says aloud, "Wow, what a stressful time" (NITTI).

    He *zooms out* yet further and employs the SOS practice.

- ATTENTION: He *shifts* to a non-triggering Sight (the license plate of the car ahead).

  After he *shifts his* attention, he *opens* his awareness sequentially—world, body, mind—and then he *stays*.

- INTENTION: He *stays*, zooming in and out, attuned to the moment.

  Zooming in and *out*, he monitors and modifies the focus and stability of his attention and the openness of his awareness. He drives home and the urge passes.

This example reveals the skillful and conscious management of awareness and attention using the mind training system SkillfullyAware. It also demonstrates the essential unity of the five basic techniques: focus on positive, prime ahead of time, NITTI, SOS, and zooming. This system and these techniques will work under any circumstance or with any distressing physical or psychological condition.

But please remember, life as we know it includes some amount of pain. You're not practicing SkillfullyAware to *erase* pain. You're practicing SkillfullyAware to *lessen* suffering. There's a big difference between the two. Remember, your only job is to not make things worse. That's the game you're playing.

CHAPTER 9

Slaying the Dragon

*"Get up, stand up (Stand up for your life)
don't give up the fight!"*

Bob Marley

I was mugged in Los Angeles a long time ago. A car pulled up while I was standing on the street outside my fraternity brother Carter's house, waiting for him to get back from the bar. Three guys about my age got out and formed a semicircle around me. The guy to my right asked me if I knew where Lincoln Street was. At the same time, a guy on my left coldcocked me, breaking my jaw. For the next six weeks, jaw wired shut, I ate everything through a straw.

Years later I had a dream where I found myself in a situation that was much worse. Four cowboys, each brandishing a Bowie knife, had me surrounded. After that mugging in LA, I had decided to take up martial arts, and by the occasion of this dream, I had been practicing for ten years. Even while dreaming, my martial instincts told me that something was amiss here. Yes, my assailants were armed and they had me outnumbered, but why was each one twice my height? Added to that, violence such as this usually tends to focus the minds of all involved, yet these cowboys were the embodiment of cocksure carelessness. Their lackadaisical manner implied that they thought I would give up and give in. They were wrong. Their leader took his eyes off me for just a second, time enough for me to slip behind him and press my own knife to his throat.

Feeling the power dynamics shift so suddenly in my favor was a pleasurable rush to be sure. My first instinct was a humble one, to work out a negotiated settlement. That's typical for me, to seek a win-win. There's some aspect of my ego structure that always wants to prove I'm a fair and decent person, and that's what I did—I struck a bargain with the villains. But not a moment after I released my knife from the leader's neck did they reassert their strength and dominance over me, and I found myself back in a position of weakness. The last thought I had before I woke up was, *I should have killed that SOB!*

In the years after the blowup with my business partners and even after a two-month retreat at Chenrezig, a roiling conflict still raged inside me. On one side was my ego ideal of a wise and kind person, on the other a wild and emotionally unstable beast whose presence I vehemently resisted acknowledging. The reedy boundary between my conscious and subconscious minds was sometimes a battleground between these opposing temperaments and thus the perfect environment for dream confrontations.

At the time in question, I'd done enough dream work to know that "healing the night" dreams like the one detailed above recapitulate material that a person has not fully dealt with. So, what did that cowboy dream point to that was unresolved in me? What was the message?

The day after I had that dream, I retold it to members of a community meditation group I regularly sat with at the University of Arizona. I was interested in the other meditators' feedback. Was the dream bidding me to step into my power more fully? Was it offering the opportunity to remove another obstacle blocking a more authentic expression of myself? Kill or be killed—what should I have done? The teacher that day, Jeffrey Brooks, wouldn't answer those questions directly, but he did offer some advice. "If a dream like that presents again," he told me, "remember that nothing in it can hurt you."

His words cycled through my mind later that night as I lay in bed waiting to fall asleep. As I peered into the depths, bands of sunlight streamed past me, illuminating three sleek and menacing forms gliding below: great white sharks! I've seen enough nature documentaries to know that great whites frequently attack from below, and so as not to suffer the same fate as do seals swimming at the surface, I dived deep. Once below them, I felt more at ease. I then became aware of how free I was to breathe underwater. The visibility was matchless, too. I've dived hundreds of times in pristine waters of the Caribbean and the Great Barrier Reef, but this experience was superior to both, rather like looking through fresh air. Far in the distance I could make out the barnacle-encrusted footings of a pier, so I swam toward it.

The water brightened as I made it to the shallows. Wet with sea foam, I emerged onto land and found myself at the bottom of a long concrete staircase. Soon after starting the climb, I felt the presence of a large figure looming above me. *Oh no*, I thought.

Looking up, I saw a huge naked yellow-green Shrek-like ogre blocking my way. The way it flaunted its claws and sharp teeth caused a momentary irritation to rise in me. Sharks and now *this*? Suddenly I became lucid, remembering Jeffrey's words. "Nothing in a dream can hurt you."

With that, all fear vanished. Showing no mercy, I reached up and viciously ripped its cock from its body. The massive monster deflated into something that looked like a blob of pizza dough. Without hesitation, I threw the blob over my shoulder, dusted off my hands, and proudly ascended the staircase. The next morning I woke up with more energy than I'd had in years. The phlegmatic spell of my depression was broken!

That dream, and Jeffrey's timely and prescient advice, served as the "magical support" I needed to break through what had seemed like an impenetrable barrier to my growth and development. Up to that point, the losses I had endured after the contentious split with my business partners still loomed large. The story line I'd previously clung to—me as a successful entrepreneur—was long over, and there was as yet no resolving plotline to replace it. Even after I'd spent two months on retreat at Chenrezig, there were months-long periods when I found myself slogging through confusion and hopelessness. I'll tell you the truth—until that moment I'd experienced no meditative ecstasy that felt as good as ripping the prick off that dream figure. He was my dragon to slay. After killing him, I became the beast! Exercising that life-affirming aggression cut the ties binding me to the past. Finally, I was free to move forward with my life.

Mythological characters like those in epic tales, dreams, and imagery in our minds frequently arise to block a person's access to higher perspectives and zones of magnified power. Why? Because no one succeeds in ascending the ladder of development without first defeating a host of nemeses, otherwise referred to as threshold guardians. Every classic story has them. In *The Wizard of Oz*, the Wicked Witch of the West's flying monkeys opposed Dorothy and her entourage. In *Star Wars*, the ever-present stormtroopers fought Luke at every turn. In the Harry Potter series, the initial obstacles to Harry's advancement were the Dursleys. Their investment in ignorance—"Don't ask questions"—kept Harry in the dark about the truth of his birthright and destiny. In each case, antagonists tried to block the aspirant from gaining insight.

The motif that development is never effort-free is so universal that it probably imbues the character of God and flows down into the physical laws of the universe and, finally, into the code of evolution itself. Putting forth effort on one's own behalf places a person where they need to be to receive such magical support, and often at just the right time.[88] Jeffery's words of wisdom were the words I needed to hear to make a different choice.

A parallel endeavor of individuation, the process of developing into a more whole and truer version of yourself, is equally arduous. Advancement up this hill is taxing precisely because it requires the acknowledgment and embrace of all aspects of your being, unique and universal, virtuous and venal. That is no easy task either. Mastery, and specifically mastery over one's darker impulses, involves venturing into discomforting environs and enduring trials. Only after surviving epic and morally consequential conflicts does one eventually find a way back to oneself. That's the path every noble person must tread in order to resolve the paradox of self and not-self, of fullness and emptiness. How does it happen then that coming to know the truth of oneself negates the self? On the other side of these contradictions are love and freedom, the great boons of the spiritual journey.

No threshold guardian will permit free access to life's most meaningful treasure without first subjecting you to tests and trials. Spiritual growth, therefore, is not for the faint of heart. Because for something to grow, something often has to die. The fear of that confrontation, of killing or being killed, is often enough to deter those who are unwilling to fight the adversities that their development demands they overcome.

My threshold guardians were demonic and aggressive, but they can present as friendly and well-meaning characters, too. Overly accommodating family and friends who keep a person from experiencing the consequences of their choices will block progress just as readily. When a person steps up and shoulders responsibilities that are the protagonist's to bear, they drain them of power.

Situations can be threshold guardians as well. Clinging to the paycheck of a life-sucking dead-end job or the security of a lifeless marriage can also dampen immolating fires and prevent them from clearing deadwood and opening space for new growth. Habits, too, are formidable threshold demons. How many of us engage in the daily overconsumption of alcohol, TV, or other vapid distractions? Who could we become if we could temper such anesthetizing rituals? Distorted emotions can also keep people from seeing themselves, their lives, and life circumstances more clearly. Beliefs are some of the strongest and most immovable sentinels at the gate. Believers often cling to views for reassurance, for a sense of security that the otherwise chaotic world does not offer. But growth and development require self-reflection, which demands holding even one's most cherished beliefs up to the light of truth.

Thus there are no limits to the varieties of threshold guardians; any person, circumstance, habit, emotion, or belief that thwarts you from moving forward and remaking your life will do. In that same vein, there are limitless ways you may overcome your present challenges, through physical effort, or intellectually, creatively, by force, guile, wit or dogged determination. But in each case, victory over difficult challenges and circumstances demands you act unflinchingly on your own behalf. Be assured you will receive divine support, but it will be left to you to kill the guardian at the gate!

Have you ever watched Animal Planet and seen a pride of lions feasting on a fresh kill? There is a law of the jungle operating here, plain for anyone to see. Dominant male lions eat first, and next to the table are the female lions that made the kill. The adolescents eat next, and the cubs are most often last to dine. So even the youngsters observe a social order. Have you seen what happens when one lion jumps the line and eats ahead of its turn? Instantaneous and ferocious retribution, that's what. Our distant mammalian relations observe communal rules, and this evolutionary heritage still resides in us.

Social rules hold their occupants in containers of safety, the same as they do the lion's pride. We humans also grow up in a collective construct. Our ego, or sense of self, develops in that milieu, where we learn to cultivate acceptable personality traits that help us relate to, negotiate with, and assimilate into a world of other people. Adaptation to life as a social being—in a family or a society—requires that individuals learn their culture's roles, rules, and responsibilities and then act in harmony with them. But when rules limit self-expression, they can constrain your development as well.

What happens when an adolescent male lion comes of age? There is a natural drive, a *call*, that arises in him to individuate, split from the pride, venture out into an unforgiving world, do battle, claim territory, and eventually lord as king over his own harem of lionesses. None of it is given to him, however. If he is to answer nature's call, he must violently assert himself and take it.

Much as we may dismiss or disdain it, our aggressive animal nature exists and requires expression, too. That instinct often comes into conflict with social norms, living as we do with others. In order to hold both opposing poles in our consciousness—the civil self and the feral self—the psyche must split. Consequently, on one hand we evolve a persona, or social mask, with whom we identify and prefer to show the world. From the time we acquire language, we start "scripting" an acceptable self-image, with the persona playing the lead role in our psychological drama. On the other hand, with the lead role taken, our selfish, primal, and brutish parts are forced to play the understudy. Thus we relegate our darker impulses to the backstage of the unconscious. Although we're mostly comfortable ignoring those deposed, aggressive qualities, they still remain and continue to live on in us as *shadow*. Growth and development, therefore, proceed along two distinctive tracks within the same person: persona and shadow. Inside, there is more than just me. Instead, there are we.

Sigmund Freud was not the first psychologist to expound on it, but credit goes to him for launching the notion of the unconscious mind into the public domain. Freud saw the unconscious as that part of the psyche not directly accessible to awareness, where lie hidden the life and death instincts embodied so viscerally by the example of the lions. Unconscious drives include those that deal with basic survival, pleasure, selfishness, scheming, manipulation, competition, sex, and aggression.

Freud conceptualized the whole of consciousness to be much like an iceberg. To him, the visible portion above the waterline represents the conscious mind, those aspects of ourselves and our stories of which we are aware. The rest of the iceberg, hidden from view below the waterline, represents the unconscious. But this analogy falls far short of the immense reservoir of material that was Carl Jung's conception of the unconscious.

Jung was a student of Freud's who broke with his teacher by proposing a view of the unconscious that was transpersonal—in other words, not only existent inside individuals but also present between and beyond them. His was, therefore, a *collective* unconscious. Jung used the term *shadow* to differentiate his idea of the unconscious from Freud's.

Like Freud's, Jung's unconscious includes all aspects of the self of which we are unaware. But Jung's unconscious goes much farther, containing a vast archive of archetypes. To Jung, archetypes are nonphysical, eternally existent, mythic forms that inhabit and animate the collective unconscious. Think of them as instinctual psychic themes that activate and influence our behavior.

Earlier in this book, I appealed to two archetypes inside you—the warrior and the artist—to encourage you to activate those inherent shadow energies for the benefit of your transformation.

Jung postulated that twelve of these energetic ideals live in each of us.[89] Our subconscious pull-and-push drives draw strength from some combination of warrior, sage, explorer, ruler, magician, artist, outlaw, lover, trickster, dreamer, realist, and caregiver. Thus the dynamism of archetypes serves as the wellspring of all human eros and pathos. They are the reason that stories have so much spiritual juice and why narrative medicine is so necessary and effective. Imagine that God is the creator and keeper of all archetypes and, in that way, acts as a cosmic puppet master. How "he/she/it/they" pulls on our emotional strings is through the activation of the resonant archetypic energies in us. Wherever God is, the archetypes are, in the same transcendent realm of the collective unconscious. When you feel an intuitive pull to do something, understand that archetypes are operating on you from within and without.

Jung famously wrote, "One does not become enlightened by imagining figures of light, but by making the dark conscious." Thus we gain salvation or enlightenment through coming to fully illuminate, acknowledge, understand, accept, and temper our animal instincts. In Jung's view, the boundary between the conscious persona and the shadow unconscious serves as the psychic battleground where the archetypical forces of good and evil fight for control over a person's soul. The angel that lives in each of us is sometimes referred to as "constructive" shadow. Alternately, the devil inside is "destructive" shadow.

When you feel safe, accepted and loved, you're more likely to be open to the positive influence arising out of your constructive shadow. When you feel unsafe or defensive, you're more likely to resist change and fall under the influence of your destructive shadow. Constructive shadow brings out the best in us. It's the positive influence of constructive shadow that strives for more beauty, goodness, and truth. When under the influence of destructive shadow, however, we lose perspective and act out our worst impulses. The net result of this internal push and pull between constructive and destructive shadow is ultimately what determines the shape of a person's personality, their consequential choices, and ultimately their destiny.

Framing this battle in such black-and-white terms, between the forces of good and evil, is far too simplistic, however. In mythology as in life, a higher good is sometimes reached through debatable means. Which is why at times you must use awareness and discernment just as a bug uses its antennae, to *feel* your way forward. There will be times when the aggression of destructive shadow may be necessary to bust through an otherwise impenetrable threshold. Mark my words, you will encounter rare circumstances where the greater good is done by letting wildness be wild. Understand, then, when dealing with archetypical energy, there are no rules except for one: do your best to lessen the harm you cause in reaching toward your fulfillment.

So, what did the leader of the cowboys represent in the dream I previously recounted? Was he an evil oppressor, or instead a savior, daring me to murder him so that I might reclaim a lost part of myself? Whatever he signified, that night I failed the test. But the very next night, in an additional expression of tough love, mythic collective unconscious offered up a similar test in the guise of that malevolent Shrek. The gauntlet was thrown down again: kill in order to live.

As I faced the monster, it was fierce animal energy, innate wildness inside me calling, "Claim your life!" Two options were in play: violently slay the threshold guardian or be submissive and retreat, tail tucked, back into the cell of my victim mentality. Which was the higher good? For me, the choice was clear. In that moment, the symbol of the phallus was there for the taking. In a transposition typical of myth, the better choice was to wield the violence of destructive shadow in a life-preserving way. I became the lion, and the outward appearance of destruction became in fact a creative act. Had I not activated that animalistic shadow energy, who and where would I be now?

I can't tell you how to channel your creative aggression, but I do know you'll need to do just that to escape the sucking gravity of your current challenge. Framing your life as a mythic journey may give you the strength needed to keep going. What if everything you're experiencing right now is happening for a reason? Is the spiritual lesson you're learning now enough to goad you to get up once again and stand up for your life? If you believe life has presented you with your current challenges for the lessons they offer, you won't feel like a victim. Instead, you'll feel like the strong and creative warrior and artist you are. If you're with me on this, let's start doing the hard work.

CHAPTER 10

Chasing Shadows

*"The pride of the peacock is the glory of God.
The lust of the goat is the bounty of God.
The wrath of the lion is the wisdom of God.
The nakedness of woman is the work of God."*

William Blake

Marion Woodman once said, "Creative suffering burns clean; neurotic suffering creates more and more soot." Neurotic suffering is the kind of suffering that presupposes *one solid self*—in other words, one story with very few options. Holding tightly to such a view effectively puts a person in a box, which restricts the range of creative responses to a given situation. Creative suffering is vastly different. Woodman suggests that creative suffering holds open the potential for many perspectives on one's story and situation.

Suffering creatively means making a conscious choice to work with difficulties for the purpose of adapting and evolving. Suffering creatively makes the best of situations and is therefore an indispensable means of healing, change, and transformation. You may rightly ask what's necessary to accomplish the spiritual transformation you're seeking. The simple straightforward answer is to start self-reflecting. If it's right for you, meditation can help. The stable attention, open awareness, and distress tolerance that meditation provides are exactly what development demands.

Start a meditation practice and begin engaging in shadow work—the practice of plumbing the depths of the psyche, either alone or with the help of a competent guide. One engages in shadow work by deciding to illuminate, accept, balance, and integrate all parts of oneself. Shadow work recovers lost passion and playfulness, power and purpose. It also expands the breadth of one's being, depth of intimacy, and peace of mind. It takes courage, self-discipline, and patience to discover these hidden aspects of one's personality, but the reward comes in the form of greater authenticity, integrity, creativity, and emotional balance.

KNOW THYSELF—THE MANY BENEFITS OF SHADOW WORK

- Experience the truer, more authentic self-expression that springs from actualizing the fullness of both the light and dark aspects of who you are.
- Observe and work through distorted negative emotions triggered by daily interactions with your own thoughts and feelings, with others, and with the world.
- Achieve mastery over your emotions, obsessions, and compulsions. Only those who are aware of their extremes

of desire and aversion can choose to regulate these energies and channel them in more wholesome directions.
- Experience freedom from guilt and shame that comes from extinguishing the inadvertent and harmful expressions of destructive shadow.
- Recognize your projections as projections the moment they spring from your subconscious.
- Enhance your capacity to set appropriate boundaries in your life.
- Repair your most cherished relationships through the hard work of self-reflection, compassionate communication, and the acceptance of yourself and others.
- Integrate your disowned parts and use their energy to foster strength, creativity, and spiritual development.

SHADOW AT THE BOUNDARIES

Even now, shadow is emerging from within you. Whatever thoughts and judgments surface as you read this sentence are coming from your shadow. By doing shadow work, you determine to meet all such spontaneously arising stimuli with an eye toward development. You do that by repeatedly setting conscious intentions to direct your attention toward the "boundary spaces" of your experience. In other words, skillful awareness starts by becoming aware of the energy and information arising at the interfaces of the world, body, and mind.

Your body exists in the middle of these three "parts." Let's start with the body-world interface. A shadow interface is "feel-able" by sensing into your body and out to the world at the same time. Do it now. Feel both in and out at the same time. If you get triggered by a hot chick or dude, smell a freshly baked chocolate cookie, read a disrespectful e-mail, or hear a screaming child at 2 a.m., you'll feel this boundary space light up with shadow activity related to the push and pull of craving or aversion.

She can be dead asleep on the other side of the house, but whenever my cat Rumi hears the sound of a can opener she jumps up and runs to the kitchen. If you're not attuned to the triggers in your life, you'll behave just like Rumi. Animals are compulsively drawn to or away from whatever sights and sounds activate them. But you're a human, not an animal. Set the intention to attune whenever objects in the world trigger you, activating craving or aversion. Attunement turns into shadow work when you observe with equanimity the flow of triggering emotional energy at the body-world interface.

Next, let's explore the body-mind interface. With shadow material, you can observe "where" your body's sensations meet the thoughts in your mind. Start by imagining the "boundary" between the body and mind. There really isn't a boundary, but it's the best metaphor I can provide. Once you're attuned to that "location," observe how your thoughts mix with your feelings. With your mind's eye, see in. With your mind's ear, hear in. And with your body, feel in. Notice all spontaneous Image, Talk, or Feel activity that arises. Be careful to observe these arisings with detachment. The body-mind interface is especially active when your body feels pain or your mind is troubled. If you're emotional for any reason, you can observe feelings and mental activity writing a passion play inside you.

Often when I feel vaguely uncomfortable at home, I unconsciously start to clean. I even have a name for that shadow-based alter ego, Helmut Klienstein. Whenever Helmut takes me over, shadow work involves attuning to my body-mind interface and opening to the emotion(s) I'm suppressing. The dishes may still need washing or the floors cleaning, but I'd rather do those jobs consciously than compulsively.

You can "metabolize" your shadow that way, too, by monitoring and modifying such robot-like motor programs. By attuning to the body-mind interface, you also increase your distress tolerance and capacity for conscious choice. Shadow work at the body-mind interface entails meeting all arising sensations and thoughts with acceptance and equanimity.

Finally, shadow reveals itself when triggers in the world meet your critical mind. Right now, look and listen, see and hear what's in the room you are sitting in. Do these objects trigger glee or disappointment, or do they just leave you flat? Liking, disliking, or caring less about the objects in your world reveals your shadow, too.

Pause and become aware of the *awareness* that resides right behind your eyes and between your ears. Take a moment and do that. Now look around. See out, but see in, too. Listen out, but listen in, too. Be keenly aware again of the room you are sitting in, but also remain aware of your awareness as you do it. See in and out. Listen in and out. Perceive all the subtle mental impressions and feeling tones cycling through your awareness. Can you accept and calmly relate to whatever might be your current relationship with the stuff in the room? If so, that's shadow work, too.

One more time: Close your eyes and open your awareness. See if you can place your attention at any of the previously mentioned boundary spaces between world, body, and mind. Use your conscious attention to probe into the mysterious "edges" of your existence. Shine a light on your hidden judgments, impressions, sensations, defenses, feelings, memories, stories, agendas, and intentions. All those myriad spontaneous reactions reflect your shadow. Shadow emerges in all the relationships you have with yourself, your body, others, and the world.

In January of 2005 I participated in the Scientists Retreat held at the Insight Meditation Society (IMS) in Barre, Massachusetts. The retreat was led by Joseph Goldstein and Sharon Salzberg, senior meditation teachers of the IMS, and two scientists associated with the Mind & Life Institute, Jon Kabat-Zinn and Richie Davison. I was one of about a hundred attendees. Every person there was working in some way in the fields of brain science or behavioral health or was a graduate student in the broader field of "mind" sciences. It's a great understatement to say this was a heady group.

Barre is bone-cold in the winter. So, too, were our private "yogi" rooms at the IMS. At a formal meditation retreat like that, a person arrives expecting austere accommodations. Accordingly, mustering the requisite spartan attitude to deal with a bit of bother is part of the price of admission, so I was well primed and willing to handle whatever discomforts came my way. I was happily surprised, then, on discovering the sumptuous amenity of the beds. Each room was outfitted with a luxuriously comfy mattress and a European 100 percent feather duvet. So comfortable was the bedding that it crossed the line to indulgent coziness. I took full advantage on the afternoon of my arrival by nestling in a cocoon of contentment while watching snow fall outside the window.

The format of the retreat was similar to those of other traditional meditation retreats I've attended: a gong sounds in the hall to wake everyone up at five fifteen. The forty-five-minute morning meditation begins at five thirty. Then comes breakfast. Next, everyone does their assigned "yogi" chores. After that comes more meditation, both sitting and walking. Then lunch. More meditation. Dinner. Meditation. And finally, lights out at 10 p.m.

The whole program was conducted with participants observing "noble silence." Obviously, noble silence means no talking, but it goes further than that. When engaged in noble silence, you're not even supposed to look anyone else in the eye. The end result of practicing this stricter form of silence is the achievement of clear and undistracted mindfulness that enables a person to sense even the subtlest trigger, thought, or sensation.

Maintaining such rigorous mindfulness 24/7 for seven days primes a person to see clearly. At five fifteen on the sixth morning of the retreat, I was blissfully asleep inside the womb of my feather comforter when the wake-up gong broke the quietude. The ensuing moments changed my consciousness forever after.

It was as if I were two people in one body. From a dead sleep, one part of me was immediately awake, calm, and able to witness the other, more primal part project a fierce defense against the sound, like a cat hissing and baring its claws. The higher awareness had caught that negative appraisal the moment it arose. As if to argue against the idea of getting up to meditate, a weaker part spoke to the higher awareness in the second person and feebly offered, "But you're *tired*."

The higher awareness thought, *Okay, if you're tired, what is tired?* Awareness curiously explored the body-mind interface looking for evidence of "tired." It found warmth, pressure, tingling, and sensations, but it did not specifically find any so-called "tired." A realization arose in awareness, that "tiredness" is a constructed thing. For it to exist, the parts of it have to be put together. The awareness wasn't interested in doing that. Sensations without a story are just sensations. Full of inspiration to practice, I threw off the covers and ambled downstairs to meditate.

All of that happened in the blink of an eye, and, almost two decades ago. Yet so profound was the experience that I remember it as if it were yesterday. Not more than a second passed on the clock before awareness shone light on a lifelong shadow habit of mine, which was wanting to quit before a job is fully complete. That pattern has a long history, showing up variously in relationships, school, work, exercise, meditation, food choices, and more. I'm not saying I'm a slacker, but there have been innumerable times in my life when, if I'd just shown a little more grit, I'd be far better off for it.

That gong story perfectly exemplifies the ongoing tension between constructive and destructive shadow. It took mindful attunement for me to see that subtle internal dynamic with such clarity. Indeed, it was the exquisite granularity of those moments that enabled determination to rise above a habit and for me to align with my integrity and a deeper intention. Destructive shadow was pleading with me to give up on the last morning's meditation. Its implicit message was, "You've done enough already. Give yourself a break." How many times have I given in to that seductive invitation?

Destructive shadow will always argue for a quick fix over a more fundamental solution. I'm not saying that since that experience I always choose the fundamental solution. I don't. There are many times when I still fall short. But the clarity of the insight I gained that morning prevents me from fooling myself anymore. At least now I'm aware of it when the battles between constructive and destructive shadow do rage inside me. And that, at least, is progress.

Such clarity enables choice. Therefore, the way to begin working through destructive shadow is by attuning. Sensing into yourself, others, and situations with acceptance, care, and a wish for a higher good begins with opening your awareness and placing your attention on the boundaries between your conscious and unconscious minds. You know how to do that now. So guess what—you're already doing shadow work!

All development happens at the boundary between conscious and unconscious. When your conscious mind interacts with emerging unconscious material, you're in a position to influence the flow. Shadow energy and information arise out of the unconscious in less than a tenth of a second. That's fast. So, unless you set a conscious intention to attune ahead of time, your conscious mind will always be a step behind.

Woefully, people who don't live intentionally stay stuck, repetitiously acting out destructive shadow patterns, which will reliably sow negative karmic seeds in their experience. But karmic results can and will turn positive should you start setting more virtuous intentions, which will shift the power dynamic in favor of your constructive shadow. Immediately after attuning, you're aware, curious, and accepting of whatever comes up. Thus empowered, you're in a position to skillfully monitor and modify the arising triggers, thoughts, and sensations. It's through conscious intentions, therefore, that you create the habit of priming yourself to stay awake. That's how mindful attunement enables people to work through challenging emerging shadow material in the wisest and most compassionate way.

HALF OF SHADOW WORK—BALANCING SHADOW ENERGIES

Romantic poet William Blake once wrote, "He whose face gives no light, shall never become a star." But it's also true that brazenness drove Icarus to his death when he flew too close to the sun. The often-forgotten converse moral of the myth of Icarus was the reverse admonition "Do not fly too close to the sea either." In the drama of human life, flying too high or too low in relation to the eight worldly concerns—gain and loss, pain and pleasure, fame and insignificance, praise and blame—will generate suffering. Achieving the right "altitude" between extremes, therefore, is the aim of a spiritually attuned person.

"Tuning" one's personality is somewhat like tuning the derailleur on a road bike. Tightening the adjusting screw too much creates friction as the chain runs over the lower cogs. Loosen it too much and the chain slips and jumps from one cog to the next when in the higher gears. Correctly adjusting the tension on the derailleur screw allows the rider to enjoy the functional benefit of all the gears without chafing or sloppiness. Similarly, to fully capitalize on the myriad potentials of one's personality, it is desirable to balance the complementary energies of constructive and destructive shadow.

In a like manner, your warrior and artist are archetypal energies that need balancing through expression and self-regulation. Artists are drawn to beauty and authentic expression. You might rediscover inner artistic bliss through music, learning a new language, travel, gourmet cooking, or writing. But the warrior spirit inside you must also consciously express its darker tendencies with equal vigor. You can ventilate your destructive shadow by kickboxing, letting loose at a boys' or girls' night out, yelling "Fuck!" at the right time and place, playing Rambo in a paintball war, enjoying standup comedy, or, better yet, doing standup yourself. If you feel the urge, sit for a tattoo or a body piercing, watch a horror flick, or get kinky with your partner. Use your imagination. There are a million other ways to air out destructive shadow without causing yourself or anyone else harm. Doing so consciously will balance your psyche and you'll feel better for it.

Shadow—all of it—needs expression! This first half of shadow work is letting your primal energy liberate itself in a safe and appropriately vitalizing way. So pay close attention to the visceral reactions you had to any of the shadow-releasing suggestions above. Take special note of any that you were overly drawn to or repulsed by. Remember, we often discover shadow in ourselves through what triggers us the most.

My sometime running partner Jimmy is a special person. I know him to be one of the most spontaneous, unselfconscious, undefended people I know. It's refreshing to be in his company because with Jimmy there is no mask. He is authentically himself, and he is also one of the funniest people I know. His humor is a medley of dark and light shadow, raunchy and refined, delivered without a scintilla of shame. Thank God no one can record our conversations as we run together—the PC police would certainly have us arrested.

Bawdy humor aside, Jimmy is also one of the most moral people I've ever met. He was a world-class professional triathlete during a time when the use of performance-enhancing drugs (PEDS) was at its peak. In his day, most of the top athletes were doping. I assume their reasoning was that if everybody was doing it, they were all even. For the most part, the system that supported the athletes—the athletic associations, doctors, and sponsors—turned a blind eye to the shadowy activity that everyone knew was taking place.

Jimmy was good without drugs and doping, but not one of the best. Despite his successes, it's likely you've never heard the name Jimmy Riccitello. A name you *will* recognize, however, is Lance Armstrong. Ironically, Jimmy and Lance, two athletes who made diametrically different choices regarding doping, are best friends. How is that possible? I credit Jimmy's good character for seeing and understanding the shadow dynamics of the time and the moral dilemma it forced on the athletes. What to choose when competing in an unfair system?

Sure, Jimmy would have preferred to have won more races. The fact that he's not full of righteous indignation is a testament to his well-balanced temperament and broad perspective. I also believe Jimmy and Lance can be friends because Jimmy accepts the destructive shadow part of himself. If doping could have made him a top contender like Lance, maybe he would have done the same thing. Under certain conditions, everyone is susceptible to bending the rules.

As far as I can see, Jimmy lives his personal life with equal steadiness. I've been his friend for decades, and in all that time, I've known Jimmy to be a devoted husband and an exemplary father. From the outside looking in, Jimmy appears to have a knack for balancing and expressing dark and light shadow energy in a healthy way. He chooses the high road but still lets himself get down and dirty occasionally. If only we could all feel as free to be ourselves as does Jimmy. That's what shadow work is about: finding yourself, being yourself, and finally forgetting yourself.

One last caveat about harmonizing and releasing shadow energy: I encourage you to ventilate pent-up shadow energy, but that said, be conscious about when, where, and how you do it. It is never a good time to let feelings fly when you're raw, scared, angry, ashamed, or defensive. It's in our genetic code to protect ourselves when we feel under threat. At such times, destructive shadow is probably dominating your psychic landscape, and it's best to resist your first impulses, whether they be to punish your kids, fire off an angry e-mail, quit your job, or cheat on your spouse and leave your marriage. Instead, take whatever time is necessary to regulate your emotions and get perspective. Employ NITTI, SOS, and relaxation breathing. Get help from a wise and kind person. Any and all will help. When you're in a more balanced place, it's easier to cultivate attunement, which allows for the higher good you're seeking to engender.

THE OTHER HALF OF SHADOW WORK—MEETING YOUR SHADOW

The other half of shadow work is resolving one's internal conflicts and distortions. Ironically, to disown and discard one's dark side is to accumulate it. Neglected shadow always squirts out sideways in the form of stress illness, chronic pain, mood and personality disorders, rage, unexplained accidents, rocky relationships, bad choices, or any other of the innumerable ways people suffer.

Meeting your shadow and metabolizing it can be such a frightening, even shocking experience that most people are not naturally inclined to take up this challenging type of psychological work. Instead, they do the opposite and defend against the acknowledgement of such material. Conflicted aspects of one's personality, like those revealed in me in the Scientists Retreat story, are impossible to rectify without concerted self-reflection. Without the resolving power of super-granular mindfulness, you might not even be aware of such subtle countercurrents flowing inside you. More often than not, addressing internal shadow material requires the assistance of a wise and kind friend, therapist, or coach.

We glimpse shadow only indirectly:

- By observing our exaggerated feelings and judgments about ourselves, others, objects, and circumstances
- When we find ourselves lying about choices we made
- Through the negative feedback we receive from others, especially if we receive the same feedback from multiple people
- By noting our "Freudian" slips of the tongue
- From instances where we have the same negative effect on other people
- By observing our impulsive and inadvertent acts
- By observing our obsessions and compulsions
- By noting situations that trigger anxiety, rage, defensiveness, and shame in us

The reason we often need help doing shadow work is that others can plainly see our shadow even when we are blind to it. One of my old business partners openly complained about and was often very critical of the way other therapists did their job. As one of the senior therapists, she did not hesitate to correct her juniors, even in front of patients. That habit of hers made me bristle, so I took it upon myself to offer her some unsolicited feedback. I remember taking her aside and inquiring if there was a better way to coach our less experienced professional staff. If looks could kill! She took great offense at my impertinence. She was in full denial of her controlling and demeaning behavior while simultaneously hotly resisting my advice. I could plainly see her shadow hypocrisy, but she was blind to it herself.

And yet in that moment my shadow was dancing with hers, because I hadn't asked permission to give her the feedback. I felt justified in correcting her, and that was more than a misstep on my part. It was equally unrecognized shadow in me—thinking, just as she did, that I knew better than someone else.

That's an example of how easy it is to see shadow in another and how hard to see it in oneself. So, yes, shadow work is challenging internal work. But to become fully authentic and integrated, you must explore and release all the conflicts and distortions you are carrying inside.

Throughout our lifetimes we all acquire distorted and disturbed views from others. Psychologists refer to all views we absorb from outside ourselves as "introjections." Introjections are beliefs that either come to us distorted or, once inside, are distorted by us and then held as true. In certain contexts, everyone is naturally receptive to incoming information. Children, students, employees, and anyone strongly identified with a religious community, spiritual or cult leader, or political party are all vulnerable to introjected material. In such contexts, there is a sloping power dynamic in which information flows from a transmitter down into the receiver.

The same holds true whenever someone finds themselves subordinate to another person. For instance, parents often introject distortions into their children. Recall the story of Sophie, from Chapter 6. She grew up unsure whether she could trust her primary caregivers to meet her basic needs of safety and love. The low-touch, ultra-strict parenting style Sophie grew up with implicitly introjected into her a belief that at her core something was wrong with her or, worse, that she was unlovable. That traumatic introject eventually led to debilitating insecurity, depression, anxiety, panic disorder, and a lifelong habit of berating and second-guessing herself.

Introjections are distortions that flow into a person from the outside, but that's not the only direction in which distortions flow. They also come *from* us, flowing out into the world of people, places, and things. All judgments spewing out onto others and the world are known as "projections."

I'm a reasonably well-educated and integrally informed person. Before I took Harvard's online Implicit Association Test (IAT),[90] I would have told you that I didn't have a racist bone in my body. Much to my horror, the survey results proved that assumption false. Although the negative bias it found in me was small, it was significant enough to trip the trigger of the test's sensitivity. The IAT woke me up to an unconscious bias I carry and probably still project unconsciously onto numberless people whose only fault is to look different from me. Just like me, you are also projecting your unconscious biases out onto the world. The other part of meeting shadow is learning to recognize and rectify all such similarly pernicious preconceptions.

Like introjections, projections are naturally occurring. The first view anyone has of the world is a fully narcissistic one. Toddlers are wholly incapable of taking another person's perspective. That's why you can't reason with a toddler. They're *pre*-rational. Hence, they assume their perspective on the world is absolutely true. Thankfully, though, as we mature, most of us learn to take a higher perspective, acquire a truer understanding of cause and effect, and can put ourselves in the shoes of others. But just because we grow up and develop higher, truer, and more inclusive perspectives doesn't mean that our lowest, least true, and most exclusive perspective evaporates. Remember, development is a *transcend and include* activity. That means that under the right circumstances, the immature and myopic shadow part of us can still rise up and take over.

When I was seventeen, I had a motorcycle accident. While riding on the back of my friend Paul's bike, a blue Mercedes turned left in front of us and we hit the front driver's side of it at about 30 miles per hour. Flying through the air was serene—it was the landing part that was violent, like being a frog in a blender. We were both lucky not to sustain any serious injuries. Later that night, however, I felt intense knee pain—I'd landed hard on both of them—and ended up needing crutches.

I remember standing in the school gym leaning on my crutches the next day when a few gorgeous cheerleaders gathered around me, curious to know what had happened and how I was feeling. Their attention felt good. *Really* good. And so it happened that days of *needing* crutches turned into weeks of *using* them.

It didn't take long for my guy friends to target me with growing outrage and invectives. They could plainly see what was happening. Like a child, I was milking the crutches for attention. Defensively, I thought, *How the hell do you know what I'm feeling?* Apparently they could, more than I realized. They could see my shadow angling for attention while I could not.

At that point in my life I'd yet to develop the self-awareness to see how an infantilizing introjection was influencing my behavior. Like Sophie, I grew up painfully insecure, believing that at core something was wrong with me. That introject was the primary shadow driver that led me to use the crutches long past needing them. I couldn't see my shadow, but the guys could, and they let me know it. In defending myself, I judged them for being thoughtless assholes. And yet had any one of them done what I had, I would have made a similar stink. That's because, more often than not, we react vehemently to the behavior of others that lies latent within ourselves. The whole episode was a shadow dance.

My issue with insecurity was, still is, the result of an introjection. The animosity I directed toward the guys was a projection. Becoming conscious of both types of unconscious material is the first step toward resolving shadow. One becomes conscious of shadow material through five stages: [91]

1. Unaware
2. Symptom-aware
3. Trigger-aware
4. Process-aware
5. Conscious conceptualization

As the name implies, a person living through the unaware stage of the shadow resolution process is completely unaware of shadow's impact on their life. The story of the crutches exemplifies a time when I was in that stage. Shadow insecurity drove me to lean on crutches long past their usefulness. The story also demonstrates a lack of awareness of my shadow projections.

You might find this hard to believe, but there are young people today who play video games all night long while wearing diapers so they don't miss any action. Incredibly, sitting for hours in a dirty diaper doesn't raise any red flags for them. Alcoholics in the unaware stage are similarly oblivious of any of the internal or external drivers of their exorbitant drinking. Any addict in the unaware stage is blind to the excesses of their behavior. But sooner or later, the negative karmic consequences of destructive shadow behavior increase to a point where symptoms arise that turn on the light of a person's awareness.

As you well know by now, I was full of anger and resentment after the breakup of my business. In the aftermath, I came down with a slew of stress-related conditions: insomnia, depression, chronic pain, restless leg syndrome, and atrial fibrillation. At the time, I was ignorant of any connection between anger and the symptoms I was feeling. For me the symptoms were my only problem. Consequently, I put all my effort into relieving them. Conventional medicine and big pharma were more than happy to assist me in that endeavor. A few trips to the doctor and I had prescriptions for all those maladies.

The power of medicine is that it lessens the intensity of symptoms. Unfortunately, relief is not a cure. A person stuck at the symptom-aware stage keeps employing the same tired remedies but gets diminishing benefit for their effort. What people at this stage have in common is the way they think about their issues. Since they view their symptoms as the problem, attacking and alleviating them seems like the logical solution. But only attacking symptoms just makes the situation worse.

My daughter often watches Netflix or plays video games using her iPad. When she does, she sometimes sits for a half hour or more, cross-legged on her bed, absentmindedly hunched over the screen. Frequently, after she finishes, she complains about back and neck pain. I have often suggested that Alana put her iPad on a TV tray so she can sit up straight, but the problem is, Alana hasn't yet connected her absentminded slouching with the pain. As of this writing, Alana is in the symptom-aware stage with regard to this issue. She sees only the pain as the problem, not the poor posture that causes the pain. As with anyone in the symptom-aware stage, before behavior can change it will take a higher perspective that connects cause with effect.

People transition to the next point in the process, the trigger-aware stage, in unpredictable ways. It took a fateful run and a feather hitting me in the chest for me to connect seething anger—the trigger—with the symptoms I was experiencing. But mini-awakenings like that aren't always easy to come by.

A friend of mine who experienced extreme trauma as a child occasionally cycles through long periods of depression that rob them of emotional strength. This friend saw a well-meaning therapist who advised them to limit contact with people and situations that trigger their discomforting emotions. Awareness of their triggers, and contriving ways to limit them, does relieve some suffering, which gives my friend a modicum of control. So in that sense, the advice my friend received was good and sensible.

But you know what they say about too much of a good thing. Feeling emboldened by the power that boundary-setting provided, this friend came to the misguided conclusion that anyone who triggered them was a problem. One wrong word at the wrong time and this person would hit the eject button. Consequently, the parameters of their life got progressively smaller.

Sadly, this approach has not made my friend feel any better. Instead, like all downward spirals, it's only made them more sensitive. Limiting or eliminating all triggering people was their primary solution, but for anyone in the trigger-aware stage, it's an inadvertent mistake to view triggers as the sole problem. Eliminating triggers might make a person feel better in the short run, but it's a shallow solution. You can't resolve shadow from the trigger-aware stage.

To resolve shadow, you have to dive deeper into the inner dynamics of the psyche. For me it took a feather hitting me in the chest before I finally saw that my struggles were part of a much larger process in which my story was playing a decisive role. I began meditating soon after the feather woke me up out of that raging fixation. Gratefully, the budding practice opened a window into my interior experience. For the first time, I was able to discern how the whole effause-and-caufect stream of sights and sounds, thoughts and sensations coalesced into stress and illness.

Through meditation, I became process-aware. A shift in emphasis also came with this stage. No longer was the objective to eradicate the external triggers of my symptoms. Instead, I started employing internal work to discover the causes of my internal shadow issues. The focus shifted to changing the unskillful patterns coming *from* me.

The systemic process that self-organizes into shadow patterns includes symptoms, triggers, and habitual responses. While retreating at Chenrezig, my teachers taught me about the five micro-mental events: contact, feeling, discrimination, attention, and intention. You know these five mental factors as a person's karmic (self-making) pattern creators. With the help of that incisive instruction as well as diligent meditation, I became increasingly aware of the process that cobbled all the macro-habits in my life together.

For example, at the time, one of my macro-habits was a dependency on Ambien. After my business blew up, I took it for two years to help me sleep. But once I became process-aware, I could see how shadow was putting the "parts" of my insomnia together. I was able to see the whole linear string of events. Step by step, triggering resentments led to mind-racing, which caused me to think, *I'm not going to be able to sleep tonight.* Then I would get anxious. That was the process that *self-made* my insomnia.

Once I could see it, I was in a position to do something about it. It came to pass that I retrained myself to sleep without Ambien. Cutting pills in halves and then quarters, it took me a few weeks to wean myself off the medicine. Finally, the night came when I didn't take any more, and as I lay down in bed, I let go of all fear of not sleeping. That night I committed to not chasing sleep. Instead, I was going to meditate and be satisfied with whatever happened. I closed my eyes and set the intention to joyfully and gratefully attune. Maybe I made it twenty minutes before I fell asleep.

Once I became process-aware, I began to cope differently with all manner of issues. I'm not special in this regard. Far from it. People who take responsibility for how they feel inside accept the lot of it and are determined to work through life's challenges to empower themselves. That's all I started to do. After that, the world changed. It's not that lousy stuff stopped happening to me, but I started handling all the lousy stuff in better ways.

A process-aware person no longer tries to anxiously control their symptoms or triggers. Instead, they get ahead of the process by doing the stitch-in-time work that resolves internal contradictions and distortions. That internal work deactivates triggers, which eases symptoms. Coping with an internal locus of control is what halts the downward spiral and initiates the upward.

People at the process-aware stage value healthy self-soothing. They relaxation-breathe and get adequate rest, nutrition, and exercise. In the process-aware stage, people start seeing the karma of their actions and start cleaning up their thinking, speech, and behavior, too.

SkillfullyAware practices from Chapter 8 work best for people in the process-aware stage. When a person is finally process-aware, they enter a zone of amplified power. By this time, they've overcome enough threshold demons to earn their T-shirt. No one is ever perfected, and more missteps are bound to happen, but process-aware people can at least begin to safely trust themselves again. It's also important to understand that thorough resolution of shadow requires that a person work through a final completion stage, referred to by my colleague Kim Barta as conscious conceptualization. Conscious conceptualization is where a person begins to appreciate the impact of metaphor, perspective, and story on their development. Like an editor refining a script, the recovery of a person in the conscious conceptualization stage takes on a more pointedly narrative approach. In that way, conscious conceptualization is synonymous with shadow work.

Do you remember the guy I mentioned in Chapter 8 whose wife cheated on him? Instead of making her into his enemy, he chose an ennobling story that allowed him to let go without resentment. That's conscious conceptualization. The conscious conceptualization part of shadow work reminds us that we all have choices. No matter what happens to us, we can frame the situation in a way that minimizes the negative impact. Indeed, when we're conscious, we can orient around a perspective that will eventually turn something painful into a gift.

In the next three chapters, I'll explain how human consciousness grows up through a series of stages. Each progressive stage raises a person's perspective. That higher view then enables shifts in appraisals and, therefore, more adept management of emotions and relationships. Whether you've had trauma, were born highly sensitive, or have just been under a lot of stress lately, working to raise your perspective is a direct way to attune more skillfully to each moment, change your story, and open yourself to more potential peace.

CHAPTER 11

Raising Your Window: The Concrete Tier

"Loving people live in a loving world. Hostile people live in a hostile world. Same world."

Wayne Dyer

Coming to understand themselves as individuals is a developmental task all young children work on. They're desperate to figure out how to fit into a large, sometimes confusing world of relationships. As an inquisitive five-year-old, I was actively engaged in that process of constructing my identity, which is why, sitting in church one Sunday, I was driven to ask, "Daddy, what's a Methodist?" I knew we *were* Methodists, but I had no idea what that meant exactly. After a brief pause, my father shot me a sideways glance, shrugged his shoulders, and said, "I have no idea."

I left church that day confused and chagrined, wondering what distinguishes Methodists from all the other people we knew. When I was with my mom and Joe, we sometimes went to a Lutheran church. What's a Lutheran? My friend and next-door neighbor Bruce and his family were Mormons. Same question.

My stepgrandparent Richard and his extended family were Catholic. My stepmom Klaire's family was Jewish. At the age of five these labels made no sense to me. How were Methodists different, I wondered. What was the point of giving up valuable play time every Sunday morning to get all dressed up to go to church when we didn't even know what a Methodist was?

As mentioned before, a person's perspective climbs through a series of stages as they mature. In this context, a stage is like the window through which a person views the world. The higher a person's stage of development, the higher their window. The higher their window, the more they can see. The more they see, the clearer and truer their perspective.

Imagine living in a ground-floor apartment in an iffy neighborhood in a bustling city. Roiling right outside your living room window is round-the-clock sidewalk and street traffic, noise, and pollution. Undoubtedly it would be hard to filter out all that disturbance. Worse, the unrelenting ruckus could easily overwhelm your nervous system. Moving up just one floor would feel like a little blessing, would it not? One floor higher still and the commotion would be even less in your face. You'd feel a little more secure, not so exposed. Move another floor higher and you'd probably feel even better. Making it all the way up to the top floor could feel the best, affording the most impressive view of all. That's precisely why penthouse apartments cost more. Their occupants pay for the view *and* more peace.

Higher stages of consciousness offer the exact same reinforcing benefits—more peace and perspective. I don't want to promulgate the false belief that pain and suffering will magically end someday, but raising your window will help to minimize them.

It's not just young children who grow their perspectives. We adults are actively engaged in that same process. All the way up, as we advance through each stage, we're all raising our windows to a higher level of consciousness. Some of us faster, some of us slower, we're all evolving depending on the wisdom and compassion we accumulate from our life experiences.

Emotional, social, moral, cognitive, and spiritual development is a process of maturing yourself. The driver of this inner evolution is the tension we encounter as we attempt to resolve two primary "confusions."[92] These confusions inevitably involve two complimentary questions: "Who am I?" and "Who is in my tribe?" The word *tribe* here very loosely relates to a person's group identification, which includes their family, race, culture, religious and political affiliations, profession, nationality, all sentient beings, the planet, and on and on. As a person grows up through the stages of development, their "tribe" expands to include more and more beings within their circle of compassion until that expansion extends to the Kosmos universally.[93]

But development won't happen if you just sit on the couch. It is through formative experiences that we gain the insights necessary to work through our confusions. The process unfolds iteratively, one contrasting experience after another. As we go through life, sometimes we act out of our best self. At other times, our destructive shadow rules our behavior. Over time, and if we're reasonably self-reflective, we slowly accumulate enough contrasting data points to eventually triangulate a sense of self. In other words, through the good and the bad, we develop a lived sense of ourselves in the form of a narrative foundation that becomes our self-story. At any particular moment it is your evolving "story of me" that tells you who you are and where you fit.

I keep reiterating this point, but it's important. The unconscious story-making happening inside you right now is a *system* dynamic. As such, it is happening all by itself, like your heart beating and fingernails growing. Therefore, it's imperative to set conscious intentions if you want to influence the trajectory of your story going forward. The trick in all of it is to develop the conscious habit of directing your attention toward beauty, goodness, and truth as you grow, change, and heal. Remember the "cloud of probability" I mentioned in the chapter on karma? Although nothing is determined, you can incline your world-body-mind system toward more positivity. There's a correspondence between your subtle interior and the outer world. That's especially true in your relationship to others. Work on changing yourself on the inside first, and then the probability is higher that your outer world and the people in it will seem to change for the better as well.

The narrative foundation of your ego is built one floor at a time and from the ground up. Sadly, no one gets to skip floors. A child's self-story is unavoidably elementary. That's the sine qua non of innocence. A child's outlook lacks the depth and breadth of experience that a more mature adult viewpoint can offer. Even so, no matter where a person finds themselves on the tower of development, the game is always the same: resolve the confusion of your current stage!

Growing up and accepting, processing, and overcoming your challenges is attunement in action. Attunement is *the* one thing you can do to help resolve the cyclic conflicts that may be keeping you stuck. Trust me—it's still working that way for me, too. We're all still unfinished works of spiritual art. Learning more about these stages and their confusions continues to hasten my development. It will do the same for you.

The title of this chapter is "Raising Your Window." *Develop* is a verb; you have to *do* something to become something. It also bears repeating that everything you experience internally is karmic "feedback" arising out of the way you relate and related with people and things. Recall the circle of three: subject, object, and the interaction between the two. Again, that's the developmental crucible. *Everything* happens within that space. How you interact with the world of objects determines not only the way you feel inside but also the ultimate speed and height of your development.

With the help of many others who came before her,[94] consciousness researcher and teacher Terri O'Fallon, PhD, identifies six pairs of broad stages of development. She calls each of these stages "person perspectives." O'Fallon's work borrows from and is compatible with prior research in differentiating these developmental stages using a numbering system of 1 through 6.[95] To make the model more accurate and robust, she divides each stage into two. She refers to the first part of each person perspective as the immature phase. She calls the second part of each person perspective the mature phase.

Dr. O'Fallon assigns decimals to differentiate the immature and mature phases. She chooses ".0" to represent the immature and ".5" to represent the mature phase of each stage. That numbering format follows the same pattern through all six person perspectives. Dr. O'Fallon also gives each stage a one- or two-word descriptor to help readers get a broad sense of the psychological nature of each. So, all told, Dr. O'Fallon identifies twelve progressive stages, or windows, up through which consciousness grows. Each provides a view of the self and its relationship with the world.

>
> **Concrete Tier**
> 1st Person Perspective
> Immature phase = 1.0 "Impulsive"
> Mature phase = 1.5 "Egocentric"
> 2nd Person Perspective
> Immature phase = 2.0 "Rule-Oriented"
> Mature phase = 2.5 "Conformist"
>
> **Subtle Tier**
> 3rd Person Perspective
> Immature phase = 3.0 "Modern"
> Mature phase = 3.5 "Achiever"
> 4th Person Perspective
> Immature phase = 4.0 "Pluralist"
> Mature phase = 4.5 "Strategist"
>
> **Metaware Tier**
> 5th Person Perspective
> Immature phase = 5.0 "Construct Aware"
> Mature phase = 5.5 "Transpersonal"
> 6th Person Perspective
> Immature phase = 6.0 "Universal"
> Mature phase = 6.5 "Illumined"

If you'd like to learn more about "stages theory" from Dr. O'Fallon (which I highly recommend), connect with her via her website, www.stagesinternational.com.

Before I explain them all individually, one thing I should say about these perspectives is that each is perfect as it is. Babies are not defective because they're so needy. Similarly, the joy and mayhem that toddlers and children exhibit are just and right. Each stage is beautiful in its own way. So please don't generate the false impression that something is wrong with the lower stages of conscious development. There are issues to resolve and therefore something to learn at each stage. In essence, no matter the stage, we're all doing the same thing: developing.

1.0 IMPULSIVE

When infants are born, they are mostly powerless. They cannot take care of their needs, though they can summon their caregivers by crying. Thus the first and most essential challenge at this point in their lives is to attach to their caregivers and develop basic trust that their survival needs will be met. Attachment bonds develop between a child and their parents through attunement and lovingly tending to the child's needs. Furthermore, the infant's lifelong growth and development depend on their parents' nurturing this foundation of security so they feel safe enough to explore their surroundings. Indeed, consistent and sustained parental love and attention is what enables the infant's sensitive nervous system to open up and receive the rush of input that flows into them from the new world into which they were born.

At this early point in life, babies have no sense of themselves or the world. In other words, from their viewpoint, they appear to fuse with the world. Indeed, that's their primary confusion—they have no sense of the boundary between themselves and the outside world. They have no idea where they leave off and the world begins. Thus a baby's perspective is described as oceanic. Newborn babies exist in the ocean of the *now*.

Before they're six months old, a baby's eyes can't focus well enough to distinguish the edges between themselves and anything else. For that reason, they have a hard time seeing the contrast between their body and the outside world. Put another way, the circle of three has yet to constellate in them. At this point in their development, self and other are completely indistinguishable.

After six months of age, however, a baby's eyes do mature and synchronize well enough to allow them to appreciate the border between themself and other objects, as well as the space in between. It's a tall order, but clarifying a world of concrete objects, which includes themself as a concrete person (as in, I am my body) is one of the first tasks a baby's immature nervous system must work out. Accordingly, and related to the "fusion confusion," at stage 1.0 babies are all trying to work out the question "Who am *I* in this concrete world?"

Incidentally, I keep writing the word *concrete* because Dr. O'Fallon's stages theory further divides the six pairs of stages into three "tiers." The tiers are "concrete," "subtle," and "met-aware." Dr. O'Fallon, in alignment with previous research on conscious development, uses these three additional classifications to help her organize an individual's development based on their capacity to *relate* to objects—concrete objects, subtle objects, and awareness itself.[96]

A concrete object is what it sounds like, something solid that you can see and touch and put a fence around. Contrast that with a subtle object, which is something that exists only on the subjective interior of a person or group of people, like a thought, visualization, plan, feeling, intention, or principle. Last, a met-aware object is not really an object at all; it's awareness itself.

No infant has the ability to relate to anything other than concrete objects. The solid contours that exist between its body and the outside world must be built and understood by its nervous system first. When Alana was just a few months old, I could see her puzzling through the confusion of constructing a self and a world. Wide-eyed and cooing with receptivity, her attention was naturally drawn to various sights, sounds, and tactile sensations. Her delicate and curious fingers and mouth left nothing unexplored. With the help of her parents' love and through repetition and mimicking, her nervous system eventually began to make sense out of all the sensory noise. She began to make gross distinctions and clarify the boundaries between herself, us, and every other solid thing.

Thus, through the first stage, which Dr. O'Fallon calls the 1.0 Impulsive Stage, a baby works out that it's a separate person (a body) in a world of separate, solid objects.[97] Because an outer world is just beginning to come into focus for them, a 1.0 Impulsive baby lacks any notion of social boundaries and conventions. Appreciating that other people even have a perspective is way over its head. It will take years before a child's developmental window moves up another couple of floors so it can appreciate that other people have a perspective, too. Instead, infants believe that everyone sees just what they see (physically).

Throwing a fit when things don't go their way is the one universal tool in every infant's emotional toolbox. A chief reason 1.0s are so overly emotional is because they don't yet have language. Crying is the primary way they attract the attention to get their needs met. In most instances, parents respond to the child's cry with caregiving. That nurturing exchange helps the child learn to trust itself and the world, creating the foundation for a life of emotional stability. Without that foundational connection to a caregiver, shadow defenses will begin emerge in the baby. How extreme an infant's behavior must become to get a parent's attention has a direct impact on its budding personality.

For example, let's say an infant is hungry and responds to that drive by crying. If their parents are responsive, the baby learns to trust their feelings and learns that communicating leads to intimacy and connection. On the other hand, if there is no response from their parents, the child might start to feel anxious and cry a little louder. If the louder cry finally gets attention, the baby may learn that a little more drama does the trick, and a lifelong shadow pattern is born. Should the anxious cry not work, at some point the baby might become angry and cry louder still. If anger gets the baby what it wants, it learns two things: that aggression is a strategy it can use to get its needs met and that its parents, and by extension other people, can't be trusted. If nothing works to get attention, at some point the child gives up and falls into a depressed state to conserve energy. In this way, *some* types of anxiety, rage, and depression that appear later in life may be conditioned shadow responses to attachment wounds sustained at the 1.0 stage.

Being preverbal, the 1.0 infant has only its body sensations to inform it of its needs and emotions. When big feelings arise, ventilating them through a purifying scream is all they know to do. Children who grow up in repressive and violent homes often find themselves in a no-win situation: they can express their feelings and face the neglect or wrath of their parent, or they can choose to suppress their needs and feelings. After the child grows up, these shadow imprints become part of the adult's story and behavioral pattern. Then, when under extreme stress as an adult, a person carrying trauma from the 1.0 level can "shadow-crash"[98] all the way back down to the first floor in an inconsolable emotional heap.

Yelling at a baby to stop crying, leaving them to cry, or, worse, spanking them sets a child up for a life of emotional confusion and collapse. Infants can't tell the difference between healthy and unhealthy parental responses. In the latter case, an implicit shadow message gets introjected into the infant, that expressing the full range of their emotions is not acceptable and, worse still, that they're on their own when it comes to sorting out their feelings. Therefore, if you break down emotionally or struggle with anxiety, depression, or an addiction or in any other way find it impossible to express or manage your feelings, you *may* have experienced developmental trauma at the 1.0 stage.

1.5 EGOCENTRIC

The typical developmental time line sees a child slowly transitioning to the 1.5 Egocentric Stage starting at around eight months. A toddler will fully embody the 1.5 stage by twelve to fourteen months. At this point in a child's development, they have resolved the confusion of fusion of the 1.0 stage. To a 1.5 Egocentric toddler, objects on the outside are now distinct. They know they are a solid, separate person in a world of solid and separate objects. In fact, their conception of themself is so concrete that they identify themself with their body—i.e., "my body is me." Egocentrism seems to peak somewhere between eighteen to thirty-six months, which is why this period in a child's life is also sometimes referred to as the "terrible twos."

A growing fetus in its mother's womb has its needs met instantly, like magic. After it's born, and if it's born into wholesome circumstances, that pattern of having its needs met almost instantaneously continues. From such a child's perspective, therefore, it seems that the world actually *wants* them to have what they want when they want it. An active toddler takes that implicit message, turns it around, and transforms it into a projection that all their needs and desires *should* be met. A primary goal of the 1.5 Egocentric Stage is to become an active agent in the world. Toddlers do this by exciting, exploring, and expanding their personal power. For this reason, toddlers turn into what are sometimes referred to as little "power gods." They're on a mission to learn how to meet their own needs and begin working on their budding autonomy in four domains: physical, intellectual, emotional, and social.

Toddlers mostly exercise their power in these domains by engaging the world through play. Play teaches young children how to use their bodies. Toys stimulate their minds. Manipulatives like blocks, Legos, Lincoln Logs, and Magna-Tiles serve to develop both their body and their mind. Playing alongside others challenges them emotionally and socially. All that active engagement allows kids to create, initiate, follow through on their intentions, complete projects, and, finally, celebrate. "Mommy, look at the Lego castle I built!"

When parents greet their toddler's action orientation with love, support, and healthy boundaries, the child begins to develop a healthy idea of themselves as an active agent, which serves them as they grow. But if a toddler's blossoming life energy is met with a controlling or abusive parental response, the child's action orientation can again warp toward patterns of anxiousness, anger, or depression.

We've all seen this before—the child in the grocery store begging for what it wants. A skillful parent knows how to rein in a child's impulse through attuned dialogue without damaging its action orientation. Unskillful parents, however, routinely dismiss or dominate their child, which can wound their child's action orientation. Broadly speaking, children who grow up in homes with less well-attuned parents tend to feel more anxiety, learn to sneak around to take what they want, and use anger to dominate and pain behaviors to manipulate.

We all have internal will, and that's especially true for toddlers. Teaching a young child how to exercise its will in a healthy, socially acceptable way is the nut of skillful parenting. But toddlers can still only see the world from their immature viewpoint. Their sense of *social* boundaries is either nonexistent or nebulous, which sets them up for near-constant power struggles with their parents, siblings, and friends.

Uninhibited as they are by social constraints, these lovable little narcissists are still predominantly ruled by their emotions. If there are mantras for a child at this age, they are "I want what I want when I want it" and "What's mine is mine, and what's yours is mine." The chief confusion of the 1.5 stage is puzzling out how to get and keep what they want in the face of all the boundaries. Thus the balancing act of parenting a toddler is allowing a child to explore and exercise their power while at the same time holding firm boundaries in a loving way. [99, 100]

Additionally, a toddler's sense of right and wrong is largely determined by whether they get their needs met. Consequently, they have a rudimentary self-oriented sense of morality. Although there are studies that document nascent empathy and compassion in infants,[101] it's also accurate to say that through the 1.5 stage, toddlers see the world primarily from the perspective of how things affect *them*. Thus the capacity for remorse in children from the ages of two to five years is slight. Instead, they tend to regret only the behavior that gets them into trouble.

Consistently held parental boundaries and the challenges of sharing, caring, and being fair inevitably begin to conflict with a toddler's belief in their magical hegemony. At 1.0 there were no boundaries, physical or social. Now, at 1.5, boundaries are everywhere the child turns. Some parenting experts estimate that toddlers may hear the word *no* more than a hundred times a day! Talk about boundaries. It's through this clash of wills with their parents, siblings, and friends that the 1.5 Egocentric toddler slowly begins to learn the social lessons that represent the dawning of the 2.0 Rule-Oriented Stage. But fully embodying all those social lessons will take three to four years, sometimes longer.

At the 1.5 level the merest rudiments of inner self-talk and visualization are barely beginning to emerge. Have you ever asked a three-year-old what they're thinking? They can't tell you. If they respond at all they will point to something solid outside themself, like "that tree." 1.5s easily confuse what seems real to them on the inside for the "truth" of what's happening on the outside.

Additionally, toddlers have no understanding of time. Conceptualizing seconds, minutes, hours, days, weeks, months, or years is impossible for them. It is precisely these early blind spots that create the many characteristically crazy, utterly humorous distortions we associate with young children.

Because they can't visualize and have no sense of time, they also can't grasp cause and effect. They live in a magical world where if it's true for them, it's true. We have a pool in our backyard. I began teaching Alana to swim when she was only two years old. From the time she was two until she was four or five, Alana was convinced she could breathe underwater. While we swam together, she would declare that "fact" over and over again with conviction. I made the mistake once of trying to reason with her about it. That just upset her. For me, it was mind-boggling to witness how impervious her magical thinking was to any and all contrary evidence.

Because they can't visualize well and have only an elementary understanding of cause and effect, it's also difficult for them to picture the consequences of their behavior. Thus, learning from their mistakes is well-nigh impossible. To adults, learning from mistakes seems obvious, but not for 1.5s. For years we couldn't get Alana to understand that getting scratched or bitten by the cat was an inevitable consequence of her rough handling. I was incredulous that it took her so long to put two and two together. She eventually did learn that lesson, step by painful step, but it took a couple of years and a lot of antiseptics and band-aids.

Another strange consequence of a toddler's narrow, first-person view is that they are unable to recognize that other people can see them from the outside. We call this particular blind spot "one-way seeing." By the age of three, toddlers are keenly aware that nose-picking in public is inappropriate. Truly, they're the first to point it out if they see someone else picking their nose. But because they don't yet realize that other people can see them, you'll often see a toddler blatantly digging in their nose with no sense of shame. That's a kid for you.

The challenges and confusions at the 1.5 stage are many, but undaunted toddlers work at activating their autonomy in spite of all the obstacles. They puzzle through the discrepancy between what they think and what is real, and they learn the difference between right and wrong and the consequences of their behavior.

Everyone viewing the world from a higher perspective gets this stuff, but people who were traumatized as toddlers and grow up with a warped action orientation may carry reactive shadow patterns hidden in their subconscious. As they grow and their developmental window rises from floor to floor, the shadow pattern moves up with them. Later, if a person is carrying a 1.5 shadow pattern inside them, stress can force it out into the open, causing the person to "shadow-crash" down to the 1.5 level.

An adult experiencing a 1.5 shadow crash will prioritize their ego needs above everything else. Accordingly, they will bust through social boundaries and established norms to get what they want. Unlike toddlers, however, adults have a lifetime of experience to draw on and are therefore more devious in accomplishing their goals. When under the influence of 1.5 shadow, a wounded adult is completely self-serving and emotionally fragile, focuses on getting and keeping, makes up their own reality, doesn't learn from their mistakes, lies without remorse, judges right and wrong and good and bad solely based on how it affects them, won't take the advice of experts, doesn't understand cause and effect (science), solves conflict with "tantrums" (harming others), and has no idea that others can see them, all of which makes them shameless.

2.0 RULE-ORIENTED

At some point, the physical, intellectual, emotional, and social methods toddlers use to exercise their power mostly stop working. Their siblings and other kids begin to hit back. Their parents can't be outsmarted. Their temper tantrums bring them consequences. Indeed, all the interpersonal boundaries toddlers encounter force another shift in perspective. All that resistance causes these little narcissists to begin to see other people differently. Finally, children awaking to the 2.0 Rule-Oriented Stage realize—and this may sound strange—that other people are people, too. It dawns on them, "They're like me!" That realization engenders empathy, which widens the child's circle of compassion.

The emerging empathy of a person at the 2.0 level isn't mature enough to fit the definition of attunement yet. Rule-oriented kids and grownups still can't really sense into another person's subtle interior—at this stage, the interpersonal cues they respond to are outward and concrete—what they can see and hear. People at this stage still only relate to concrete objects. Attunement as I've defined it is a subtle activity.

People at the rule-oriented stage are driven to adhere to rules by their overwhelming need to fit in. Therefore, second-person perspective is a *collective* stage, which focuses on relational *reciprocity*. When a person moves up to 2.0, a beautiful thing begins to happen: real friendships, where there is genuine give-and-take, start to blossom. While 1.5s play alongside each other, 2.0s start to play *with* each other. For the first time in a child's life, the impulse to care, share, and be fair becomes important. It's through this type of social learning that sacred principles like the Golden Rule develop.

Because of the intense desire to fit in and do right, the emotion of guilt comes up at this stage as well. *Healthy* guilt is a huge driver of social learning. Thus there's an emergence of abundant goodness at 2.0 in the form of traditional values like loyalty, honor, service, and sacrifice. Although it is a slow process, valuing the perspective and needs of others will raise a child's developmental window, and most kids make the transition to 2.0 by about seven or eight years of age. But not until the age of twelve or fourteen will they fully settle into this stage.

In our apartment building analogy, one floor higher at 2.0 offers a better and more expansive view of kinship. But even as they move up developmentally, the child takes its internal 1.5 narcissist with it.

At 2.0, a child can begin to imagine and *relate* to an angel on one shoulder and a devil on the other. That sets up a split, a tug-of-war in the child's ego. "Should I listen to the angel or the devil whispering in my ear? I still want what I want, but I also want to fit in with the group." Thus, at 2.0, two ego states argue inside the same person.

Shadow patterns that arise out of the first-person perspective grow up with and affect the 2.0 child into adulthood. Think of a time you had to negotiate with someone else. What patterns of thought, speech, and behavior did you display in those intimate situations where you had to balance reciprocal relations? Were you open to working through the tension or did you fall into a defensive pattern? Both are shadow; the former is constructive, the latter destructive.

Realizing that other people also have a perspective leads to another interesting insight, that of two-way seeing. The infant and toddler only see from their perspective outward. At 2.0, children realize that other people have a mind like they do and, therefore, can see them back. "OMG, other people can see me pick my nose!" When a person recognizes that others can see them, they begin to feel social pressure. But the rules, roles, and responsibilities are still new for the child just entering the 2.0 stage, and they still mostly look to others for social cues and align their behavior accordingly. Thus, when acting out of the 2.0 perspective, they often follow "leaders" and adopt and accept the rules that those leaders define, even if doing so conflicts with their internal sense of what's right. Anyone at this developmental level is exceptionally susceptible to peer pressure. Therefore, rule-oriented people follow *principals* more than their *principles*. Challenging a person at 2.0 to courageously stand firm on their principles in the face of peer pressure is a behavioral intervention for this type of shadow pattern.

A blessing of the 2.0 perspective is that the rules, roles, and responsibilities create a structure children can grow into. When healthfully embodied, the moral and ethical foundation developing in a 2.0 child holds them in a container of safety. But a child's ability to "hear" themselves think (internal auditory sense) is still relatively immature at this stage. One difficulty for anyone at 2.0 is remembering the rules. It takes a lot of mistakes and consequences, or what are called "concrete operations," [102] for children to finally mind all the rules. As a result, people at this level need, indeed desire, structure. O'Fallon postulates that adults at this developmental stage are greatly supported by fundamentalist churches, which help them remember ethical rules and, in general, goodness. Similar concrete institutions, like the military and team sports, offer codes of conduct and fulfillment through collective participation.

Beyond peer pressure, another curse of the 2.0 stage is that the rigid container of rules, roles, and responsibilities can trap a person. Being caught in a container of rules can lead to groupthink and all the myriad shadow dynamics that go with that. "Everyone in my group is good. Everyone outside my group is bad. My religion, political party, race, team, etc., is good; all others are bad." Add the coercive effect of rewards and punishments to group pressure and the feedback created can bind isolated cultures to this perspective for generations. Anyone shadow-crashing down to the 2.0 level from a higher perspective will insist on following the rules and enforcing fairness, even if they cause more harm in the process.

It follows that the morality of a person looking out a 2.0 window is rigidly concrete. At this stage the rules aren't seen as a human construction but instead are handed down from higher authorities. Therefore, the veracity of such authority figures as God, presidents, priests, rabbis, imams, strict fathers, AA sponsors, or commanding officers isn't questioned. Similarly, rules are broken by "bad" people, which justifies heavy-handed punishment. Even today we live with a penal system largely structured around a 2.0 ethos. How else do we explain why many millions of people still languish in prison for years simply for the crime of medicating their pain with drugs?

2.5 CONFORMIST

By the end of the rule-oriented stage, kids are able to wrap their heads around clock time and the whole personal space thing. What pops them up into the next stage is acquiring the ability to see patterns that result from their interactions with others. It's a big trick of consciousness, to zoom in and out and develop the two-way seeing that allows them to manage their own presentation and accept the presentation of others. At the 2.5 Conformist Stage, a person can visualize the consequences of their behavior.

Conformists can remember in their "mind's eye" what happened earlier and hear the words of authority figures internally. This gives them the capacity to learn from their mistakes and not repeat behaviors that got them into trouble. The result is a fully integrated set of principles and culturally synchronous morality. After having fully fleshed out the pro-social lessons of 2.0, young adults and others at this stage are able to function well enough to maintain reciprocal relations in most interpersonal interactions.

But this isn't attunement yet. Attunement is sensing into oneself, situations, and contexts with acceptance and care and a wish for a higher good. Asking a person at this level to attune would be like asking them to ride a unicycle while juggling three balls. It's not going to happen. A lot more practice is required to pull that off.

That said, the 2.5 Conformist Stage represents the maturation of the second-person perspective, but it doesn't mean conformists are thinking for themselves yet. Far from it. Indeed, a confusion that arises early in this stage is believing they're making individual choices, when in actuality their thinking and behavior conform to their particular in-group ethos.

At this level of development, a conformist will think they're following *their* principles when in actuality the principles they live by were introjected into them by their family and their in-group and its ethos. Consequently, anyone shadow-crashing to the 2.5 level will tend to fall on the sword of these introjected principles no matter the cost. Only at the end of this stage will a conformist be able to stand on their own principles in the face of group pressure.

It's not uncommon for people holding a second-person perspective to embrace one set of rules for their group and yet another set of rules for everyone else. "Don't tread on me, but excuse me while I tread on you." A 2.5 person brought up within a particular faith tradition will hold a view of God that closely aligns with *their* religion. Furthermore, questioning their faith's sacred stories and beliefs won't readily occur to a conformist, nor would it be easy for them to do so. Indeed, the act of questioning strongly held group norms results in extreme cognitive dissonance for them.

As the label for the stage suggests, conformists are often unduly compliant. In social situations, they are reticent to criticize anyone inside their immediate circle. "Rocking the boat" or appearing disloyal is anathema to them, as it puts them at odds with the primary objective of this stage, which is to blend in. For that reason, shame is an emotion prevalent at this stage.

The time frame that conformists live within includes *their* past up to the present day; a person at this developmental level can't adequately visualize things they haven't yet directly experienced. Consequently, they don't think too far into the future. At one time, before I understood this, I was incredulous when I asked myself, *Why isn't global warming the top issue on everyone's mind? We all have children, for goodness' sake!* After learning about these stages, I finally understood why not all of us care about the impending global catastrophe. One reason is that conformists are not able to picture a future world that's markedly different from the one they live in today. Another reason is that myth, not science, informs their cosmology. If you find that rare conformist who acknowledges that the earth is warming, they reckon it's happening either because God is pissed at us or because these are the "end days." When it comes to climate change, many conformists believe that God, not man, is in charge.

Once a person reaches the 2.5 Conformist Stage, they're aware that other people can see them. But that two-way seeing only applies to "concrete" seeing—in other words, what is happening on the *outside*. Concrete two-way seeing doesn't apply to subtle internal processes like thinking. Consequently, anyone at this stage won't know that other people can see *how* they think. Ignorance of that fact tees up a treasure trove of ironies.

For example, a 2.5 liberal landlord will rail against a conservative's politics but choose to rent his apartments to churchgoing families. An astute observer would notice the inconsistency. One might also notice a conservative friend rail against liberal secularists at home but prefer that their geopolitical adversaries be ruled by more liberal governments. And indeed, fundamentalists of all stripes believe they are right and everyone else is wrong. That's irrational stuff, but it speaks to the primary blindness of 2.5 conformism. People at this stage readily see the error in "others" but can't or won't see it in themselves.

I have a client who identifies himself as a conservative. While I see the world differently, I love this guy. He's exceedingly thoughtful and generous. Every time he comes to visit, he brings a bounty of fresh eggs and vegetables from his farm. We'd be pleased if this guy were our neighbor—he's trustworthy and socially minded, and we wouldn't have to lock our doors. I'm comfortable around him because my internal conformist also strongly resonates with his "traditional" values. That part of me relaxes in the presence of honest, hardworking, and selfless people. And as with me, the healthy sense of shame he carries motivates him to do good. I appreciate that. In all these ways this man personifies the beautiful qualities of 2.5.

The reason he's working with me is that his anxiety has become intolerable. The source of his fear, from his telling, is the tearing down of the social fabric of this country by violent, radical leftists. This is the quintessential "us vs. them" dynamic that can trap a conformist—my group good, others bad. As kind and giving as he is to me, he has no love for liberals. What's more, no part of this good man can see or admit to the violence coming from his side of the political aisle. He's certainly correct to point out that we have a major problem with hate and violence in this country, but what he's missing is that it's not just coming from the left. There is at least an equal share of anger coming from the right.[103] Indeed, as of the writing of this book, the Department of Homeland Security is warning of a "heightened threat environment" created by violent right-wing domestic extremists.[104]

The rage *he* carries mirrors what he hates about liberals. He just doesn't see that yet. Gently and respectfully sharing ideas that titrate just the right amount of cognitive dissonance is an intervention that can work for someone at this stage. Indeed, a validating conversation about the similarities of the two sides of the political divide may serve to expand compassion and engender a move up the tower of consciousness.

A 2.5 Conformist's internal self-stories play an outsize role in shaping the perspective they hold of themself, in part because a person at this stage doesn't easily reflect on their thoughts. At this stage, people know that they think—they just don't think much about their thinking. Conformists won't spend a lot of time inquiring into their thoughts and feelings. But gently asking them to reflect on their thoughts and feelings can sometimes open the door to a higher perspective.

Late in the stage, another confusion arises that can set up some conformists for up-shift to the next level. Early in 2.0, a child may still regard their parents as all good and all-knowing, but by late 2.0, a child's perception of their parents is more realistic—they start seeing their parents as fallible people, too. At the latter part of 2.5, teenagers are able to "zoom out" and see the contradictions between what their parents (or other authority figures, including the church) say and what they do.

Visual and auditory thinking is also finally coming online at the end of 2.5. Conformists start mulling over the contradictions they see, both internally and externally. As mentioned, people at this stage solve problems by staying true to their principles. But eventually adding a new principle or bending principles to fit new circumstances creates conflicts.

Noticing the hypocrisy in oneself and in authority figures can begin to create a disabling cognitive dissonance in some people, which can resolve itself in one of two ways. To remain comfortably ensconced within the safety of their group, a 2.5 may simply deny all their internal conflicts and press ahead with a new enabling principle. Sadly, if that type of self-deception becomes a pattern it can trap them at this stage, and within the concrete tier, for the remainder of their life. The other possibility is that they begin to acknowledge the contradictions they see within themself and others in their group. That courageous act of self-reflection then permits the dissonance to gain momentum and, if it should reach a critical threshold, spit them out of the vortex of the conformist perspective. What lies ahead for such a person is the upward movement of the developmental window, and the dawning of a new, inner, *subtle* world.

CHAPTER 12

Raising Your Window: the Subtle Tier

"The best things in life aren't things."

Art Buchwald

3.0 EXPERT

My stepfather, Joe, was the consummate disciplinarian. His strictness was especially evident at the dinner table. Should I forget to chew with my mouth closed, he might stab the back of my hand with his fork. But masquerading as the paragon of virtue, as he often did, can be a dicey proposition. Playing that game can lead to displays of hypocrisy, and by the time I was fourteen years old I was able to zoom out and measure the man's behavior by *his* standards. Needless to say, I found gaps. The example that most readily leaps to mind is the time he nearly choked on a breakfast roll after cramming the whole thing into his mouth. Unaware that there was such a thing as the Heimlich maneuver, I sat bug-eyed, watching him struggle, mouth agape, crumbs tumbling out, as if doing his best snake impersonation, trying to swallow the entire wad of dough whole. Oh, the duplicity!

But it wasn't just Joe and his hypocritical rigidity that felt like a straitjacket. That same sense of wanting to break out was a reflection of the time, too. In the early to mid '70s, a fresh new countercultural spirit was flowering. "Turn on, tune in, drop out" was the mantra of a generation of young people determined to think for themselves.[105] Although I was too young to protest the Vietnam War and partake in any free love, I did my part by wearing purple bell-bottom jeans and puffy flower shirts and questioning authority at every turn.

The first institution this newly emerging doubt began to scrutinize was my faith. Ten years after asking my dad what a Methodist was, I still didn't know. Add skepticism to confusion and I began to view all religions differently. It finally dawned on me: *Oh, the point of these sacred stories is the moral message; they're not meant to be taken literally.* For a 2.5 Conformist transitioning to a 3.0 Expert perspective, that was an expansive, freeing, and simultaneously anxiety-producing realization.

Dare I think for myself? Despite the fear of being different, I was drawn to find the unique "Mark," separate from all the familial and cultural programming. I didn't know it then, but what I was experiencing was the reappearance of the same confusion that comes up at the 1.0 Impulsive Stage. At 15, I was again wondering, *Who am I?* But this time, the question was in relation to *Who am I separate from my tribe?* I didn't know it at the time, but I was about to dedicate the next decade to finding the answer.

Around the time I turned seventeen, the lifelong practice of going to church stopped making sense. A new me was in the process of becoming. Concurrently, and like most American teenagers, I spent hours a day worshiping at the altar of another shrine, that of 1970s TV. *Kung Fu* [106] was a show I found particularly captivating. The weekly portrayal of warrior monk Kwai Chang Caine, a guy on a hero's journey [107] through the Old West, spoke directly to my soul. I didn't realize it then, but that show was spiritual nourishment. Every episode saw Kwai Chang Caine turn inward for strength and wisdom, which made me yearn to train my mind and body in the same way. It's humorous to recall now, but to emulate Kwai Chang, I invented small austerities for myself, like walking barefoot across blazing hot asphalt parking lots. Although I would be a college sophomore before I began to study Eastern mysticism and the martial arts in earnest, I credit *Kung Fu* with planting that seed of inspiration in the soil of my consciousness.

My first college roommate was enrolled in Officer Candidate School for the Marine Corps. There exists in my family a long proud military tradition, so it didn't take much arm-twisting for him to persuade me to enlist myself. Following his lead, I spent six weeks during the summer before my sophomore year of college attending Officer Candidate School in Quantico, Virginia. I completed boot camp and, by the judgment of my superior officers, fared well and was asked to complete the training the next summer.

I returned home to Tucson full of pride and esprit de corps, believing I would continue to pursue a commission. Since my other college buddies were all intending to go to law school, I imagined I'd seek a parallel path and become a JAG lawyer in the Marine Corps. I chose an appropriate major to fulfill that ambition, political science. After that, I was on the treadmill to graduation. It wasn't until four years later, after the commencement ceremony, that I realized I was way off track.

Who was I kidding? I wasn't cut out to be a lawyer, a Marine Corps lawyer no less. I shy away from confrontation. Add to that the fact that I weigh about 130 pounds soaking wet. To get a drop of respect in that environment, I'd need to spend two decades puffing out my chest. How could I have been so confused? What I didn't see growing inside me at that time was the conflict between convention and invention. My still-strong 2.5 Conformist who still wanted to fit in was standing in direct opposition to the emergent 3.0 Expert who was aspiring to find his own way.

Recognizing that I'd spent all that time, energy, and money earning a degree that I didn't want shook me with angst and guilt. What had I done? Worse, what was I going to do? I admonished myself for making a huge mistake. But looking back, those five years of exploration, learning, and fun were far from a waste. With the benefit of hindsight, I can now appreciate that time in my life for what it was, a sumptuous smorgasbord of experience. Throughout, I sampled a variety of jobs and classes and got to know myself better. I stocked shelves at a grocery store, studied history, and learned how to write. I minored in astronomy and took a class on self-hypnosis. I tended bar and did the *est* training.[108] Occasionally, I experimented with mind-altering substances. Regularly, I kicked ass in the dojo. I earned an EMT certification and drove an ambulance. And, as you already know, I worked on a dive boat in the U.S. Virgin Islands.

After graduation and spending one season in the USVI, I returned to Tucson and went back to driving the ambulance.

One day a nurse joined us for a ride-along. Like me, she was a student of the martial arts, which prompted a discussion of sports injuries. Both of us had had many. "Why don't you go to physical therapy school and learn how to take care of your aches and pains?" she asked me, and something about that felt right. Never one to let careful deliberation get in the way of a hasty decision, after that one conversation I decided to return to school and become a physical therapist.

When a person's developmental window moves up one floor, from 2.5 Conformist to the 3.0 Expert perspective, in most cases the box of conventional roles, rules, and responsibilities becomes so tight that it compels a person to bust out. Accordingly, the emergence of the 3.0 perspective is a time of passionate receptivity to new ideas and inward searching. My story exemplifies what the emergence of the 3.0 Expert perspective looks and feels like.

The 3.0 Expert perspective is also an advancing iteration of what went on at the 1.0 Impulsive Stage. When we compare these two perspectives, a pattern starts to take shape. Just as 1.0 is the beginning of the concrete tier, the 3.0 Expert Stage marks the start of the *subtle* tier.

The world appears external and concrete to everyone in the concrete tier. The new and unfamiliar world that dawns for the 3.0 Expert is an internal and subtle one. Thus a person awakening to what's also referred to as a "modern" perspective has access to two worlds: the old outer one and a new inner one.

As a person matures through all the stages of the concrete tier, they accumulate a penetrating understanding of how the external world works. The task is very similar for a person awakening into the subtle tier. They begin to learn the ropes of a new world, except this time that world is an internal one. Where a 1.0 infant uses echolalia to copy its parents and learn new behaviors, a 3.0 Expert searches for mentors and seeks to emulate their thinking.

The dawning of the subtle world is also what triggers a person's interest in subtle objects, such as thoughts, plans, and abstract ideas. In young adulthood, the brain is mature enough to generate beta waves that enable a person to focus on and clarify these evanescent phenomena and to visualize things they've never seen before. If your developmental window has already grown up to this level, you'll remember the excitement you felt zooming in on, examining, and philosophizing about novel subjects and future possibilities. The universe is awash in infinite subtle ideas a person can engage with.

Like a 1.0 infant, early on in the 3.0 stage a person has a hard time prioritizing subtle objects to focus on. In the same way an infant uses its mouth and fingers to explore everything, the expert samples subtle objects. Additionally, 3.0s have a distinct interest in understanding and explaining how things came to be the way they are and how they work.

Where a 2.0 Rule-Oriented person or a 2.5 Conformist might eschew science and "intellectualization" for fear that rationality might conflict with their beliefs and erode their faith, a modern person relishes it. That doesn't mean this opening to new values and ideas arises anxiety-free. Indeed, dissolving connections to one's conventional past is usually unnerving. Consequently, newly minted 3.0s instinctively look for people to help them through the transition. Dr. O'Fallon writes that at 3.0, "expert advice operates like a cradle for the mind." Like our parents did for us early in life, experts help 3.0s navigate through this turbulent time.

Not surprisingly, colleges and universities become gathering places for young people at this stage. It makes sense that once their studies are complete, a 3.0 wants to become an expert themself. Graduation from college or university becomes a ceremonial rite of passage, which confers a diploma or certificate to signify their achievement. Just as trophies and flags are tchotchkes for the second-person perspective, framed diplomas and certificates become the outward symbols of the third-person perspective.

All those diplomas on a person's wall can convince the bearer of the superiority of their technical abilities. Woe betide the colleague with the temerity to challenge their thinking or way of doing things. I remember being a newly minted physical therapist and believing there was one right way to mobilize a joint and, further, how prideful I was in defending my views. Wow, was I full of myself.

As with a 1.0 Impulsive, a 3.0 Expert's primary focus is on themself. They're still in the immature part of the third-person perspective so can't yet sense well enough into the subtle interiors of others. These shortcomings prevent people at this stage from attuning. That incapacity can and does cause problems in relationships.

Despite all their internal focus and technical ability, 3.0 Experts struggle when it comes to prioritizing subtle decisions. I had a client who was a brilliant scientist and an innovator in a growing multibillion-dollar market, yet this genius couldn't pull the trigger on the simplest marketing decision. He tied himself into knots wondering whether or not to advertise at an upcoming convention. What stops 3.0 Experts like him from moving forward is the clash of competing scenarios bouncing around their minds. A useful intervention for a person at this stage is making a list of pros and cons of competing ideas or decisions and having the expert do the work of prioritizing decisions in order to bolster the upside and minimize the downside.

Although a person with a modern perspective is a capable thinker, they're not yet well-adapted to think about their thinking. Much like fundamentalists before them, 3.0s can get caught in the trap of their beliefs. Most of our modern problems stem directly from groups of arrogant experts, entrenched in separate silos, defending their dogma. Fortunately, systemic solutions do exist, a few floors higher up the tower of consciousness.

3.5 ACHIEVER

There was a tremendous upwelling of curiosity when the window of my consciousness moved from 2.5 to 3.0. I was on fire to learn and to get to know myself better. Despite spending five years and umpteen thousands of dollars on one degree, I was still so eager to absorb knowledge that I didn't hesitate to jump right back into school, this time to study physical therapy.

A full-time student once again, I felt confident I was following my heart. But the lesson of these perspectives is that a person can only see what they see. So my decision, consequential as it was, was based only on the limited information I had at the time. Throughout my whole physical therapy program, the vague sense that I had made another mistake in choosing a field of study lingered in the background of my mind. Fortunately, the profession of physical therapy offers numerous subject areas in which to specialize. Learning to treat my sports injuries was what initially sparked my interest in the subject, so I stuck with it and chose to concentrate on orthopedics.

After graduating and passing the licensing exam, it was official: I was a physical therapist. Wanting to stay in Tucson, I took a job with a respectable private practice in town, but within a few short months that position felt like all the other treadmills I'd been on. As the enthusiasm for that job waned, I began looking for another situation and accepted a position at the University of Arizona as the PT for the Student Health Center. That engagement was initially very satisfying—I enjoyed the autonomy and the pace of the caseload—but within only two years, the same vocational wanderlust arose in me again. As it happened, I got a little shove out the door when budget cuts at the university necessitated layoffs.

Typical of any 3.0 Expert, notwithstanding being green around the edges, I did not lack for confidence in my technical abilities. The fact that all my former U of A patients were young and healthy and got better fast only served to reinforce the misconception that I was better at my job than was actually the case. After leaving the university, I clung tightly to that flattering opinion and went into business for myself.

Like all stage transitions, the movement from 3.0 to 3.5 was gradual and nebulous. I still yearned to sit at the feet of experts and continue to develop professionally, but I also sought to *own* something. That dialectic caused a foggy tension to precipitate in me. On one hand was an unsatisfied need for self-understanding and expression, and on the other a growing hunger for self-importance and expansion.

The time horizon at each successively higher perspective continues to expand. The 3.0 Expert focuses on the past, the present, and probably no more than a few years into the future. The 3.5 Achiever, on the other hand, has full access to memories of their immediate family's past and can readily picture future scenarios five to ten years out. By the time I was in my early thirties, my brain circuitry was mature enough to allow me to visualize and prioritize subtle objects like business plans and future success. Unfortunately, a little-known confusion comes along with that growing capacity to future trip. Achievers often mistake their dreams of the future for the reality they will inhabit when they get there. It's nearly always the case, however, that what arises in the future does not match the achiever's visualizations.

Even looking back now, I can't tell if it was the lingering 3.0 arrogance, the 3.5 future-fantasizing, or both. Whatever the cause, I blithely dismissed the reality that I'd only been practicing PT for three years and knew nothing about business or the complexities of medical billing. I was so hypnotized by the success I was imagining that I took out a $40,000 loan and signed a three-year lease for office space before one single doctor had agreed to refer me patients. With the cart placed squarely in front of the horse, I opened ProActive Physical Therapy on April Fool's Day, 1993.

Predictably, the flood of patients I'd imagined flowing into my clinic was more like a trickle. Luckily, I had enough on the ball to generate sufficient business to pay the bills and a small salary for myself. The economy was good and what I lacked in experience I made up for in eagerness. Within a few years, financial success was finally knocking at my door.

But the unfolding future, once I'd caught up to it, was indeed different from the one I had envisioned. Most notably, I'd thought financial security would bring satisfaction with it. That wasn't the case. My ever-present discontent with the discrepancy between where I was and what I wanted kept me on the lookout for more opportunities. 3.5 Achievers want to do something bigger than themselves. That desire was pushing me forward full on.

It's consistent with being a fledgling 3.5 Achiever that work was everything to me. And because my business wasn't where I wanted it to be, more and more of my time was spent focusing on ever-more successful goals and outcomes. These included imaginative plans for business growth and ingenious ways to earn lots of money. Like the 1.5 Egocentric toddler, the 3.5 Achiever focuses narrowly on their own individual priorities. I constructed a socially lubricious mask to help me get where I wanted to go. Like putting lipstick on a pig, that mask helped me pretty up the 3.5 self-oriented avariciousness that was present just below the surface.

The developmental vista that finally appears when a person's window rises to 3.5 is that of self-reflection. From 2.0 on, people are aware that they think, but it isn't until 3.5 that they really start thinking about their thinking. In all previous stages, thoughts have the thinker; at 3.5, the thinker turns the table on thoughts and instead can behold *them*. The word that best defines such perspectival jujitsu is *metacognition*, which roughly translates as being *above* one's thoughts. When you're metacognitive, you are the observer and the observed at the same time; subject and object exist within the same person. Although not yet attunement, metacognition is a precursor of it.

That mounting ability to hold a mirror up to my mind began revealing aspects of shadow that I had been unaware of. As my appreciation for real expertise grew, it dawned on me that I wasn't the expert I thought I was. It was now clear that developing true expertise in my chosen profession would take decades of dedicated study and practice.

In January 1996, I was feeling passion for my field as well as being excited to grow my business, and it was then that I met a Belgian man who taught for the International Academy of Orthopedic Medicine. It took only one of his classes on diagnostic orthopedics for me to know that this was the area of therapy on which I would focus and that he was the guru to teach me. As fate would have it, he and his wife were living in Tucson. Having just moved to the States from Europe, they were also earnestly trying to build their teaching business. What was holding them back was the absence of a physical location where they could treat patients.

Seeing an opening, my 3.5 Achiever sped into action by painting for them a picture of a "center of excellence." I floated the idea that if we formed a partnership, I would offer my clinic as the new home of the American Academy of Orthopedic Medicine. Notice how the 3.5 Achiever in me was working all the angles on the subtle plane. That's what achievers do—they use their minds to construct plans and visions that influence others. Once my teacher and his wife had endorsed the plan, she and I went further and enlisted a colleague with extensive referral relationships in the community to join our team. The four of us formed OrthomEd.

What enlivens a 3.0 Expert is the desire to absorb information and become someone. The 3.5 Achiever, on the other hand is determined to *use* that knowledge and expertise for personal gain. Both of those motivations were driving me psychically and spiritually when I met my business partners, and the same was true for them. So on the surface, and at least regarding these two concerns, it would seem that the partnership was synchronized. Yet almost from the start our partnership was on the emotional rocks. Combine the individual focus of 3.5 with the blindness of one-way seeing and you get a person who talks *at* you rather than with you. My partners and I did a lot of talking at each other. We were all so stuck in our heads, envisioning our individual futures, that we missed every opportunity to sense into ourselves, each other, and the situation with acceptance and care to manifest a higher good. Had we been able to do so, I'm convinced we could have worked out our differences and built an amazing business, but all that potential was lost because our developmental windows were one or two floors lower than the situation required.

As a blossoming 3.5, I began to notice how different I was from my partners. They were still interested in becoming narrow-domain experts. Me, not so much anymore. After two years of in-depth study, I began to notice the shortcomings in the theory and techniques we were teaching. Where they saw ever increasing opportunities to treat intractable pain syndromes with their hands, I had reservations about that narrow approach.

As part of our work, the group of therapists I hung out with were all trying to develop the most ultrasensitive palpation skills. One weekend we were testing whether we could feel the negligible one- to two-degree "spin" of a thoracic vertebra (mid-back) when you bend a patient sideways. Standing back, I watched as each of my colleagues professed that they could feel it. Here I was, a person who played the classical guitar, but when it was my turn I could not feel it. Mind you, all the research was on my side—mostly clinicians fool themselves when they rely on palpation skills to render a diagnosis.[109] Being a part owner of the company, I was chagrined and dismayed. A portion of what we were selling was snake oil!

That experience inspired me to break out and start teaching therapists a new way of considering the conditions we treat, as a blend of physical and psychological pain. Our business, however, had to function within the established health-care insurance system. That required me, as a physical therapist, to limit my focus to treating the body. Eventually, it was too much effort to push the river, and I lost all interest in the type of work we were doing. As a 3.5 who could only see one way—from my side out—I wasn't aware that my partners were able to observe that attitudinal shift in me. But they could, and it put me on the outs with them. My behavior put additional strain on the partnership when I cut my patient caseload and started writing a book.

Who could blame them for voting me off the island? Even so, when that decision came down, it was a total shock. You already know the abbreviated version of that story—I shadow-crashed and fell into a fiery rage that lasted a couple of years. It took a white feather hitting me in the chest to break me out of that bitter fixation. Since the 3.5 perspective enables a person to think about their thinking and feeling, it follows that it also allows a person to reflect on their behavior. I did a lot of that during the next decade.

3.5 is the mature phase of the third-person perspective, where the capacity to resolve and clarify subtle thoughts and sensations really comes on line. Consequently, meditation and mindfulness become key interventions for people with an interest in accelerating their development. Indeed, meditation threw open the door to my subtle interior. The more mindful I became, the more I could see my part in the breakup and take responsibility for it. It's no exaggeration to say that internal spiritual work has been the bedrock of my recovery.

In the near aftermath of the collapse, I would never have thought I could forgive my ex-partners. But as I reflected on my part in the fiasco, compassion replaced rage, especially when I began to see my shadow in them. Their arrogance was my arrogance, their greed was mine as well. We were all doing the same thing, looking out for ourselves and creating our own selfish visions of the future. Self-dealing is what 3.0 Experts and 3.5 Achievers do. At least that's the destructive shadow aspect of these stages. When destructive shadow is in play, the coercive patterns that the 1.5 toddler uses to get its way—dominate, obsess, collapse—show up at 3.5 again. But constructive shadow that facilitates self-reflection is available at the achiever level as well and enables the arduous inner work of recovery and reconciliation.

Approaching life as a spiritual journey keeps you in the practice. A person's daily practice then continues to push the window of their conscious development higher. Raising my window enabled me to amend my story and thereafter suffer less. My story of self-change and healing also exemplifies the power of narrative medicine. Happily, there's even more goodness available to the intrepid folk who push still higher into the stages ahead.

4.0 PLURALIST

I started meditating in earnest after the disintegration of my business and, as a result, became conscious of more of my unconscious patterns. For the first time in my life I was able to appreciate many more of the previously hidden expectations, judgments, and assumptions I was making. I was a story machine.

At the same time, I was studying Buddhist teachings on the nature of mind. I could confirm the validity of those teachings by observing my mind while meditating. Those firsthand observations led me to conclude that everyone shares the same human consciousness. I know it sounds like a stretch, but there was no other way to explain how I, too, could see the exact same system dynamics that countless other meditators reported seeing while they meditated.

It's a provable fact that when meditators set up similar practice conditions—local attention and a global awareness—they all observe the same thing. Sure, the flow of thoughts and feelings cycling through each individual's mind varies, but the mind itself is a system, and that system follows the same rules of cause and effect in everyone. After witnessing that truth for myself, I put two and two together. Just like me, numerous narratives are running through everyone else's mind. We're all story machines!

The insights that arose in me while sitting on a cushion didn't stop after I got up. I began to consciously attune to other people and sense what was going on inside of them. It's not like I could read their minds, but I was becoming much better at reading the feelings behind their outward expressions and emotions. A person has to raise their developmental window to 4.0 before real attunement becomes possible. 3.5s can sense into other people's subtle interiors, but at that lower stage, they do so to serve their own ends. At 4.0, subtle reciprocity, which is the essence of attunement, is a goal in and of itself.

Sometimes, without a word being spoken, I would notice myself feeling what another person was feeling. Often, I would ask and confirm these impressions. Then, more often than not, an intimate dialogue would follow. Through many such heartfelt exchanges, it became clear that if another person attuned to me, they could see into me as well. I came to realize that I wasn't the black box that I'd thought I was. Just as the 2.0 Rule-Oriented child realizes that others can see them on the outside, the one-way seeing of the third-person perspective evolves into the two-way seeing of a 4.0 Pluralist. I see into you, and you see into me, too.

The 4.0 Pluralist level is an upshift of the 2.0 Rule-Oriented Stage, but instead of focusing on concrete rules, the pluralist focuses on subtle ones. The subtle rules that honor the notion that we all share the same human consciousness are these: respect the rights and dignity of everyone, and protect the rights and dignity of everyone. This pluralistic celebration of individual authenticity and diversity is expressing itself all over the world today with an increasing acceptance of gay marriage and LGBTQ rights. It exemplifies the fact that the higher a person's perspectival window rises in the tower of conscious development, the wider their circle of compassion becomes. Indeed, naming this stage "Pluralist" reflects this specific character trait of folks at this level.

All that said, the shadow of this stage is that pluralists don't see how judgmental they can be when people don't pay attention to *their* subtle rules. Just as 2.0 Rule-Oriented folk are quick to ostracize rule-breakers, pluralists will also "cancel" someone for breaking subtle rules. Referring to a person by anything other than their preferred pronoun and you're out! Diversity of opinion is highly valued at 4.0—unless you disagree with them. Indeed, people at this level invented cancel culture. Pluralists are often referred to as "mean greens" for just this reason.

What people at 4.0 really want to do is come out of hiding and be who they are. I wanted that for myself too, and knew it was going to take some work on my part to sort myself out. Therefore, when my first wife suggested I attend a week-long group therapy workshop at a retreat center in Tennessee, I was amenable to the idea. I got the sense, however, that this was another one of her well-meaning attempts to help me remedy more of my blind spots. She was right—quite frankly, I had many legitimate issues to work on. More than that, my sincere wish was that we could make our marriage work. Instead of going just for me, this time I was retreating for us. So with no quibbling or sniveling, I packed up and headed off to Tennessee.

The program I attended was called the Living Centered Program.[110] I'd done therapy before, but the LCP was my first experience doing *group* therapy. There were eight people in our cohort, and there was one other person who'd never done anything like this before. Happily, the six other veteran group processers far outnumbered us, and the old-timers didn't hesitate to show us two newbies how to venture into highly personal topics that I had no courage or interest in exploring.

Truth be told, the first day I felt like I was eavesdropping on a confessional. Every part of me was loath to hear what was clearly none of my business. It was weird that I should feel shame arise in me while overhearing what others were admitting to. When it was my turn to share, I balked, and then my inability to even modestly self-disclose filled me with more shame. My mind raced, my skin crawled, my body fidgeted. It was awful.

But strangely, by day two, I was somehow adapting to the process. By the afternoon of the second day I felt less exposed to the glare of all that personal sharing, somewhat as if I were developing a protective tan. After that point it was like "Shine on you crazy diamond,"[111] and I was able to appreciate the brilliant authentic sharing. As the week went on, I also finally found my voice. All the dialogue we engaged in enabled the blossoming pluralist in me to realize that the previous view of myself, others, and the world was just that, a view, and as such, it represented only a small part of a much bigger picture.

The higher 4.0 perspective begins to transform the me-oriented 3.5 person into someone who's more concerned with the well-being of others and the whole. In time, that leads pluralists to recognize the importance of respecting subtle boundaries. Their practice of spirited reciprocal exchange will ultimately enable and reinforce a 4.0's ability to stand back and appreciate the energetic vibe flowing through people and situations. Perceiving those ultra-subtle dynamics is a pluralist's superpower.

During the weeklong group therapy retreat, I came to realize that we're all a collection of multiple selves, existing on a spectrum of virtuous and venal, and that each version of ourselves is valuable and doing the best it can in a given context.

The whole experience began to open me to the core lesson of 4.0, that genuine self-expression met with compassion allows people to live their truth openly and in peace. As these revelations came to me, I felt more and more love for my wife. I called her every day, eager to share my experiences. I was also fast coming to the conclusion that we were going to be able to work out our differences and save the marriage. Then, on the last day of the retreat, our group engaged in a modality known as psychodrama.[112]

If you're not familiar with psychodrama, it was developed in Vienna in the second decade of the twentieth century by a young follower of Sigmund Freud, Jacob Moreno. Moreno was an imaginative innovator. In 1910, he created the Theater of Spontaneity, a setting in which his clients could act out their unconscious impulses. Then, while studying at the University of Vienna, he gathered together a number of prostitutes and conducted group therapy sessions that were the first of their kind. Shortly thereafter, he combined these two approaches and named the technique *psychodrama*. His method crossed the Atlantic and became popular in the United States after he immigrated in 1925.

When my time for psychodrama rolled around, our group facilitator gave us the instruction to pick an experience from the past for which we still carried some emotional charge. Psychodrama uses people and props to produce a spontaneous reenactment of a particularly poignant formative experience. We divided ourselves into small troops and set to work envisioning a replay of the event, something referred to as a "sculp." After some preparation, we brought each of our performances to life.

For the life of me, I can't remember the details of my own sculp. I'm guessing it had something to do with resolving my marital dilemma, but to this day I can't say for sure. I do vividly remember one other group member's sculp, however. His reenactment had him lying on the ground with his "mother" standing above him. I can still see him reaching out to her, desperately trying to grab her hand. As he struggled, the minor players put large blankets on top of him. By the end of his sculp, the blankets concealed his entire body, completely cutting him off from any connection to his mother.

Through my colleague's sculpt, I was finally getting a glimpse, however indirect, of a conflict arising in me. The whole of my life up to that point was a social construction. Build a business, make lots of money, attract a beautiful woman, get married. Where was "Mark" in all that? When I looked at it that way, I saw my marriage as social construction as well. It was probably the same for my wife. I had been pushed by reasons other than love to get married, and so had she. I was experiencing the principal confusion of the pluralist: they cannot differentiate their personal authenticity from their social construction. In light of that realization, it seemed that marriage was yet another treadmill I'd placed myself on.

I also saw in my group member's psychodrama his desperate attempt to maintain a loving connection. More than that, I saw a man *needing* love. No matter how hard he tried, the love he sought was unavailable to him; there was a barrier in the way.

Suddenly, I woke up to the truth, like the feather hitting me in the chest all over again. My wife was dear to me, but as much as I wanted our marriage to work, I could see it was a union of two incomplete people seeking completion through the other. The answer I'd been hoping to receive revealed itself through the penetrating metaphor of that sculp. So clear was the message that the dilemma solved itself. The Rubicon was finally crossed. Our amicable and loving divorce took place soon after my return home, all without a single harsh word spoken between us.

Eventually, an issue will arise that is not solvable with the tools available to a person at a particular level. Doubling down and using more of the tools of that stage won't be enough. For pluralists the tool is dialogue, and they won't notice when endless talking about feelings inhibits forward progress. Endless reciprocal exchange is not a problem for pluralists. But if you're a hard-driving 3.5 Achiever, working or living with a pluralist can drive you crazy at times. A 3.5 Achiever is a master of prioritizing tasks and employing the 80/20 rule. Achievers know how to get things done. In situations where pluralists lose perspective, a couple or a working team needs a 3.5 Achiever to gently point it out.

The operative word here is *gently*. Achievers are self-oriented—they tend to overvalue their opinions and undervalue those of others, and because of their one-way seeing, they have a hard time acknowledging their blatant control orientation. A pluralist will see all of that and demand an equal say. Should a pluralist get on their soapbox, however, they will probably want to stay "in process" long after the 3.5 wants to pull the trigger on a decision.

Whether it be an intimate relationship or a business partnership, when experts, achievers, and pluralists come together in co-creative activity and learn to interact cooperatively, everyone benefits. We need the detail orientation of the expert, the efficient goal orientation of the achiever, and the reciprocal approach of the pluralist. Each operates from their strengths and minimizes the weaknesses of the others. In the end, balancing all these perspectives produces the best outcomes. Raise the developmental window one floor higher still and it becomes possible for a single person to hold all of the foregoing perspectives, concrete through subtle. When that happens, a rare individual may share the full spectrum of benefits possessed by each.

4.5 STRATEGIST

Siddhartha Gautama lived twenty-five hundred years ago, before there existed anything remotely resembling systems science, and yet using meditation alone, he worked out a cosmology remarkably close to that of the modern systems view. Strategists see systems, and we can deduce that his insight into deep interdependence marks him as one of the first humans to reach the strategist's level.

How can we infer this? Without saying so explicitly, his teachings express his understanding of systems and expose his perspective on them. The quintessential Buddhist teaching on karmic causality, the twelve links of dependent arising (Pratītyasamutpāda),[113] epitomizes his systemic worldview.[114] Dependent arising was his way of explaining how a systemic flow of energy, information, and matter creates the patterns of thinking and behavior that bind a person to perpetual cycles of suffering. Think of Siddhartha's twelve links as one side of the coin and my effauses and caufects of healthful change as the other. The former explains suffering and the latter a means of release.

Strategists are aware that all phenomena exist as a result of multiple causes and conditions and that nothing exists independently of the system of which it is a part. For Siddhartha and the strategists, the window of consciousness is finally high enough to enable them to see that all physical and mental states depend on, and arise from, a causal stream of preconditions—outer and inner worlds arise together in an interdependent flow of effauses and caufects.

Therefore, a person at 4.5 can consciously open their awareness, zoom out, and see the whole system. This outsider's view allows strategists to stand back and *behold* systems and contexts, enabling them to deconstruct and reconstruct them as they see fit. Their higher perspective reveals both the deep actuality of interdependence and the profound inner workings of systemic evolution.

Strategists are also able to turn the laser beam of their attention inward, onto their own subtle patterns of mind, zoom in, and then influence them as well. In zooming in and zooming out, it becomes clear to strategists that body and mind, biology and meaning, objective and subjective have always been and will forever be entwined in a co-creative dance. That enlightened view brings with it a wellspring of power and wisdom to change human systems, both internally and externally.

I had a lot of time on my hands after losing the business and splitting with my first wife. Couple loneliness with mental and physical pain and you get a sense of what the turn of the millennium was like for me. You'll recall that I struggled with depression, chronic pain, heart palpitations, anger, addictive issues, and more. Thankfully, all that pain also motivated me to do something about it. After returning from Chenrezig, I stuck to a consistent spiritual practice. My morning routine consisted of coffee, a small square of dark chocolate (definitely spiritual!), reading dharma, and meditating for an hour. In the evening I'd repeat the whole process, sans the coffee and chocolate.

Reading and flooding myself with new healthy ideas was developmental. Living alone with no one to talk to, I devoured a lot of books. Add suffering to that relative isolation and it's easy to see why the topic of Buddhist mind training was at the top of my reading list. It quickly became clear to me that the teaching on the twelve links of dependent origination was central to the philosophy. One book in particular described an evidence-based cosmology that perfectly connected the outer objective and inner subjective worlds that I was beginning to unify. It was a dense read, but Joanna Macy's *Mutual Causality in Buddhism and General Systems Theory: The Dharma of Natural Systems* explained how the philosophical psychology of Buddhism, specifically the teaching on the twelve links, maps perfectly onto the meta science of self-organizing systems. This one book, more than any other, gave my developmental window a hefty shove upward.

But book learning can only take a person so far. Cultivating a firsthand experience of the twelve links by meditating is what pushed my learning curve higher still. Dispassionately watching the call and response of thoughts and sensations slowly—slowly—induced an indwelling appreciation of both the twelve links and systems science to arise in me. Like an echo bouncing off a canyon wall, one spontaneously arising thought would reflectively initiate a feeling in reply. Then a feeling would likewise spur another thought and so on. Taking a detached observer's perspective, I watched thoughts and sensations, and self-perpetuating cycles of suffering, arise and pass without any effort on my part.

It hit me that I was witnessing karmic "self-making" in action. I could see the circle of three. The meditating "me" was the subject, the spontaneously arising thoughts and feelings were the objects, and then there were also the subtle interactions between them. That multipart, zoomed-in and zoomed-out perspective *is* a systems view. Strategists in that privileged position can unscramble knotty riddles unsolvable by folks at lower levels. Take the riddle of the chicken and the egg. A person who can see both the inside and the outside of systems holds the key to unlocking such paradoxes. Seeing further than people at lower levels, strategists grasp that neither the chicken nor the egg came first. Instead, they see the how the system itself produces results. The epiphany at 4.5 is that both arise *together*, entangled as they are in vastly interdependent evolutionary feedback loops. To a strategist, everything dependently arises.

I remember reading Macy's book while working as the director of the pain program at the psychiatric hospital. By the time I'd taken that position, I'd worked in the field for twenty years, traveled the world with some of the best diagnosticians and manual therapists alive, and had just recently earned a doctorate and certifications in orthopedic manual therapy (COMT) and strength and conditioning specialist (CSCS). And yet, despite all that experience and education, I was not adequately prepared to help these chronic pain patients with their multifarious mind-body symptoms. They all had intense pain. The vast majority were also addicted to their pain medicine. And every single one was depressed and anxious.

There are no boundaries, evolutionarily speaking, between a chicken and its egg. The same can be said for the body and the mind. As a physical therapist, I was licensed to treat the body. I had to leave the mental pain to the psychiatrists and psychologists. But to the brain, pain is pain. In other words, roughly the same brain circuits light up whether a person is suffering from physical or psychological pain. To a one, my pain patients were suffering with both. The arbitrary boundary that the medical system places between the body and the mind would have me focus on the body and leave the mind to someone else. But reading Macy's book gave me scientific cover and the courage to shift away from solely focusing in on hurting parts to focusing out on the broader system. Thus I started looking for a unifying theory that would explain the essential cause and remedy of both types of self-perpetuating pain.

I didn't find the answer in a book—instead, it was hiding in my mind all along. I could see that there was always one mental state behind every case where stress turns into a mental or physical illness. That mental state is "attentional fixation." The tunnel vision of attentional fixation always causes awareness to dim. When that happens, a negatively distorted story and amplified emotions come with it. Restoring awareness, on the other hand, provides additional perspective, which changes the story and the emotions and ultimately can restore health. Upon realizing that, it became clear that all stress-related illnesses share the same creation story and the same remedy. Exactly as Siddhartha said, "When this is, that is; This arising, that arises; When this is not, that is not; This ceasing, that ceases." [115]

My own traumas certainly primed me for pathological fixation, big emotions, and stress-related illnesses, and it was obvious that these same system dynamics were at play in my patients. The more my patients opened up and shared their stories, the more I understood how, like mine, their families also affected their health, both for good and ill.

A strategist's time frame expands to include multiple generations. That expanded time line enables the understanding of how epigenetics [116] (biology) and transgenerational trauma (story) permit the transmission of stress-related illnesses through families. Even beyond what was found by the ACEs study on disrupted development from Chapter 6, there is a substantial and growing body of evidence that supports the idea that children can be affected by their parents' traumatic experiences that occur *before* their birth and even before their conception! [117, 118, 119, 120, 121, 122, 123] As unbelievable as that sounds, it means that stories travel through time and pass from parents to their children through epigenetic factors.

These data suggest that having depression, anxiety, or an addiction later in life is much less about the genes you carry than about the *memes* you inherit.[124] That transgenerational arch of development becomes clear to strategists. Indeed, it was that insight and all the corroborating data that helped me create a pain program that favored a person's story over their biology.

Sadly, the clinical model operating at the psychiatric hospital where I worked was coming from a lower developmental level. In that conventional model, the body and the mind were treated as separate entities. Buddhist psychology and system science lay bare the error in that way of thinking. A patient's predispositions and preconceptions—in other words their story—shape their current reality and, simultaneously, the future that is on its way to becoming. Their mind-body carries the historical markers of their story and will continue to do so unless they shift the script.

Ignorance of the causes of healthful change becomes the primary reason why a person cycles in suffering. In other words, if you don't know what to do to help yourself, you're stuck. So, instead of having my patients lie back while I try to fix their broken parts, I required that they learn something new and take up their own cause. As Macy wrote, "the doer, by the doing, is done unto." In that same spirit, the pain program's curriculum focused squarely on education and self-care rather than pills and procedures. I couldn't reach inside my patients and directly change their biology. What I could do is jigger the system by upgrading their understandings and beliefs—i.e., their story—and in so doing indirectly achieve the results we were after.

The three skills that strategists employ to address systems issues are deletion, addition, and alteration.[125] Deletion is recognizing and actively removing some aspect of a system process that is deleterious to a particular goal. For example, most of my back-pain patients don't realize that repeatedly forward-flexing and stretching their backs is a major reason they continue to hurt.

Understanding that ligaments take months to heal, I instructed them to stop stretching, which enabled their torn discs to form scar tissue and recover.

Addition is the opposite of deletion. With addition, you add something to facilitate the goal you're working to achieve. For this reason, I suggested that all my patients add meditation to their self-care routine. It's the mind that creates the world. Logically, then, anyone who wants to influence their system has to become a better witness to their subtle internal mental dynamics. When you add skillful awareness to any healing process, you accelerate it.

Last, alteration is modifying some aspect of a system so it works better. We all have to communicate with each other, but some communication styles work better than others. That's why everyone who takes my SkillfullyAware class learns the four steps of compassionate communication: facts, feelings, needs, and requests. Compassionate communication helps people step into a 4.0 Pluralist's shoes and remain attuned to each other even during stressful conversations.[126] Alter and upgrade the way people communicate with each other and you set the stage for betterment.

As with all the previous stages, at this level the circle of compassion widens again. But here it extends beyond the human dignity of 4.0 to encompass the larger dignity of the ecosystem that creates the conditions in which we all live.

O'Fallon and Barta teach that some suffering is necessary for development to progress. If someone has it too easy, why change, right? As I've said before, pain is a great motivator, but it's also true that some suffering is completely pointless. Understanding how to allow for growth-inducing suffering while eliminating pointless suffering is the master stroke that rewards the strategist level with its name.

I used the strategist's perspective to create my pain programming and, after that, SkillfullyAware. Other people who shared this view of the world used their "vision logic" to "re-wild" Yellowstone. More strategists will be needed in the decades ahead if we're going to solve intractable problems of systemic racism, political polarization, income inequality, population overgrowth, climate change, and ecosystem collapse.

But for all that is possible at this level, strategists still have their blind spots. Although strategists can see when others are judging them, they can't yet see themselves judging others. The reason they can't see themselves judging others in the moment that it's happening is that strategists are still operating from *inside* the subtle tier. That means they are still identified with, thus inside, their story. Elevating one's sense of self above and beyond story is what happens when a person transitions to the metaware tier. For the rare and fortunate people who make that leap, the four remaining higher perspectives continue to offer the potential for more peace.

CHAPTER 13

Raising Your Window:
The Metaware Tier

"In the beginning was the Word, and the Word was with God, and the Word was God."

John 1:1 KJV

The concrete world that we're all so familiar with seamlessly merges with another, more intangible, ultra-subtle one. Whether you know it or not, it's happening right now, all around you. Your eyes have a shape, but the space into which they see does not. Your ears have size, but the sounds they register do not. You can discern the boundary of your body, but the sensations you feel are as edgeless as fog. Our three primary senses of seeing, hearing, and touching seem to create boundaries between subjects and objects, but as a person's perceptual capacities mature—from concrete to subtle to ultra-subtle—what they see and where they look from evanesces into space.

At the highest levels of awakening, all boundaries dissolve, even those between subject and object, and melt into a unified whole, making easier the heroic task of reshaping the patterns of one's karma. For the person who raises their window this high, emptiness and fullness, boundaries and boundlessness, time and timelessness, self and not-self all exist at once. That ineffable universe of paradox begins to reveal itself at the threshold of the metaware tier.

5.0 CONSTRUCT-AWARE

When a person meditates, they use their consciousness to observe their consciousness. That's the essence of perspective-taking—to turn yourself back on yourself. By the time I started meditating, the window of my consciousness was already firmly ensconced in the subtle tier. If I had to guess, the perspective I had on myself and the world was hovering around the 3.5 Achiever and 4.0 Pluralist levels.

I began teaching the SkillfullyAware program five years after I started meditating. The time and effort I devoted to studying living systems, lecturing on the topic, and watching the interior of my own living system seemed to push the window of my consciousness even higher, to the 4.5 Strategist level. Thus a wider horizon came into view.

Observing causality from both the inside and the outside, I began to fathom the effauses and caufects of stress and illness. Energy, information, and matter were cycling through a living (world-body-mind) system. The driver of the self-sustaining feedback loops that I was observing was the energy of emotion, always culminating in a story or, if things got worse, a stress-related condition.

Meditation revealed that causality flows the same way on the inside as it does on the outside. To convey that truth to my patients and students, I wanted to create an analogy that would help them see it for themselves. What both realms have in common is that objects pass through a space. For that reason, in my teaching I began to use the words *objects* and *space* a whole lot more.

I used the word *objects* to stand for concrete nouns on the outside and subtle nouns on the inside (i.e., thoughts and feelings). I used the word *space* to stand for actual space on the outside. But when speaking about the subtle interior, I used *space* to stand for awareness. My intention was to make clear that whether a person has their eyes open or closed, they see the same thing: objects perpetually arising and passing through a space.

The fact that sense objects arise, abide, and pass through the space of awareness becomes clear to anyone who meditates with any amount of precision. Furthermore, you'll quickly discover that each arising bit of subtle information leads to the next momentary arising bit, in an everlasting and unbroken flow. Tibetan meditation teachers advise their students to do analytical meditation on what they call the "mind stream," which encourages this insight. They have their students watch how each thought and feeling connects to the next. Then they have students imagine their stream of thoughts and feelings flowing back into the past and forward into the future. The conclusion that students come to is that all their thoughts and feelings are, have always been, and will forever be connected to each other in an unending stream.

Check it out. Every time you care to look, you'll witness a steady and uninterrupted flow of thoughts and feelings. Sit quietly for a moment with your eyes closed and you'll observe all the subtle "objects" (thoughts, feelings, and sensations) pass through the "space" of your consciousness.

The main takeaway is that objects are passing through space, whether you focus in or out. To solidify my patients' and students' appreciation of this phenomenon, I began encouraging them to notice the space around them. In other words, I asked them to hold the intention to be more "space-aware" as a part of their daily practice. We're all enculturated to pay attention to objects. Few of us, on the other hand, are aware of *space*.

A way I found to encourage people to contemplate space was to ask the question "What's the most important thing in this room?" In all the times I asked that question, I never did hear the answer I was looking for, which was "space." Without space, where would objects fit? Nothing can exist without the space in which it resides. That truth holds for your inner world as well. There would be no "room" for the subtle objects of thoughts and feelings to arise and pass through your interior without the space that consciousness provides.

This analogy, connecting the outside and the inside worlds, was working well for my patients and students. They started to see the flow of effauses and caufects, which empowered them to make changes. But unbeknownst to me, the programming was working on me at the same time. Noticing space, pointing it out, and teaching and talking about it eventually had a profound effect. I remember dining at a favorite neighborhood Thai restaurant when, unexpectedly, it seemed the space behind my eyes shot back to infinity. I was looking from very far back, like when you turn binoculars around and look through the wrong end. So far back did the perspective recede that my ego—the sense of self made up of thoughts, feelings, and story—became apparent in the foreground of my consciousness. Suddenly, and very strangely, I was looking *at* my ego instead of *through* it. Every object, even my subtle self, was in the forefront of this space.

That experience was a classic example of what people report feeling at the 5.0 Construct-Aware Stage. When consciousness breaks through the ceiling of this stage, awareness becomes "conscious awareness," which means it starts observing itself. In other words, awareness is aware of awareness as well as all the objects arising in it. Like the effect of putting on corrective lenses, subtle seeing becomes ultra-subtle.

Often when people first open to this stage, they report feeling disoriented. That's because the subtle self loses its moorings as the boundaries between the inside and the outside seem to disappear. At 5.0, awareness feels utterly spacious. A person also begins to recognize that awareness operates much faster than thought. As world-body-mind boundaries appear to dissolve, a roiling stream of perceptions, words, and reflections floods into consciousness. That torrent of cycling sense data can make it difficult for a person new to this stage to string a coherent sentence together. Talk to a person who's new to 5.0 and you'll watch them struggle to communicate because they are constantly being interrupted by their own perceptions. The primary confusion that can arise out of these recycling conceptions is wondering if the meaning that is making itself is *meaningful.*

Since I'd been playing with the practice of space awareness for some time, I didn't find the experience at the Thai restaurant as disorienting as that. Instead, it was at once thrilling and paradoxical. What I found most fascinating was the sense that "I" was behind myself. My familiar sense of self, the one constructed by story, the one that seems to live in my head, lost its location.

Actual locations are findable in the concrete world. Middle school math teaches us that we can plot the location of anything in the external world on an x, y, and z graph. But try as you might, you cannot plot the location of a thought anywhere in the domain of awareness. Likewise, there is no "place" from which your ego views the world from inside awareness either. At the restaurant, those two inscrutable facts were poignantly evident to me. As the spacious feeling of being untethered from any location overtook me, my ego felt as if it had evanesced into space.

At times, and for those without proper understanding or guidance, emergence into 5.0 can be overwhelming and disruptive. Indeed, a compulsive drive to open to the fullness and fascination of the metaware experience can overtake some who enter this stage. When that happens, it can cause them to want to let go their conventional lives, leave their relationships, quit their jobs, and otherwise drop all worldly pursuits to follow the spiritual calling of a metaware life. Still others who poke into Construct-Aware don't trust stepping into the expansive freedom; nor do they want to sacrifice everything for a spiritual vocation they don't yet fully understand. Instead, consciously or not, they pull back, lower their sights, and settle back down into the practicality of their previous 4.5 Strategist's existence.

Now is a good time to tell you that the augmented and spacious metaware state that opened up for me at the Thai restaurant did not last. Within a few minutes the state dissolved and I noticed myself looking through my ego once again. Instant enlightenment was not in the cards. What happened to me—a getting-it-and-then-forgetting-it kind of thing—is actually the norm for most people who break through the boundary between the subtle and metaware tiers. It usually happens that way because the metaware perspective is so transcendent that it's challenging to integrate with normal life—in other words, to embody.

But an experience like that was impossible to forget. Given my work and interest in peak spiritual experiences, I was drawn to try to repeat it. Also, by this time in my career, I knew that just like any other spiritual experience, recreating a metaware state was doable. Since everything, even peak spiritual experiences, emerges out of conditions, re-creating a metaware state would only require that I reestablish those particular conditions. That's exactly what I decided to do.

I was energized to explore the boundarylessness of the metaware self and rest in the timeless *now*. Initially, when I began to consciously shift into the metaware state, I felt like I had at the Thai restaurant—somehow out-of-body, where there was no here or there or up or down. It took a few years before those transient states congealed into a trait that felt more natural, enduring, and embodied. What I experience now can be described as a seamless blending of world-body-mind into one boundaryless aware space where the three-tiered perspectives of concrete, subtle, and metaware all exist at once. I'm not sure if everyone who shifts into metaware shares this experience, but for me what works best is a hybrid view that permits having both one foot in the conventional world and one in the metaware.

You'll recall that people at the 4.5 Strategist Stage understand how systems operate. They have an appreciation for the way society, culture, and family systems create and recycle patterns that affect how people live. Thus they can observe the social construction of reality on a mass scale. Strategists also understand that there is no way of stepping outside of the systems and contexts that construct, condition, and hold us. At the 5.0 Construct-Aware Stage, that profound systems view reaches a deeper level still—it becomes apparent that systems are just a collection of stories.

Boom! Flickering micro-bits of data construct everything! Seeing structures arise out of awareness with lucidity enables the construct-aware person to witness the projections coming from them the moment they arise. That super-quick seeing further assists them in perceiving how the mind makes the world out of appraisals, words, and boundaries. Finally, a construct-aware person groks how the external world of form and the internal world of formless information interpenetrate and reflect one another—informational effauses and caufects flow in and between each realm, with all affecting all.

As happens with every other upshift in perspective, time and space expand at 5.0. The vastness of space extends to edge the cosmos, and time reaches back to the beginning of the universe. From the big bang forward, it's clear that recursive, cycling patterns of matter, energy, and information self-make everything. From a practical point of view, that enhanced awareness helps construct-aware folk better observe the habits of mind that until then largely controlled their thinking and behavior.

5.5 TRANSPERSONAL

The 5.5 Transpersonal Stage is animated by a passion to do something with the vast expansiveness of the metaware playground. Instead of deconstructing everything as it arises, transpersonals begin to appreciate, prioritize, and utilize constructs to create models that improve experience for themselves and others. Transpersonals can also take advantage of their enhanced awareness to engage in shadow work to amend any remaining bad habits. The Transpersonal Stage can be where wholesale change and healing get a booster shot.

As a general rule, the particular words a person uses indicate what they relate with. That fact provides evidence that words and the way they are used reflect a person's developmental level.[127] For example, someone is probably viewing the world from the window of the concrete tier if you repeatedly hear them discussing concrete values. Hearing a person talk about their devotion to God, tradition, loyalty, rules, and law and order hints at their developmental level.

3.0 Experts are perfectionistic, so if you hear a person say something like, "I gotta get it right," you can assume that's important to them. Consequently, you'll also hear someone at the expert level say *details*, *technical*, and *perfect* a lot. In the same vein, they also want to give "110 percent." Since coming to embrace their new subtle self is largely what the 3.0 stage is all about, you might also hear someone at this level use the word *unique* in reference to themself.

The correlation between word choice and stage level appears all the way up and down the spectrum of consciousness. For instance, 3.5 Achievers reveal their individualistic action orientation by talking incessantly about *focus, opportunities, goals, outcomes,* and the *future.* Fascination with their deep and multifaceted inner life leaks out through the words of 4.0 Pluralists. They want to discuss being *aware* of *parts of me,* their internal *reactions, judgments,* and *defenses,* and their effort to *grow* and *evolve.* The 4.5 Strategist's perspective hovers over the all stages below, concrete as well as subtle. That higher perspective leads them to use the words *contexts, systems,* and *development* often. Strategists are also keenly aware of the family system dynamics working inside them—you'll hear strategists frequently say *projection* and *shadow* as they reflect on those inner dynamics.

Crossing into the metaware tier marks the first time a person finds themself "outside" of words and meanings. In other words, the construct-aware perspective hovers above the subtle ego and its stories. The notion begins to take hold that the realities constructed and solidified by words are as diverse as the people using and interpreting them.

People at lower levels generally make the assumption that words mean the same thing to everyone. Folks at 5.0 disabuse themselves of that false impression. Words paint the pictures of individual and collective realities, but what most people don't realize is that they are the artists doing the painting. Construct-aware folk *do* see that, which is why you might hear them ask, "What do you mean when you use that word?" They are also aware of the "illusion" of "constructs" that people "make up" with words. And they refer to their unique viewing platform that floats above words. They may speak of it as "aware of awareness," "presence," "attunement," or "witnessing."

The words a person at the 5.5 Transpersonal level uses don't vary much from those used by someone at Construct-Aware, but transpersonals have an orientation toward action, so you may hear them use the word *models* to describe the way they observe the mind-made world. SkillfullyAware is an example of a model refined by the transpersonal perspective. You're likely to catch 5.5s discussing their "passion" for sharing their models.

Activated as they are, 5.5s may also show an interest in pushing the window of their development higher. Kim Barta refers to this compulsion as the drive to "climb the corporate ladder of consciousness." That effort often has them reengaging in shadow work by reclaiming and integrating any as yet alienated "ego" states.

But please don't get the idea that once a person becomes meta-aware they can amend their destructive shadow habits quickly and without effort. That's not the case, not by a long shot—at least that's been my experience. Even at this level, a person's karmic programming is still their karmic programming. As such, it makes itself. Changing it is always an uphill push, like with Sisyphus and the boulder. In fact, some who reach the transpersonal level may mistakenly believe they've reached the pinnacle of human evolution. Anyone carrying an ongoing tendency toward narcissism into this stage may never resolve their lingering shadow patterns.

But for 5.5s who recognize that they are still in process, walking through daily life can become a pro-level exercise in watching and working with shadow patterns spewing out of them in real time. At first, being conscious of the tremendous upwelling of my own shadow material was hard to manage, but one gets used to it. Soon enough I began to realize that the real gift of the transpersonal experience was a keener awareness of my subtle ego scheming in the background.

The Greek philosopher Thales once said, "The most difficult thing in life is to know yourself." Assuming this is true, you now know the reason: shadow. The gift of psychological and spiritual work is in retrieving a life-enhancing supply of self-knowledge from the well of the unconscious. That well is infinite, so the work is never done. Without direct and intensive effort, shadow won't evaporate, even as a person's perspectival window rises into the metaware tier.

The transpersonal level is yet another upshift from the 1.5 Egocentric and 3.5 Achiever stages that came before. It displays many of the same qualities, chief among them one-way seeing, where a person sees others' shadow bits without realizing others see them back. Again, at 5.0, a person sees the illusion of language and meaning or, more specifically, that words don't mean the same thing to everyone. Understanding other people's worldviews allows construct-aware folk to see and stand outside theirs and others' projections.

At the 5.5 Transpersonal level, any destructive shadow that remains can take a more active stance, influencing the perceptions of others so as to get what one wants. That capacity allows a person to enact subtler forms of manipulation.

If destructive shadow patterns are not remedied at earlier stages, they can be even harder to recognize, reclaim, and put right at this level. For this reason, shadow work at the 5.5 level can be likened to walking through a maze of mirrors, where reflecting on reflections can obscure the best way forward. Receiving support from another person who also sees through the transpersonal window is an irreplaceable benefit for recognizing and resolving one's own shadow at this level.

If someone is aware and humble enough to do the work, slaying the dragon of the remaining shadow at the transpersonal level equips a person with a considerable capacity to help his fellow man. By virtue of the height of this perspective, people at 5.5 are able to discern the vein of truth that runs through disparate fields and thereby link them together. That capacity allows them to then construct, reconstruct, prioritize/categorize, and redefine models that can provide benefit to an ailing world. Eckhart Tolle and Byron Katie are living examples of spiritual teachers whose lessons come from the transpersonal level and above.

6.0 UNIVERSAL AND 6.5 ILLUMINED

Before I begin, please note that apart from brief-state experiences I've had involving the 6.0 Universal Stage, one of which I will recount, I won't be writing about the nature of the sixth-person perspective from firsthand knowledge. For that reason, the following commentary will rely heavily on accounts of others who live at these stages.[128]

One's conception of the divine continually renews and refines itself as the window of development ascends through the twelve stages of consciousness. At the start of life, infants live in the oceanic *now,* where there is no self or other, much less a God. That's not to say they don't have spiritual experiences. The beauty and goodness arising through their senses is part and parcel of their emergent spirituality. A colorful mobile hanging above their bed and joyful encounters with pets and people encourage their budding life force to enter the world more fully.

Once their senses mature, a felt sense of personhood and agency arises. That body-based sense of me and mine produces the first "power god." From their perspective, toddlers believe that they are the creator and destroyer of worlds and that the beautiful and the good are whatever they say they are. Picking a flower for Mommy and smashing their sibling's Lego castle are both sources of exaltation. But little dictators need boundaries, and the images of a devil on one shoulder and an angel on the other help guide them. The devil is selfishness; the angel cares, shares, and is fair. Kids transition to 2.0 when they can bridle their egoistic desires for the sake of friendship. Hence, reciprocal relationships become the next thruway to spirit.

Inspired to fit in, and because stories are preeminent in a young person's life, 2.0 Rule-Oriented kids adopt the mythology of their family and culture. Sacred texts and truth claims by parents and clergy become the template for their evolving spirituality. Whatever they're told is what they believe. Less immediate than the bodily feelings of beauty and goodness experienced at 1.5, the doctrinal lessons at 2.0 are more mind-based.

Both cognition and spirituality continue to evolve, and by the age of twelve to fourteen, a person can step back and reflect on what they've been taught and judge whether their actions are consistent with the morality of their group. Folks at the conformist level who subscribe to a particular faith tradition may perceive this back-and-forth as dialoguing with God. For example, God implores them to "love your neighbor as yourself." For religiously inclined people, serving God increases beauty, goodness, and truth. Secular but spiritual 2.5s are similarly motivated to amplify beauty, goodness, and truth by living in alignment with their principles but may do so by serving their family or community more directly.

Transitioning to the subtle tier can occasion a tectonic shift that reorients the way a person relates to spirit. When the subtle mind comes online, 3.0 Experts will foreground their personal spirituality ahead of the collective form they grew up with. A religiously inclined expert may continue to adhere to their faith tradition yet feel that their relationship with God is somehow now more special. Such a feeling can precipitate the yearning to be "born again."

Secular 3.0s will also want to follow their *unique* path to spirit. Experimenting with mind-expanding substances is one way they might do that. Alternatively, spirit may move an expert to explore the sciences. Such inquiry can lead to cognitive dissonance between faith and reason, and cause the expert to eschew their spiritual side altogether. They may develop an allergy to myth, give up their faith, become an atheist, or unconsciously adopt scientism as their new belief system.

The spirituality of 3.5 Achievers is just as varied. A religious achiever will feel called to enact God's plan. A New Age achiever might start pairing coincident events, leading them to endorse "Law of Attraction" strategies. A secular achiever might find spiritual fulfillment by following their passion and becoming an entrepreneur. These and many more are the permutations of spiritual expression at the third-person level.

Most people find that the transition to the fourth person perspective coincides with a renewal and deepening of spiritual sensibilities. 4.0 Pluralists are more accepting of their own and others' interior experiences. Religiously inclined pluralists drift more toward progressive, universalist congregations, where everyone is welcome and scriptural teachings are taken allegorically rather than literally. At 4.0, God is no longer perceived as an entity as much as a life force or universal energy that lives in everyone. Secular pluralists are fascinated by and want to give voice to their many subpersonalities and readily accrue spiritual sustenance from therapy and therapy groups. New Age pluralists are drawn to participate in drumming circles, solstice celebrations, and group meditations.

4.5 Strategists view the whole inner and outer experience of spirit as a dynamic social construction. Strategists understand that they're just one part of a much larger whole and, moreover, that the universe is participatory. "God," if they even use the word anymore, is the unfolding universe itself, the expression of which is observable through the interaction of all the parts. Because all affects all, spirit draws strategists to live in coherence with their values. By playing their part, they amplify beauty, goodness, and truth.

Thus we can see that each higher stage brings "God" closer. A vast and holistic perspective dawns at the threshold of the metaware tier as a person's ego becomes visible in the foreground of their awareness. A figure-ground flip occurs where, instead of having a mind, the mind has them, much like the floaty experience I described at the Thai restaurant. Instead of being in the world, the self, the body, and everything else is *in* awareness.[129] That same perspectival shift led to the boundary of my body evaporating into space. Such an expansive feeling can lead construct-aware folks to associate their consciousness with divinity.

It's not hard to re-conceptualize some ancient scripture with a metaware twist. Take the biblical verse John 5:26: "For as the Father has *Life* in Himself, so also He has granted the Son to have *Life* in Himself"[130] (capitalization and italics are mine). Also consider John 14:6, attributed to Jesus: "I am the way, and the truth, and *The Life*." If we equate *Life* and *The Life* with consciousness, the indivisibility of the Creator and the creation becomes apparent.

We see this perspective expressed in other cultures as well. Advaita Vedanta, an ancient school of thought in the Indian tradition, sees one's true essence (atman) as no different from the ultimate (Brahman). There is also this quote, attributed to Zen Master Dōgen Zenji: "Truth is not far away. It is nearer than near. There is no need to attain it, since not one of your steps leads away from it."[131]

These and countless other scriptural citations *may* express the metaware view that self, awareness, and divinity are one.[1] Then at

---

1   "Oneness" can be experienced all the way from 2.5 onwards; it is not just a met-

the 5.5 Transpersonal Stage another beautiful expansion occurs. A person begins to back awareness up in an infinite regression, like that hall of mirrors analogy, which can enable the further recognition, disidentification, and cleanup of shadow patterns.

At every stage below the sixth-person perspective, a self looks out, into the world. Even at 5.5, the eyes you look out of still feel like they belong to you. But an almost unimaginable shift occurs at 6.0. From the viewpoint of the universalist, all separate selves merge into one. In other words, the hall of mirrors of 5.5 moves out of the individual and into the collective. In this way, a universalist sees just one reflected "I" looking back at themselves through many eyes. Thus it is here, at this penultimate stage, that *I* becomes *we*.

We can't know for sure, since the data on people at 6.0 and 6.5 is still sparse, as they are the rarest of rare. But my intuition of the spirituality of 6.0 Universalists is as if their consciousness acts like a mycelial network. For readers not familiar with how mushrooms propagate, they do so through a web of ultra-delicate underground fibers called mycelium. In this analogy, think of a subterranean network of invisible, ultra-thin, translucent fibers running in every possible direction. So, like consciousness, mycelium are there, everywhere—you just can't perceive them. Consciousness, like the mycelial network, is just under the surface. Everything in both these "subterranean" realms is

---

aware phenomena. In terms of the scriptures I reference, my view on them is mine and mine alone. I want to be explicit that these views are not those of anyone at Stage International. I'm aware I'm coming to these conclusions on my own, and that they lie outside those of the established academic community to which I belong.

interconnected, which my intuition tells me mirrors a 6.0's perception that one big mind links all with all.

It is my belief that the metaware collective that emerges at 6.0 integrates the concrete and subtle into one ultra-subtle multidimensional universal consciousness. At the Universalist Stage, a person groks that the whole is an inexpressibly vast network. The new "I" that emerges is the One Consciousness itself. Harking back to the mycelium metaphor, each mushroom that sprouts at the surface represents but a single point of the One Mind, "fruiting" as another person. Thus at 6.0 a person becomes a singular perspective that the whole has on itself. The staggering realization that we all are one compels compassion to expand infinitely.

Just as all barriers to love dissolve at 6.0, so does time become timeless and space boundless. Think of eternity (time) and infinity (space) both coming with arrows, starting at zero, and then pointing outward, extending out in a line forever. The timelessness and boundlessness of the sixth-person perspective drops the arrows and the direction. Spheres of space-time expand to infinity.

Again, these are my musings, conclusions, and beliefs. But the way I see it, at this high stage, there is nothing left to hem God in. *The Life* becomes The All, and all is in The All. There is no separate Creator and created at 6.0.

At the next level,[132] that of the 6.5 Illumined Stage, even the complete unity of the 6.0 perspective may be subject to another simplifying refinement. I'll refer to the ancient Vedic metaphor of Indra's net[133] to convey this even more sublime potential for spiritual expansion. To adherents of the Vedic religions, Indra was the ruler of all gods, king of the highest heaven. As such, he was also the keeper of an infinitely large net that spanned the cosmos. Located at each of the net's cross stitches was a single perfect jewel, the reflection of which contained the reflection of all the other jewels. In that way The All was in all and yet no single jewel itself was obscured by or mistaken for any other. There were parts and the whole, existing together.

Thus, in one image, Indra's net illustrates the ultimate interpenetration, inter-causality, and inter-being seen at the level of the 6.5 Illumined stage. Not only is all in The All and vice versa, but everything is connected through one infinite stream of effauses and caufects. In his book *Hua-yen Buddhism: The Jewel Net of Indra*, Francis Dojun Cook wrote, "Thus each individual is at once the cause for the whole and is caused by the whole, and what is called existence is a vast body made up of an infinity of individuals all sustaining each other and defining each other. The cosmos is, in short, a self-creating, self-maintaining, and self-defining organism."[134]

Looking to other world religions, one might find a correspondence between Indra's net and the Bible verse John 1:1, which reads, "In the beginning was the Word, and the Word was with God, and the Word was God." Imagine how a person holding an illumined perspective might interpret that Scripture, associating "the Word" with information, and "God" with the One Consciousness. From an Abrahamic viewpoint, the Word and God also share the qualities of interpenetration, inter-causality, and inter-being. The Word and God are two inseparable sides of the same coin (my interpretation).

Thus, at this final stage, the whole metaware collective—that of the synonymousness of consciousness and information—may come into view. Illumined folk may see that the One Consciousness constructs its parts out of expanding information. From that perspective then, nothing would exist outside this dynamic. Thus, this high view may reveal the ultimate synthesis of consciousness and meaning. From the vantage point of the One Big Mind at 6.5, meaning would make everything, which follows that everything is meaningful. It's mind-blowing to realize that your individual story may lie at the heart of a participatory universe.

So there it is, my take on the full scope of spirituality, from the first stage to the last. Just as we develop along physical, cognitive, emotional, interpersonal, moral, and self lines, it's natural that we would also develop along a spiritual line. But what if your spiritual development were the one and only goal of the One Mind? To me, there can hardly be a more perfect way to achieve that aim than by coupling consciousness with information. Just as one mycelial network fruits individual mushrooms, so did the One Consciousness "fruit" you. Similarly, just as every jewel in Indra's net reflects all the others, the one causal network connects you with your life circumstances.

Consider also the One Consciousness is trending toward more beauty, goodness, and truth, spontaneously and effortlessly pairing each with the other. Consider as well that it does this in ways that best enable the propagation of the formative lessons your development requires. Eckhart Tolle, in his seminal book *A New Earth: Awakening to Your Life's Purpose,* espouses this view: "Life will give you whatever experience is most helpful for the evolution of your consciousness. How do you know this is the experience you need? Because this is the experience you are having at the moment."

That is a vision of how the whole, driven by the evolutionary code of the Universal Aspiration—to increase happiness and decrease suffering—might inexorably and endlessly develop more beauty, goodness, and truth. If all this is true, the "spiritual" task that's left for each of us is to accept our current circumstances with as much equanimity as we can muster, and then attune and endeavor to make meaning out of our suffering. I'll use the epilogue to enlist you in just such a worthy project.

EPILOGUE

"Awareness is the greatest agent for change."

Eckhart Tolle

The "stages model" we explored in the last three chapters is endlessly complex. Indeed, volumes could be written on the subject. You may well ask whether it was relevant to attunement and the overall topic of how stories make us sick. That's a valid question, especially since I devoted some 20 percent of this book delving into it. I felt it important to share the stages theory with you for two reasons. The first is that exposure to the information itself is developmental. Understanding the perspectives of each stage will help you estimate the window you primarily view yourself and world through. The second related aim of sharing stages with you is to connect you directly with the raison d'être of this book. Understanding human development will help you to better attune to yourself and your relations. That way we can all make a better world.

The tumultuous dawning of the twenty-first century has been epochs in the making. We humans have been evolving higher and higher perspectives ever since we stood up on two legs. There was a time when we lived in isolated tribal communities, feared and fought with outsiders, and worshipped magical earth spirits. Though exceedingly rare, tribes that hold that same primal perspective still exist in remote parts of the world today. Just as rare are people viewing the world from the opposite end of the developmental continuum, whose compassion is universal and experience of spirit boundless.

With those examples, you can imagine the twelve stages plotted on a bell curve. Farther out on opposite tails is where you will find these rarer distributions. On the other hand, the more populous stage cohorts occupy the central, fat part of the curve.

At different times, and depending on the circumstances, every person may exhibit a range of perspectives. For example, should I fall into a rage, I might have a state experience of 1.5. On the other hand, after having ingested psilocybin mushrooms, I temporarily saw the world through the window of the 6.0 stage. State experiences arise and pass, and after each state episode a person's view eventually resolves back to whatever is their current "center of gravity." A similar principle applies to collectives as well. Individuals and subgroups within populations exhibit a range of worldviews, but at any one time, the aggregate culture exerts a dominating influence whose gravitational pull causes all the other perspectives to orbit around it.

At present, most adults in the modern world look out of the windows of the 3.0 and 3.5 perspectives. The authority of these two worldviews overpowers all the rest. At their best, these modern worldviews, undergirded as they are by rationality and science, were able to raise humanity out of the Dark Ages. Indeed, we have modernism to thank for pulling billions out of poverty, utterly transforming the way we live and how we govern ourselves. There is no doubt that most people are freer and more prosperous than they were even one hundred years ago. But the modern worldview is not without its dark side. As you will recall, the third-person perspective centers on the explorations and goals of the *individual*. That self-oriented outlook is great for freedom and self-determination, but it has also spawned a rapacious, amoral, market-driven economy that, like cancer, is set to grow unchecked until it eventually kills its host. Indeed, the stress, illness, and blight so chronic in the modern world today are the withering effects of a system that feeds on us and nature like a parasite.

The destructive shadow of me-oriented modernism is that we believe we are separate from each other and nature and behave accordingly. But nothing can be further from the truth. As you well know by now, deep interdependence reigns. From the micro to the macro, the universe is a holon,[135] one appearing as many. This is the realization of folks who reach the sixth-person perspective.

But the vast majority of us don't see that. Instead, most of us feel isolated and cut off from larger, more inclusive holons that could offer the sustenance we so desperately need. In that way, your current distress and the concurrent unraveling of the biosphere are inextricably entwined. The future of humanity won't consist of two separate camps, one of winners and the other of losers. No, we're all in this together. In the final tally, there will be only one camp, winners *or* losers. The fact of our global interdependency consigns us to the same fate.

It's very likely the stress, trauma, or disease that sparked your interest in this book stems from the familial, cultural, and economic systems in which you reside. No question, you're caught up in system dynamics, large and small, and it's impossible for you to ever pull yourself up and out of the grip of their dominating influence. The question becomes, what do you do with the predicament in which you find yourself, existing as you do as a tiny fraction of a larger whole? As I said before, you can't change the global system. It's too big. Thus, the only option left for you is to change yourself.

What is the one thing you can do right now to raise your awareness so you can start feeling better? I'm hoping that after reading this book, your answer will redound to attunement. Think of attunement as a harmonic relationship, like syncing to the ecstasy and pathos of an opera. The highs and lows are as meaningful as they are inevitable. Your epic life is no different. Imagine yourself a member of the orchestra—your job is to adjust your contribution and phrasing to blend with, embellish, and enhance the overall production. The moment-to-moment feedback that attunement provides lets you play your individual part to make the greater whole better.

Nature herself is the conductor. But clearly, we are not following her lead. Individually, we're out of step with more healthy and wholesome ways of caring for ourselves. On a collective scale, we're marching to a beat driven largely by the vacuous values of the modern perspectives. All the racket we're generating has us on edge, relentlessly pushing our tender animal bodies to the brink of exhaustion. If we keep going, continuing to live in disharmony with ourselves and nature, we will cross an invisible line from which there will be no return. Perspectives lower than 4.5 are limited in their capacity to envision a future that is much different from what they are currently experiencing. It's for this primary reason that individuals, and indeed humanity as a whole, have such a hard time fighting against inertia and changing.

What we all need at this pivotal moment is a wholesale shift in our culture's value structure, where collectively we stop living to consume and instead live to *give*. Only at the height of the 4.5 Strategist level does a person fully realize the interpenetration of the inner and the outer and why attunement is imperative.

Most people can't picture how bad things can get. That was certainly true of me twenty-plus years ago, when I viewed myself and the world through the lens of the third-person perspective. As the calendar turned over from 1999 to 2000, the only worry I harbored was the chaos that might ensue should predictions of the Y2K global Internet crash come true. As you know, I was caught completely by surprise when my life and business collapsed only a few short months later.

Just before the fall, at the dawning of the new millennium, I was blissfully vacationing with family in Palm Springs, California. During the day, we alternately lay by the pool and played bocce ball or croquet on the manicured lawns. To while away the evening hours, we amused ourselves with a deck of animal totem cards. These are similar to tarot cards; people use them for fortune-telling. I'm not sure of their exact history beyond the fact that indigenous peoples believed that the spirit and power of animals flows in and out of a person's life. Which animal influence reigns at any one time depends on where a person is going and what tasks they need to accomplish. The idea is that the cards will answer those questions for you.

As with tarot cards, a questioner makes a specific inquiry and then shuffles the cards and lays out a "spread" to divine the answer. In my heart, I didn't believe there was any connection between the symbolic pictures on the cards and my fate, but I was fully into the lighthearted fun of trying to rouse and engage the magical forces. It was New Year's Eve, and like anyone, I was curious about what lay ahead for me.

My stepmother, Klaire, held court, acting as the chief card dealer and soothsayer. When it was my turn I asked, "Which of all the animal totems is going to rule my future?" This inquiry required only a one-card answer. Klaire carefully shuffled the deck and fanned the cards across the table. With intent, I slowly passed my open palm just above the line of cards, feeling for any ultra-subtle energy that would draw me to the right one. I thought I felt a very slight tingle as my hand passed over one particular section of the spread. Thinking I was guided by the rise and fall of vibrations, I narrowed my search and zeroed in on one card.

Before I slid the card out of the spread, I wondered if it might be a lion, the symbol of strength and leadership. Or maybe the hawk, emblematic of clear vision? I drew the card out and turned it over. My totem was a decidedly humbler creature: the salmon! *Great*, I thought. *It's my destiny to struggle against raging currents, climb torrential waterfalls, narrowly survive ravenous bears, only to make it to the spawning grounds, have an orgasm, and then die.*

I'm still here, so obviously I haven't reached the final spawning grounds yet. But it's worth mentioning, given the stress and struggle of the past twenty years, that this animal totem card was eerily prophetic. Salmon is definitely my totem; I've had to fight a relentless current to achieve whatever worldly and spiritual attainments have come my way.

I recount the salmon story because we all have some salmon in our story lines. In our own way, we are all swimming upstream against the currents of life. Like salmon, if we're to fulfill our destiny, we have to be tough.

Life does not have to be easy to be good. Truly, if someone offered me all the money I lost when my business blew up in exchange for the wisdom and peace I've since gained from struggling against the currents of life, I wouldn't take it. To bargain away the boon of self-knowledge would leave me spiritually bankrupt. It will be the same for you, too.

Salmon are also a keystone species.[136, 137] From the bottom up, the health of the whole forest ecosystem depends on them. Humans are the ultimate keystone species. Our capacity to see the big picture, which influences our values and the choices we make, affect the well-being of the global ecosystem.

My intention in writing this book was to zoom in and zoom out and to connect all the dots for you—world, body, and mind. The hope was to confer an understanding of how consequential your role is in this passion play that's unfolding. Like it or not, it's a hero's journey. Treating it as such will not only energize you and help you feel better but also raise the window of your consciousness and make meaning out of your struggles. This expanded vision and purpose will empower you to add your energy to a larger movement. The larger movement needs you! Only by our mutual effort can we create a global trophic cascade that will transform us and the world.

Keep this in mind when things get hard. Given the challenges we're facing in the decades to come, we're all salmon. Turning things around is going to take a concerted and sustained effort on all our parts. For yourself and everyone and everything else, find your strength. Your warrior doesn't need to be comfortable. Trust me, your spiritual development will be well worth the cost of the fight. Find your creativity as well. Design your life. Your artist needs to express itself. It will wither and die brokenhearted unless it is able to give its unique gifts.

My last word harks back to the beginning. Please, start practicing. When you do, you will most assuredly reach the same conclusion as have countless soul-searchers before you, that the beauty and satisfaction of living an awakened life is priceless. Your story may have made you sick, but it can also be your salvation.

ENDNOTES

1. Witt, Keith. *The Attuned Family: How to Be a Great Parent to Your Kids and a Great Lover to Your Spouse.* https://drkeithwitt.com/books/buy-book-attuned-family/

2. Lindahl, J., et al. "The Varieties of Contemplative Experience: A Mixed-Methods Study of Meditation-Related Challenges in Western Buddhists." *Plos One* 12 (5), 2017. DOI: 10.1371/journal.pone.0176239

3. The following is not an exhaustive list. Don't take it as such. Consult a well-qualified behavioral health practitioner trained in the therapeutic use of mindfulness meditation if you have any questions about whether you should start practicing it.

4. Grossman, P., et al. "Mindfulness-Based Stress Reduction and Health Benefits: a Meta-Analysis." *Focus on Alternative and Complementary Therapies* 8 (4), 2010: p. 500. DOI: 10.1111/j.2042-7166.2003.tb04008.x

5. Machelska, H. "Faculty Opinions Recommendation of Mindfulness Meditation for Chronic Pain: Systematic Review and Meta-Analysis." *Faculty Opinions–Post-Publication Peer Review of the Biomedical Literature*, 2016. DOI: 10.3410/f.726767524.793525167

6. Querstret, D., et al. "Mindfulness-Based Stress Reduction and Mindfulness-Based Cognitive Therapy for Psychological Health and Well-Being in Nonclinical Samples: A Systematic Review and Meta-Analysis." *International Journal of Stress Management*, 2020. DOI: 10.1037/str0000165

7. "Compassion and Loving-Kindness Meditation: An Overview and Prospects for the Application in Clinical Samples," *Harvard Review of Psychiatry* 26 (4), July 2018: pp. 201-215. DOI: 10.1097/HRP.0000000000000192

8. McKeown, Patrick. *The Oxygen Advantage: Simple, Scientifically Proven Breathing Technique to Help You Become Healthier, Slimmer, Faster, and Fitter.* New York: William Morrow & Company, 2015.

9. Brown, Richard P., and Patricia L. Gerbarg. *The Healing Power of the Breath: Simple Techniques to Reduce Stress and Anxiety, Enhance Concentration, and Balance Your Emotions.* Boulder, Colorado: Shambhala, 2012.

10 https://www.matthieuricard.org/en/medias/matthieu-ricard-why-are-you-called-the-happiest-man-in-the-world-1-of-5

11 https://en.wikipedia.org/wiki/Brahmavihara

12 https://www.mindsetworks.com/

13 http://chenrezig.com.au/

14 https://www.youtube.com/watch?v=8X7ZhmBEnoA

15 https://www.youtube.com/watch?v=yecJLI-GRuU

16 Ferrucci, Piero, and Vivien Ferrucci. *The Power of Kindness: the Unexpected Benefits of Leading a Compassionate Life*. Langara College, 2019.

17 Many thanks to John Peacock for his unique perspective on the social-historical context of ancient India, specifically on the origins of the Brahmanic worldview and early Buddhism. John is the director of Master Studies of Mindfulness-Based Cognitive Therapy at Oxford University. If you would like to hear his perspective directly, search for his podcasts delivered at the Insight Meditation Center, Redwood City, California, 09-03-11. I accessed and began listening to the podcasts 06-21-13.

18 The Vedas are said to be "apauruṣeya" (not of human agency). They are supposed to have been directly revealed and thus are called "śruti" (what is heard). Wikipedia, accessed 06-22-13.

19 Paraphrasing John Peacock in a talk delivered at Insight Meditation Center, Redwood City, CA, 09-03-11.

20 The first of the four Vedic texts. The Rigveda contains hymns to be recited by the *hotar*, or presiding priest. Wikipedia, accessed 06-22-13.

21 Paraphrasing John Peacock in a talk he delivered at Insight Meditation Center, Redwood City, CA, 09-03-11.

22 See Wikipedia for a full exposition of the Sramana movement. Accessed 06-22-13.

23 "Intention, I tell you, is kamma. Intending, one does kamma by way of body, speech, and intellect." Anguttara Nikaya 6.63.

24 The Second Law of Thermodynamics says there is a natural tendency for entropy (measure of disorder) to increase over time. Essentially, all conditioned things fall apart.

25 Bodhi, Bhikkhu. *A Comprehensive Manual of Abhidhamma, Pali Text, Translation & Explanatory Guide*. Sri Lanka: Buddhist Publication Society, 2003.

26 www.scholarpedia.org › article › Hard_problem_of_consciousness

27 A person without meditative training perceives only highly processed information presented to them by their narrating mind. This normal level of perception is referred to as "initial" perception.

28 Meditators gain what is called "acquired" perception, the ability to perceive the overlay of narrative construction over the raw sense data as it enters their mind system.

29 Ego development: T. O'Fallon (2011), Cook-Greuter (2002), R. Kegan (1994), Loevinger (1998).

30 https://www.cdc.gov/violenceprevention/aces/about.html

31 https://www.theatlantic.com/magazine/archive/2011/04/secret-fears-of-the-super-rich/308419/

32 The theory of Structural Dissociation (Van der Hart, Nijenhuis & Steele, 2006).

33 Panksepp, 1998; Van der Hart et al., 2006.

34 Fisher, Janina, PhD. *Healing the Fragmented Selves of Trauma Survivors, Overcoming Internal Self-Alienation.* New York: Routledge, 2017.

35 Cozolino, 2002: Teicher, 2004.

36 Van der Hart et al., 2004.

37 https://en.wikipedia.org/wiki/Strict_father_model

38 Trichotillomania (TTM), also known as hair-pulling disorder or compulsive hair-pulling. https://en.wikipedia.org/wiki/Trichotillomania

39 The term "attachment parenting" was coined by the American pediatrician William Sears.

40 https://en.wikipedia.org/wiki/Attachment_theory

41 https://en.wikipedia.org/wiki/Attachment_parenting#In_practice

42 https://en.wikipedia.org/wiki/Childhood_trauma

43 Dan Siegel's conceptualization of "earned secure attachment" reflects the view of attachment theorists (Main, Schore, Lyons-Ruth) that childhood attachment trauma can be modified through life experiences and "grow" states of secure attachment in adulthood.

44 https://en.wikipedia.org/wiki/Sensory_processing_sensitivity

45 Klages, Wolfgang (1978). *Der sensible Mensch: Psychologie, Psychopathologie, Therapie (The Sensitive Human: Psychology, Psychopathology, Therapy)* (in German), 1 ed. Stuttgart, Germany: Enke. p. 133. ISBN 978-3432898711.

46 https://opentextbc.ca/introductiontopsychology/chapter/10-1-the-experience-of-emotion/

47 https://www.gla.ac.uk/news/archiveofnews/2014/february/headline_306019_en.html

48 https://en.wikipedia.org/wiki/Contrasting_and_categorization_of_emotions

49 ibid. Damasio, 2000; LeDoux, 2000; Ochsner, Bunge, Gross, & Gabrieli, 2002.

50 The principle of excitation transfer refers to the phenomenon that occurs when people who are already experiencing arousal from one event tend to also experience other emotions more strongly.

51 Klages distinguishes between sensitive and highly sensitive people, classifying artists and "high intellectuals" as an example of the latter.

52 Transactional theory of stress and coping (TTSC), Lazarus, 1966; Lazarus & Folkman, 1984.

53 https://www.cnvc.org/

54 C. L. Cooper, ed. *Prolonged Arrest of Cancer*, New York: John Wiley & Sons, 1988. p. 32.

55 https://www.webmd.com/balance/stress-management/effects-of-stress-on-your-body

56 https://www.jimmott.com/2iaphome.html

57 Keltner, Dacher, et al. *The Compassionate Instinct: the Science of Human Goodness*. New York: W. W. Norton & Co., 2010.

58 https://en.wikipedia.org/wiki/Fractal

59 https://en.wikipedia.org/wiki/Julia_set

60 https://www.youtube.com/watch?v=K32rEfjxTGs

61 Goswami, Amit. *The Self-Aware Universe: How Consciousness Creates the Material World*. New York: Penguin/Putnam, 1993.

62 Glattfelder, J. B. (2019) "A Universe Built of Information." In *Information—Consciousness—Reality*. The Frontiers Collection. Springer, Cham.

63 Davis, P., Gregersen, N., *Information and the Nature of Reality: From Physics to Metaphysics*. Cambridge: Cambridge Press, 2014.

64 https://www.shinzen.org/about/

65 Tolle, Eckhart. *The Power of Now: A Guide to Spiritual Enlightenment*. Novato, California: New World Library, 2010.

66 Brach, Tara. *Radical Acceptance: Embracing Your Life with the Heart of a Buddha*. New York: Bantam Books, 2004

67 Kotsou, Ilios, et al. "Acceptance Alone Is a Better Predictor of Psychopathology and Well-Being than Emotional Competence, Emotion Regulation and Mindfulness." *Journal of Affective Disorders* 226, 2018: pp. 142–145. DOI: 10.1016/j.jad.2017.09.047

68 Barlow, D. H., Allen, L. B., Choate, M. L.. "Toward a unified treatment for emotional disorders." *Behav. Ther.* 35 (2), 2004: pp. 205–230. http://dx.doi.org/10.1016/j.beth.2016.11.005

69 Veenstra, L., Schneider, I., Koole, S. "Embodied mood regulation: the impact of body posture on mood recovery, negative thoughts, and mood-congruent recall." *Cognition and Emotion* 31 (7), 2017: pp. 1361-1376. DOI: 10.1080/02699931.2016.1225003

70 Coles, N., Larsen, J., Lench, H. "A meta-analysis of the facial feedback literature: Effects of facial feedback on emotional experience are small and variable." *Psychological Bulletin*, 2019. DOI: 10.1037/bul0000194

71 https://en.wikipedia.org/wiki/Hebbian_theory

72 Wiswede, D., Münte, T., Krämer, U., Rüsseler, J. "Embodied Emotion Modulates Neural Signature of Performance Monitoring." *PLoS One* 4(6): e5754. Published online June 1, 2009. DOI: 10.1371/journal.pone.0005754 PMCID: PMC2685014

73 Cuddy, A., Wilmuth, C., Carney, D. "The Benefit of Power Posing before a High-Stakes Social Evaluation." Harvard Business School Working Paper, No. 13-027, September 2012.

74 Shapira, L., Mongrain, M. "The Benefits of Self-Compassion and Optimism Exercises for Individuals Vulnerable to Depression." *The Journal of Positive Psychology* 5(5), 2010: pp. 377–389. DOI:10.1080/17439760.2010.516763

75 https://www.oxfordbibliographies.com/view/document/obo-9780195393521/obo-9780195393521-0034.xml

76 https://www.learningtogive.org/resources/jewish-philanthropy-concept-tzedakah#:~:text=Judaism%20teaches%20the%20belief%20that,of%20sharing%20the%20Almighty's%20work

77   2 Corinthians 9:6-7.

78   Bihar al-Anwar, vol. 70, p. 308.

79   Park, S., et al. "A Neural Link between Generosity and Happiness." *Nature Communications* 8(1), 2017. DOI: 10.1038/ncomms15964

80   Gentile, D., et al. "Caring for Others Cares for the Self: an Experimental Test of Brief Downward Social Comparison, Loving-Kindness, and Interconnectedness Contemplations." *Journal of Happiness Studies* 21(3), 2019: pp. 765–778. DOI: 10.1007/s10902-019-00100-2

81   But in case it's necessary, let me clarify. When I suggest that you set the intention to be more generous, I'm not talking about codependently giving yourself away. Codependency is giving with a hidden agenda to get something in return. Codependency binds giver and receiver in an unhealthy dynamic that diminishes both. That's not anything like the generosity of which I'm speaking. Rather, perfected generosity spreads goodness in both directions. It surely benefits the receiver but will also redound to your benefit as well.

82   The optimal balance between attention and awareness is my meditation teacher John Yates's definition of mindfulness.

83   My first meditation teacher, Shinzen Young, first introduced me to the six attentional targets Sight, Sound, Touch, Feel, Talk, Image. He has graciously allowed me to use these same six attentional targets in the SkillfullyAware method.

84   https://en.wikipedia.org/wiki/Savoring

85   https://en.wikipedia.org/wiki/Affect_labeling

86   Constantinou, E., et al. "Can Words Heal? Using Affect Labeling to Reduce the Effects of Unpleasant Cues on Symptom Reporting." *Frontiers in Psychology* 5, 2014. DOI: 10.3389/fpsyg.2014.00807

87   I learned about the ten "saboteurs" after reading *Positive Intelligence*, by Shirzad Chamine, Greenleaf Book Group, Austin, Texas, 2012.

88   In Joseph Campbell's formulation of the hero's journey, help is given to the hero, sufficient to make them wiser, stronger, and better able to face the challenges of the adventure. Each hero must merge the advice of the magical helpers or mentors with their own willpower and faith to carry out the quest to its conclusion.

89   https://en.wikipedia.org/wiki/Jungian_archetypes#:~:text=Twelve%20archetypes%20have%20been%20proposed,%2C%20Jester%2C%20and%20Regular%20Person

90 https://implicit.harvard.edu/implicit/takeatest.html

91 I first became aware of the five stages of shadow resolution through a class I took taught by Kim Barta, MS. Kim is a world-class expert on shadow and its resolution. I am forever grateful for his expert instruction, and all credit for delineating these five stages goes to him. If you are interested in diving more deeply into this topic for the purpose of resolving your own shadow or to assist you in working with others, I highly encourage you to contact Kim directly through the Stage International website: https://www.stagesinternational.com/about/#about

92 O'Fallon, T., PhD. "States and STAGES: Waking up Developmentally," *INTEGRAL REVIEW* 16(1), April 2020.

93 A Pythagorean term meaning the pattern or order that connects the universe throughout its many dimensions of physical, mental, and spiritual existence. 2. In integral theory, the sum total of the manifest universe when contrasted with spirit as the unmanifest, or emptiness. When used alone, the sum total of the manifest and the unmanifest, including spirit.

94 Developmental theories have been evolving for well over one hundred years, including Baldwin (1901), Freud's psychosexual developmental model (Freud, 1961), Piaget and cognitive development (Piaget, 1969), and Erickson (1997) and his psychosocial development. Others have refined Erickson's work, including Kegan (1994) and Cook-Greuter (1999).

95 Ego developmental model, Cook-Greuter (1999).

96 Dr. O'Fallon's stages theory is a developmental matrix derived in part from the Loevinger's stages of ego development.

97 Terri O'Fallon, PhD, and Kim Barta, MS

98 Kim Barta, MS, coined the term *shadow crash*. A shadow crash results when, due to stress or some other type of triggering event, a person "crashes" down and acts out of a lower perspectival level than their norm. For example, a person whose normal perspective is 3.5 crashes to 1.5 when under stress.

99 *The Attuned Family: How to be a Great Parent to Your Kids and a Great Lover to your Spouse*, by Dr. Keith Witt. https://drkeithwitt.com/books/buy-book-attuned-family/

100 Siegel, Daniel J., and Tina Payne Bryson. *The Yes Brain: How to Cultivate Courage, Curiosity, and Resilience in Your Child.* New York: Bantam, 2018.

101 Stern, Jessica A., and Jude Cassidy. "Empathy from Infancy to Adolescence: An Attachment Perspective on the Development of Individual Differences." *Developmental Review* 47, 2018: pp. 1–22. DOI: 10.1016/j.dr.2017.09.002

102 https://en.wikipedia.org/wiki/Piaget%27s_theory_of_cognitive_development

103 National Consortium for the Study of Terrorism and Responses to Terrorism, a Department of Homeland Security Science and Technology Center of Excellence. "The Organizational Dynamics of Far-Right Hate Groups in the United States: Comparing Violent to Non-Violent Organizations." Final report to Human Factors/Behavioral Sciences Division, Science and Technology Directorate, U.S. Department of Homeland Security. December 2011. Page 5.

"White supremacists and other far-right hate groups are seen as representing a significant threat. When surveyed about terrorist group presence within their state, 85% of state law enforcement agencies indicated right-wing extremist group presence, and 82% indicated the presence of race/ethnicity/hate-related groups (Riley, Treverton, Wilson & Davis, 2005). A more recent survey of state police agencies (74% response rate) found that 92%, 89%, 72% and 70% of respondents respectively indicated that neo-Nazis, racist skinheads, Ku Klux Klan, and Christian Identity groups were operating in their jurisdiction (Freilich, Chermak & Simone, 2009; see also Carlson, 1995). Simi's research demonstrates that it is important to focus on the entire universe of far-right hate groups, including both violent and nonviolent organizations. Simi has found that far-right terrorists were usually involved in the larger movement before becoming terrorists. He concludes that their decision to turn to violence is the culmination of an "extremist career." Importantly, Simi (2009: 29) argues that this finding indicates that "efforts to monitor extremist groups are important."

104 https://www.dhs.gov/ntas/advisory/national-terrorism-advisory-system-bulletin-january-27-2021

105 https://en.wikipedia.org/wiki/Turn_on,_tune_in,_drop_out

106 https://en.wikipedia.org/wiki/Kung_Fu_(1972_TV_series)

107 https://en.wikipedia.org/wiki/Hero%27s_journey

108 http://www.wernererhard.com/est.html

109 Seffinger, M., et al. "Reliability of Spinal Palpation for Diagnosis of Back and Neck Pain." *Spine* 29(19), 2004. DOI: 10.1097/01.brs.0000141178.98157.8e

110 https://www.onsiteworkshops.com/programs/living-centered-program/

111 https://en.wikipedia.org/wiki/Shine_On_You_Crazy_Diamond

112 https://en.wikipedia.org/wiki/Psychodrama

113 https://en.wikipedia.org/wiki/Pratītyasamutpāda

114 Macy, Joanna. *Mutual Causality in Buddhism and General Systems Theory: The Dharma of Natural Systems*. New Delhi: Sri Satguru Publications, 1995.

115 https://en.wikipedia.org/wiki/Idappaccayat

116 The behavior of a person's genes doesn't just depend on the genes' DNA sequence—it's also affected by so-called epigenetic factors, like stress, trauma, lifestyle, and nutrition. Changes in these factors can play a critical role in disease. The external environment's effects on a person's genes can influence disease, and some of these effects can be passed on to a person's offspring.

117 Yehuda, R., Lehrner, A. "Intergenerational Transmission of Trauma Effects: Putative Role of Epigenetic Mechanisms." *World Psychiatry* 17(3), 2018: pp. 243–257. DOI: 10.1002/wps.20568

118 Chan, J., Nugent, B., Bale, T. "Parental advisory: maternal and paternal stress can impact offspring neurodevelopment." *Biol Psychiatry* 83, 2018: pp. 886-94.

119 Bohacek, J, Mansuy, I. "Molecular insights into transgenerational non-genetic inheritance of acquired behaviours." *Nat Rev Genet* 16, 2015: pp. 641-52.

120 Ferguson-Smith, A. "Genomic imprinting: the emergence of an epigenetic paradigm." *Nat Rev Genet* 12, 2011: pp. 565-75.

121 Rando, O. "Intergenerational transfer of epigenetic information in sperm." *Cold Spring Harbor Perspect Med* 2016, 6.

122 Rakoff, V. "A long term effect of the concentration camp experience." *Viewpoints* 1966, 1: pp.17-22.

123 Sigal, J., Weinfeld, M. "Trauma and rebirth: intergenerational effects of the Holocaust." New York: Praeger, 1989.

124 A unit of familial or cultural information, as a concept, belief, habit, or practice, that spreads from person to person in a way analogous to the transmission of genes.

125 O'Fallon, Terri, PhD, and Kim Barta, MA. *Developmental Life Design, Unfolding the Living Map of Life. Stages Essentials for Therapists and Coaches: Precision in Developmental Assessment & Intervention*, 2017, p. 29.

126 https://www.cnvc.org/

127 O'Fallon, T., PhD. "Triangulating the Language Literature Supporting the STAGES Scoring Rules." Abstract. Feb. 2, 2018. www.stagesinternational.com

128 Interviews with Kim Barta and Slack Q&A with Terri O'Fallon. October through December 2020.

129 This flip can happen whenever people go from a state of awareness into a state of awareness of awareness. It just takes practice to make the shift.

130 English Standard Version

131 Born in the year 1200, Dōgen Zenji was a Japanese Buddhist monk, writer, poet, and philosopher. He was the founder of the Soto school of Zen.

132 There are four more Stages theorized in the "Unified Tier" but writing about them here is way beyond the scope of this book.

133 https://en.wikipedia.org/wiki/Indra%27s_net

134 Cook, Francis Dojun. *Hua-yen Buddhism: The Jewel Net of Indra.* University Park, Pa.: Penn State University Press, 1977.

135 A holon is something that is simultaneously a whole in and of itself, as well as a part of a larger whole. In other words, holons can be understood as the constituent part-wholes of a hierarchy.

136 https://en.wikipedia.org/wiki/Keystone_species

137 https://pacificwild.org/salmon-a-keystone-species/

ACKNOWLEDGEMENTS

Years ago, I read a book called "Outliers" by Malcolm Gladwell, which details how success most often happens. His premise is that achievement is never simply the product of one person's individual effort, and that succeeding despite major life challenges takes more than just hard work. Instead, success usually results from a network of supportive people, unplanned opportunities, and lots of lucky breaks. Sure, hard work makes a difference, but without magical assistance and serendipity, success would be far rarer.

That being the case, I'm inspired to give thanks to a responsive Universe and all of the many people who helped me finally get this book out.

Know that this list is not exhaustive, but only highlights many who have supported me at critical junctures in my life. Those who warrant special thanks include my parents, Jack, Susanne, Klaire, and Joe. I'd like to thank Lynda Skinner for all the happy years. Hearty thanks go out to my best friends, Pete Eckerstrom and Steve Emrick. Thank you, Cal and Jennifer Turner, and also Patrick Doss, for your special and generous gifts at times when I needed them the most. Frances Causey and Brian McLaughlin, thank you for helping bringing *Is Your Story Making You Sick?*

to the screen. Thanks as well to Ann Marie Chiasson. You're a dear friend and world-class colleague. I'm grateful to Anna Geller for being my first editor, and Babette Hämmerle for her help with Chapter 6. Shinzen Young, John Yates, and Geshe Tashi Tsering, thank you for your incisive teachings on meditation and the mind. Thanks to Jane Ryder, Brian Preston, Ross Browne, Doug Wagner, Julie Miller, Colleen Sheehan, and the Ebook Launch team for bringing this book to life.

Lastly, the most influential person I want to thank is my daughter, Alana. You are my biggest blessing and my most happy coincidence. Alana, I want to thank you for the gift of delight, known only by the father who holds his precious daughter tightly. I know that your loving arms will not hold me forever, so I am thanking the Universe now for the bliss of the present moment. Life is meaningful because I share it with you.

ABOUT THE AUTHOR

Mark Pirtle is an integral therapist, teacher, speaker, and author. He's also a filmmaker, having produced the documentary *Is Your Story Making You Sick?* in 2019. Combining the disciplines of living systems theory, mindfulness meditation, positive psychology, and narrative medicine he developed an evidence-based program for healing stress-related illnesses he calls *SkillfullyAware®*. Pirtle speaks professionally, consults with businesses and private clients, hosts retreats, and teaches Mindfully Overcoming Addictive Behaviors, 10-week online class for eMindful.com. He is a faculty member for the Andrew Weil Center for Integrative Medicine Fellowship Program at the University of Arizona and is a founder and Director of Life Sciences and Programming at Kenyon Valley Ranch Retreat Center, Tubac, Arizona.

www.ingramcontent.com/pod-product-compliance
Lightning Source LLC
Chambersburg PA
CBHW072141100526
44589CB00015B/2035